MAD
TECHNICAL ENGLISH

English for the Information Age

Computers Internet Mobile Phones Mathematics P... ...tion

麦德
科技英语

[美] 麦德（Michael A. DeRabo）编

北京大学出版社
PEKING UNIVERSITY PRESS

图书在版编目(CIP)数据

麦德科技英语/(美)麦德(Michael A. DeRabo)编.—北京：北京大学出版社,2009.4
(麦德英语)
ISBN 978-7-301-15070-2

Ⅰ.麦… Ⅱ.德… Ⅲ.科学技术－英语 Ⅳ.H31

中国版本图书馆CIP数据核字(2009)第042569号

书　　　名：**麦德科技英语**
著作责任者：[美]麦德(Michael A. DeRabo)　编
责任编辑：汪晓丹
标准书号：ISBN 978-7-301-15070-2/H · 2230
出版发行：北京大学出版社
地　　　址：北京市海淀区成府路205号　100871
网　　　址：http://www.pup.cn
电子信箱：xdw777@pup.pku.edu.cn
电　　　话：邮购部 62752015　发行部 62750672　编辑部 62765014　出版部 62754962
印　　刷　者：北京宏伟双华印刷有限公司
经　　销　者：新华书店
　　　　　　787毫米×1092毫米　16开本　17.75印张　490千字
　　　　　　2009年4月第1版　2009年4月第1次印刷
定　　　价：36.00元

未经许可,不得以任何方式复制或抄袭本书之部分或全部内容。
版权所有,侵权必究
举报电话：010(62752024)　电子信箱：fd@pup.pku.edu.cn

FOREWORD

Computers. The Internet. Mobile phones. All are part of the Information Age that has radically transformed our lives and greatly enhanced our living standards. The Information Age is the latest revolution in our humankind industrial and social evolution. Much more than previous revolutions, the Information Age has permeated the lives of all humanity and brought deep changes even to the metaphysical level. Suffice to say, the Information Age has ushered us into the "real" future.

If one is to fathom and keep up with the rapid technological developments of the Information Age, one needs to have a solid understanding of the functioning of its basic elements. How do computers work? How does the Internet work? How do mobile phones work? This book explains these fundamentals of the Information Age. It explains them with enough detail to allow the reader to grasp their major aspects.

The Information Age unites us. It has made our world into a "small-village" cyberspace where the lingua franca is English. Of course English-learning books abound, but there is a dearth of books about technical English. True, traditionally, English technical jargon had been boring gibberish to most people, native speakers or not. However, with the advent of the Information Age, technical English words have permeated our everyday language and become a way to show one's vogue credentials. In fact, "techie geeks" are now part of the cool crowd.

This book is about technical English for the Information Age. The author's goal is to equip readers with all the necessary tools to understand, describe, and communicate about this Information Age. With this goal in mind, the book takes a comprehensive and integrated approach so as not only to include the major building blocks of the Information Age, namely computers, the Internet, and mobile phones, but also their foundation of mathematics, physics, and data communications.

The book strikes a balance between not being too technical and not being too general. It is detailed enough for technology-savvy engineers to sink their teeth into it and illustrated enough for the non-technical readers to follow. This balance in content is quite desirable. Indeed, there are engineering books on every technical subject, but they are also so theoretical and narrowly focused that readers either get lost in the numbers maze and/or fail to understand the relevance of the contents in the big picture of the Information Age. On the other hand, there are books that touch only very superficially on technical topics and are too vague to be of much value.

This book is divided into six units. The six units are in order of coverage: computers, the Internet, mobile phones, mathematics, physics, and data communications. The units on computers, the Internet, and mobile phones take a deep and comprehensive presentation approach so as to allow the readers a thorough understanding of the topics. The units on mathematics, physics, and data communications concentrate on the communication level to give the readers the ability to communicate about the topics. All units include many exercises to enhance understanding and practice technical English communication. Also, in order to make the book a complete package, especially for self-study readers, the author has included the answers to the exercises at the back of the book.

This book can be used not only by foreign students of English, but also by native speakers of English. Native speakers, from the technology-savvy ones to the less-technology-oriented ones, can find the book's contents of interest. For example, university engineering students can use this book as a reference guide. Less technically gifted readers can garner a general understanding of the topics through the many detailed illustrations and exercise answers.

Finally, it is worth enumerating the importance and benefits of learning technical English. Technical English is essential for:

- Reading technical publications written in English,
- Generating technical publications in English,
- Giving clear and effective technical presentations in English,
- Communicating with technology-field peers in English,
- Understanding and keeping up with the Information Age.

Michael A. DeRabo
Beijing
March 1, 2009

TABLE OF CONTENTS

UNIT 1　COMPUTERS ··· 1
  COMPUTER KEYWORDS ·· 2
  1.1　Introduction ··· 3
  1.2　Types of computers ··· 3
  1.3　The personal computer ·· 4
  1.4　Computer components ·· 5
      1.4.1　Computer hardware ··· 5
            1.4.1.1　CPU ·· 7
            1.4.1.2　Memory ·· 10
            1.4.1.3　Graphics ·· 11
            1.4.1.4　Chipset and buses ·· 12
            1.4.1.5　I/O ports and jacks ··· 14
            1.4.1.6　Wireless connectivity ··· 15
            1.4.1.7　Slots ··· 16
            1.4.1.8　BIOS ··· 16
            1.4.1.9　Hard disk ·· 17
            1.4.1.10　Optical drive ·· 18
            1.4.1.11　Keyboard, touchpad and mouse ································ 19
            1.4.1.12　Monitor, screen and webcam ··································· 20
            1.4.1.13　Power supply ·· 20
            1.4.1.14　Computer hardware trends ······································ 21
            1.4.1.15　Computer hardware example ··································· 22
      1.4.2　Computer software ·· 23
            1.4.2.1　BIOS ··· 24
            1.4.2.2　Operating system ·· 25
            1.4.2.3　Utilities ·· 27
            1.4.2.4　Applications ··· 27
            1.4.2.5　Virtualization ··· 29
            1.4.2.6　Middleware ·· 29
            1.4.2.7　Malware ·· 30
            1.4.2.8　Programming languages ··· 31
  1.5　Computer scenarios ·· 33
      1.5.1　Selecting a new computer ··· 33
      1.5.2　Selecting a gaming computer ··· 35
      1.5.3　Computer usage ·· 36

	1.5.4	Computer maintenance	36
	1.5.5	Setting up a wireless home network	37
	1.5.6	Printing a document	37
	1.5.7	Going online	37
	1.5.8	Scanning	38
	1.5.9	Writing a computer program	38
	1.5.10	Comparing computer companies	38
	1.5.11	Peripherals	39
1.6	Computer exercises		40
	1.6.1	Reading comprehension	40
	1.6.2	Reading and pronouncing acronyms	41
	1.6.3	Decoding computer jargon	42
	1.6.4	Computer essays	43
	1.6.5	Speaking exercises	43
	1.6.6	Identifying computer parts	44
	1.6.7	Cloze	45
	1.6.8	Computer action words	46
1.7	Computer glossary		47

UNIT 2 INTERNET 51

INTERNET KEYWORDS 52

2.1	Introduction		53
2.2	Internet history		53
2.3	Internet architecture		54
	2.3.1	Internet network architecture	55
		2.3.1.1 User equipment	55
		2.3.1.2 Internet access	56
		2.3.1.3 Internet backbone	57
		2.3.1.4 Internet example	58
	2.3.2	Internet protocols	59
		2.3.2.1 TCP/IP introduction	59
		2.3.2.2 TCP/IP layer functions	61
		2.3.2.3 TCP/IP data packaging	64
		2.3.2.4 TCP/IP data flow	65
		2.3.2.5 TCP/IP protocol suite	66
		2.3.2.6 TCP/IP implementation	69
		2.3.2.7 TCP/IP configuration	70
		2.3.2.8 TCP/IP future	71
	2.3.3	Internet domain name system	72
	2.3.4	Internet equipment	76

2.4	Internet services and applications		78
	2.4.1	Email	79
	2.4.2	Web	80
	2.4.3	Other Internet services and applications	81
2.5	Internet issues		84
	2.5.1	Advantages and disadvantages	84
	2.5.2	Internet administration	84
2.6	Internet future		85
	2.6.1	Faster access	85
	2.6.2	Internet ubiquity	85
	2.6.3	Internet connectivity	85
	2.6.4	Internet computing	86
	2.6.5	Internet storage	86
	2.6.6	Internet telephony	86
	2.6.7	Politics	86
2.7	Internet scenarios		87
	2.7.1	Searching for information	87
	2.7.2	Downloading content	87
	2.7.3	Designing web pages	87
	2.7.4	Getting a domain name	88
	2.7.5	Wireless surfing	88
	2.7.6	Communicating online	88
	2.7.7	Personal online shopping	88
2.8	Internet exercises		89
	2.8.1	Reading comprehension	89
	2.8.2	Reading and pronouncing acronyms	90
	2.8.3	Cloze	91
	2.8.4	Internet action words	92
	2.8.5	Identifying Internet elements	93
	2.8.6	Internet essays	94
	2.8.7	Speaking exercises	94
2.9	Internet glossary		95

UNIT 3 MOBILE PHONES **99**
MOBILE PHONE KEYWORDS 100
3.1 Introduction 101
3.2 Mobile phone history 101
3.3 Mobile phone handsets 103
    3.3.1 Mobile phone form factors 103
    3.3.2 Mobile phone hardware 104

                3.3.2.1　Main board ············ 105
                3.3.2.2　SIM card ············ 107
                3.3.2.3　Display ············ 107
                3.3.2.4　Keypad ············ 108
                3.3.2.5　Antenna ············ 108
                3.3.2.6　Audio I/O ············ 109
                3.3.2.7　Camera ············ 109
                3.3.2.8　Memory cards ············ 109
                3.3.2.9　Power supply ············ 110
                3.3.2.10　Stylus ············ 110
                3.3.2.11　Projector ············ 110
                3.3.2.12　Case ············ 110
        3.3.3　Mobile phone functions ············ 111
        3.3.4　Mobile phone software ············ 113
        3.3.5　Mobile phone processing power ············ 113
    3.4　Mobile phone networks ············ 114
        3.4.1　Mobile phone network architecture ············ 114
                3.4.1.1　User equipment ············ 115
                3.4.1.2　Access network ············ 115
                3.4.1.3　Core network ············ 115
        3.4.2　2G network architecture—GSM ············ 116
                3.4.2.1　GSM user equipment ············ 116
                3.4.2.2　GSM access network ············ 117
                3.4.2.3　GSM core network ············ 117
        3.4.3　2.5G network architecture—GPRS ············ 118
                3.4.3.1　GPRS user equipment ············ 119
                3.4.3.2　GPRS access network ············ 119
                3.4.3.3　GRPS core network ············ 119
        3.4.4　3G network architecture—UMTS ············ 120
                3.4.4.1　UMTS user equipment ············ 121
                3.4.4.2　UMTS access network ············ 121
                3.4.4.3　UMTS core network ············ 121
        3.4.5　4G network architecture ············ 122
        3.4.6　Mobile phone access technologies ············ 123
        3.4.7　Mobile phone access cells ············ 125
    3.5　Future of mobile phones ············ 126
    3.6　Mobile phone scenarios ············ 127
        3.6.1　Selecting a new mobile phone ············ 127
        3.6.2　Mobile phone usage ············ 127
        3.6.3　Mobile phone maintenance ············ 128

3.7	Mobile phone exercises		129
	3.7.1	Reading comprehension	129
	3.7.2	Reading and pronouncing acronyms	130
	3.7.3	Mobile phone essays	131
	3.7.4	Speaking exercises	131
	3.7.5	Identifying mobile phone parts	132
	3.7.6	Cloze	133
3.8	Mobile phone glossary		134

UNIT 4 MATHEMATICS 139

	MATHEMATICS KEYWORDS		140
4.1	Introduction		141
4.2	Branches of mathematics		141
4.3	Arithmetic		142
4.4	Algebra		143
4.5	Calculus		151
4.6	Trigonometry		153
4.7	Statistics		155
4.8	Probability		157
4.9	Logic		158
4.10	Discrete mathematics		164
4.11	Geometry		166
4.12	Mathematics exercises		174
	4.12.1	Identifying mathematics branches	174
	4.12.2	Reading numbers	174
	4.12.3	Reading mathematical expressions	175
	4.12.4	Describing geometric figures	176
	4.12.5	Drawing geometric figures	178
	4.12.6	Cloze	179

UNIT 5 PHYSICS 181

	PHYSICS KEYWORDS		182
5.1	Introduction		183
5.2	Branches of physics		183
5.3	Mechanics and thermodynamics		184
5.4	Electricity and magnetism		189
5.5	Optics and acoustics		197
5.6	Physics exercises		199
	5.6.1	Reading physics notation	199
	5.6.2	Identifying electronic symbols	200

　　　　　5.6.3　Cloze …… 201

UNIT 6　DATA COMMUNICATIONS …… **203**
　　DATA COMMUNICATIONS KEYWORDS …… 204
　　6.1　Introduction …… 205
　　6.2　Elements of data communications …… 205
　　6.3　Networks …… 206
　　6.4　Signals …… 208
　　6.5　Transmission …… 209
　　6.6　Encoding / modulation …… 213
　　6.7　Protocols …… 219
　　6.8　Equipment …… 222
　　6.9　Data communications exercises …… 224
　　　　　6.9.1　Reading comprehension …… 224
　　　　　6.9.2　Reading data communications acronyms …… 225
　　　　　6.9.3　Identifying data communications signals …… 226
　　　　　6.9.4　Cloze …… 227

APPENDIX …… **229**
　　1. Greek letters …… 230
　　2. The periodic table of the elements …… 231
　　3. Answers to questions …… 232

Epilogue …… **273**

UNIT 1

COMPUTERS

COMPUTER KEYWORDS

API	应用程序接口	Middleware	中间件
Battery	电池	Motherboard	主板 / 母板
BIOS	基本输入输出系统	Mouse	鼠标
Bluetooth	蓝牙	Notebook computer	笔记本
Browser	浏览器	Operating system	操作系统
Bus	总线	Optical drive	光盘机 / 光驱
Chip	芯片	Palmtop computer	掌上计算机
Chipset	芯片组	Peripheral	外围设备
Chip socket	芯片插座	Port	端口 / 接口
Computer case	计算机机箱	Power adapter	电源适配器
Core	核（心）	Power supply	供电 / 电源
CPU	（中央）处理器	Printer	打印机
CPU register	处理器寄存器	Programming language	程序设计语言
CPU cache	处理器超高速缓存	Resolution	分辨率
Cursor	光标	Scanner	扫描机
Desktop computer	台式机	Screen	屏幕 / 显示屏
Device driver	设备驱动程序	Server	服务器
Firmware	固件	Slot	插槽
FSB	前端总线	Software	软件
GPU	图形处理器	Software application	软件应用
GUI	图形用户接口	Software utility	软件公用程序
Hard disk	硬盘	SSD	固态磁盘
Hardware	硬件	Supercomputer	超级计算机
Icon	图标 / 像标	Tablet notebook	平板笔记本
IGP	整合显示芯片	Touchpad	触摸板
Interface	接口	Touchpad button	触摸板纽扣
I/O	输入 / 输出	USB	通用串行总线
Kernel	核心 / 核 / 内核	USB disk	U 盘
Keyboard	键盘	Video card	显示卡 / 显卡
LAN	局域网	Virtual memory	虚拟内存
Laptop computer	笔记本	Virtualization software	虚拟化软件
LCD monitor	液晶监视器	Virus	病毒
Mainframe	主机	Webcam	摄像头
Malware	恶意软件	WiFi	无线网络
Memory	存储 / 内存	Wireless	无线的

1.1 Introduction

Since its introduction into our daily lives about two decades ago, the computer has risen to become one of our daily life necessities. In today's society, a day without access to a computer leaves one feeling disconnected from the rest of the world, even feeling left behind. We use our computers to find out what is happening in our world, to keep in touch with friends, to work, to shop, to do research, to entertain ourselves, and all kinds of things.

1.2 Types of computers

Since the computer has to satisfy different kinds of requirements and environments, it has evolved into a few types such as the awesome number-crunching supercomputer, the corporate workhorse server, and the ubiquitous laptop. The different types of computers are listed in the following figure.

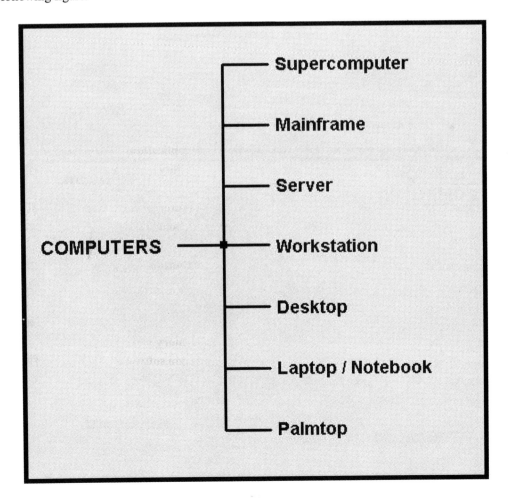

1.3 The personal computer

The personal computer has evolved into two main shapes, the desktop and the laptop (the Ultra Mobile Personal Computer [UMPC], the netbook, and the palmtop computer may also be thought of as derivations of the personal computer). The two figures below show the different components of the personal computer.

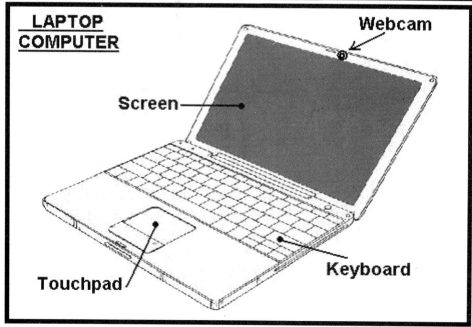

1.4 Computer components

A computer is made of hardware and software.

COMPUTER = HARDWARE + SOFTWARE

1.4.1 Computer hardware

The computer hardware mainly consists of the elements shown in the following figure.

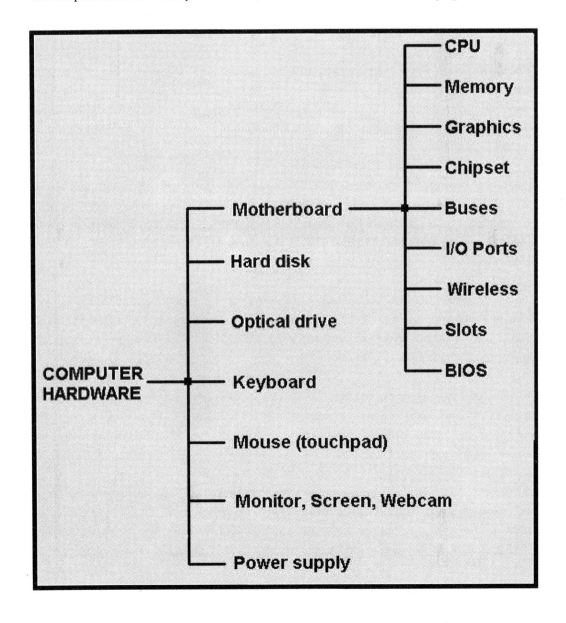

When talking about computer hardware, the motherboard, also called the main board, is the key component of a computer. It is a printed circuit board that holds all the main chips inside the computer. For example, the Central Processing Unit (CPU) is on the motherboard. The CPU could be directly soldered to the motherboard, or use a socket that is soldered to the motherboard.

The motherboard also holds the Dynamic Random Access Memory (DRAM) chips that are necessary to store data for quick access by the CPU. Another important chip on the motherboard is the Graphics Processing Unit (GPU), which is responsible for rendering graphics on the computer. And finally, another essential chip that resides on the motherboard is the Basic Input/Output System (BIOS) chip which makes the booting, i.e. starting, of a computer possible.

Since these different chips and others need to communicate with each other, the motherboard is printed with a bus, which is a set of wire circuits that connect all the chips. And in order to make sure the bus is used properly and efficiently, a chipset is used to control the bus.

In addition to chips, the motherboard may also contain slots, ports and jacks. Slots are used to insert additional hardware, such as a video card. Ports are used to connect the computer to peripherals such as printers. Jacks can be used for audio input and output, as well as for Local Area Network (LAN) connection. A recent LAN connectivity addition on the motherboard is wireless LAN chips.

Besides the motherboard, a computer includes one or more hard disks. The hard disk is the main, long-term, data storage place inside a computer. Over the years, the hard disk's physical size has shrunk while its capacity has increased tremendously. A recent addition to or rather competition to the Hard Disk Drive (HDD) is the Solid-State Drive (SSD), which uses flash memory and has no moving parts.

The next computer hardware component is the optical drive. The technology of the optical drive has kept improving up to the present where it allows for easy reading and writing of optical disks. Today's optical drives can read and write optical disks of various formats, from the pioneering CD-ROM to today's Blu Ray.

Powering all of the computer hardware is the role of the power supply. Today's computer supply is very convenient in that it can adapt to different countries' power sources such as 110V and 220V. In addition to the AC power supply, a laptop also uses a rechargeable battery that can last for up to a few hours.

The above computer hardware parts constitute the inner components of a computer. The outer hardware components constitute the interface between the computer and the user. These outer hardware components include the keyboard, which is used for input, the monitor or screen, which is used for display, and the mouse, which is used for easy navigation on the screen.

1.4.1.1 CPU

As its name implies, the Central Processing Unit (CPU) is the heart of the computer. This chip, also called a microprocessor, is the main chip on the motherboard. It operates by interpreting various instructions and executing them according to the basic fetch-decode-execute cycle illustrated below.

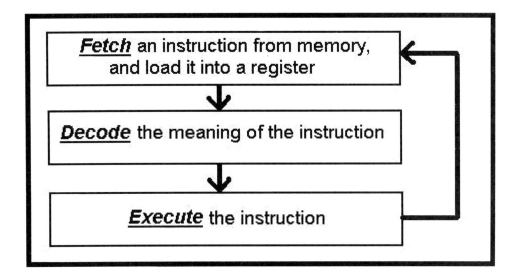

Over the years, as technology allowed for the cramming of more transistors on one chip, engineers integrated into the CPU previously external functions such as a math coprocessor to do floating-point calculations and cache memory to speed up data access. Today's CPU may consist of the following parts:

- **Control Unit (CU)** to control the function of the CPU

- **Arithmetic/Logic Unit (ALU)** to do arithmetic and logic operations

- **Floating Point Unit (FPU)** to handle decimal-number operations

- **Registers** to load instructions for decoding

- **Cache** for fast access to data

- **Clock** to synchronize the CPU operations

- **Interface** bus to interface with outside computer components

In most of today's computers, the CPUs come from two companies, Intel and AMD, with Intel holding a commanding market share. These two companies update their CPU offerings frequently. Based on Moore's Law, which states that the number of transistors that can be crammed onto a chip of a certain size can be doubled every eighteen months or so, one can get the feel for the breakneck speed at which the CPU technology is evolving. Intel and AMD are able to keep up with Moore's Law by using newer and newer chip manufacturing technologies that manipulate the chip circuit design at the nanometer level. For example, in early 2008 Intel started shipping CPUs using the 45-nanometer (nm) technology. Using the newer technology brings many benefits to the CPU. For example, the CPU circuits are smaller, thus allowing for faster communication between them. Also, the smaller size means that the CPU is more power efficient. Another added benefit of using the newer technology is that Intel and AMD can manufacture more chips per wafer, thus reducing their manufacturing costs. The following figure shows how chip manufacturing has been and will be keeping up with Moore's Law.

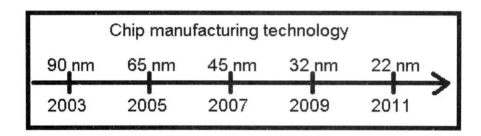

Since CPUs come from different manufacturers and each manufacturer produces so many families of CPUs, some performance benchmark tests have been devised to compare them. These tests compare the CPUs' processing power under different sets of conditions. As of early 2008, there was a consensus that Intel was the leader in laptop CPUs, whereas in the desktop CPU area, Intel and AMD were basically equally matched.

It used to be that the most popular way to evaluate a CPU was by its clocked speed in either megahertz (MHz) or gigahertz (GHz). However, that way of evaluating a CPU has been changed after the CPU speeds started reaching around 4 GHz and the CPU heat dissipation became a limiting factor. Since then, Intel and AMD started getting more performance from their CPUs by using multiple cores inside the CPU, and running the CPU at relatively lower speeds. In 2007, the two-core CPU became very common in laptops, and some desktops even featured four-core CPUs.

In addition to multiple cores, AMD engineered an additional way to boost the performance of its CPU architecture by integrating the memory controller inside the CPU. As of early 2008, Intel had not adopted such a design but was planning to use it in future CPU generations.

One example of a popular CPU for the laptop in early 2008 is the Intel Core 2 Duo. This CPU has two cores as the name "Duo" implies (some CPUs come with the designation "Quad", which means four cores). In early 2008, Intel started shipping this CPU using the newest technology of 45nm. A top-rated such CPU is the Intel Core 2 Duo T9300 running at 2.6 GHz.

The following figure shows the Intel Core 2 Duo CPU from two sides: the front view with the Intel logo and the back view with the pins.

The following figure shows the physical dimensions of the Intel Core 2 Duo CPU package.

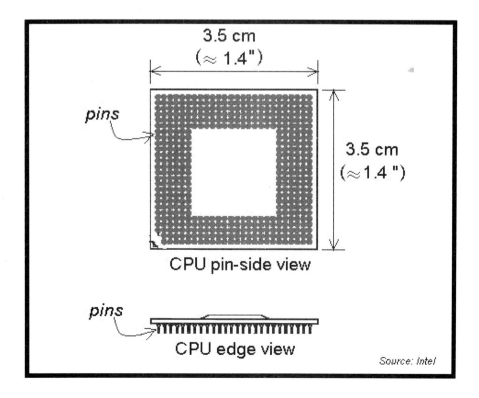

1.4.1.2 Memory

Dynamic Random Access Memory (DRAM) chips serve to hold data for quick access by the CPU. The term "dynamic" refers to the fact that this type of memory loses its data when the power is cut off. Because of its direct impact on a computer's performance, DRAM technology has continued to improve in order to keep up with the speed of the CPU. Today's most common generation of DRAM chips is Double-Data Rate DRAM, or just DDR for short (note that as of early 2008, DDR II was widely used and DDR III was also becoming available. DDR II and DDR III can also be written as DDR2 and DDR3). DDR DRAM is more efficient than previous generations of DRAM such as Synchronous DRAM (SDRAM) because it transfers data to the CPU on both edges of the clock signal, not just the rising edge.

However, data still cannot be transferred fast enough from the DRAM chips to the CPU. Therefore, a memory hierarchy has been adopted to try to remedy this situation. The memory hierarchy looks like the following pyramid.

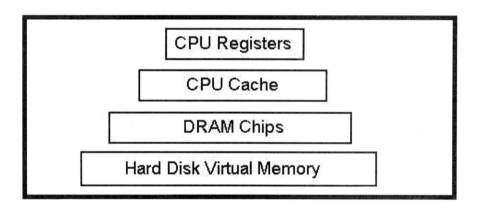

The higher the data is in the pyramid, the faster it can be accessed and processed by the CPU. The CPU registers and cache are inside the CPU itself and are the ideal places to hold the instructions that need to be processed by the CPU. However, their size is much smaller than that of the DRAM chips, where the program that needs to be executed resides, and they may not readily hold all the program instructions that the CPU needs. Thus, computer engineers have to come up with designs that try to fill the CPU cache and registers with the instructions that the CPU needs next. Also, the capacity of the DRAM chips themselves may not be enough sometimes and thus the computer operating system may have to create a virtual memory in the hard disk, which has much more capacity.

The amount of DRAM that needs to be installed in a computer depends on the operating system and applications requirements. A computer with two gigabytes (GB) of DRAM should be ideal for operating systems like Apple Mac OS X and Microsoft Vista. Memory chips are sold in modules such as the Dual In-line Memory Module (DIMM) and the Small Outline DIMM (SO-DIMM).

1.4.1.3 Graphics

When it comes to graphics processing, a computer will usually rely on either an Integrated Graphics Processor (IGP), or a separate Graphics-Processing Unit (GPU). The choice depends on what the computer is used for. If the computer is used for such tasks as word processing, Internet surfing, DVD-movie watching, and playing simple games, then an IGP is sufficient. However, if a computer is to be used for 3D graphics and video intensive applications such as computer games, then a GPU is a necessity. The figure below shows one of the latest Intel IGPs.

IGP example "Intel GMA x3100 for laptops"	
Maximum resolution	2048 x 1536 at 75 Hz
Display support HDMI S-Video DVI	Yes Yes Yes
HD video playback Blu-ray MPEG-2	Yes 1080p
Video memory	up to 384 MB
DirectX 10 support	Yes

Source: Intel

As can be seen in the above figure, this IGP supports a very high screen resolution of 2048 by 1536. It provides the latest interfaces to LCD monitors, such as High Definition Multimedia Interface (HDMI) and Digital Video Interface (DVI). It can play high-definition movies as provided on Blu-ray DVDs. It supports fast video memory. And it also supports DirectX 10, which is a standard in the computer game industry.

Thus, the latest IGPs are much more powerful than their predecessors. In addition, IGPs are much cheaper than GPUs. Still, for heavy-duty computer game playing, a GPU is required. The top of the line GPUs are provided by Nvidia and AMD (which acquired ATI). These GPUs require fast GDDR III video memory. In early 2008, an example of a top-of-the-line GPU that can handle any game is Nvidia GeForce 8600 with 512 MB of GDDR III.

1.4.1.4 Chipset and buses

The multiple chips on the motherboard communicate with each other using buses. A bus is a set of wire circuits connecting different chips and allowing for digital communication between them. Obviously, bus communication needs to be fast and efficient. The task to fulfill this job falls to the chipset. The following figure shows the chipset and bus configuration inside a computer.

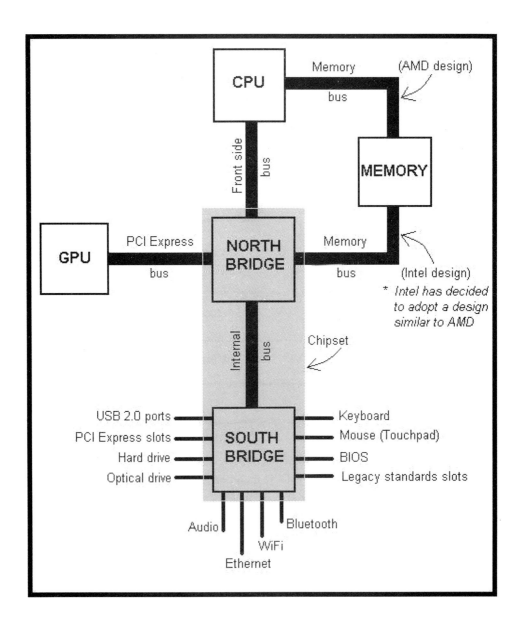

As can be seen in the above figure, a chipset in today's computers is made of a North Bridge and a South Bridge. The CPU and GPU connect directly to the North Bridge through buses. The memory also connects directly to the North Bridge in the Intel design. However, in AMD computers, the memory connects directly to the CPU.

The CPU connects to the North Bridge via the Front Side Bus (FSB), which is a 64-bit wide bus. The FSB in recent computers can run at speeds of 1333, 1066, or 800 MHz. In the case of AMD CPUs, this bus interface is called the Hypertransport Interface.

The memory bus connects directly to the North Bridge (Intel design) or CPU (AMD design). Thus, the memory controller is in the North Bridge for Intel designs and in the CPU for AMD designs. The AMD design has proven superior and Intel plans to adopt a similar design in the future. The memory bus is 64-bit wide; however, today's computers use double channels to double this width to 128 bits. The speed of DDR2 memory has been ticking up and at the present DDR2 is available in speeds of 800 / 667 / 533 MHz. Some DDR3 are becoming available in even higher speeds of 1066 and 1333 MHz.

Also connecting to the North Bridge is the GPU, if it is added to a computer. The GPU used to connect to the North Bridge via a dedicated high-speed interface called the Accelerated Graphics Port (AGP). However, in the latest computer designs, Peripheral Component Interconnect Express (PCI Express) has replaced AGP.

The South Bridge, also known as the I/O Controller Hub (ICH), interfaces with the computer's many I/O devices, ports and slots. The following table shows the South Bridge connections.

South Bridge Connections	
I/O device or Port or Slot	**Interface**
USB 2.0 ports	USB 2.0
PCI Express slots	PCI Express
Hard Drive, Optical Drive	SATA (Serial ATA) UATA (Ultra ATA)
Keyboard, Mouse	USB 2.0 LPC (Low Pin Count)
BIOS	SPI (Serial Peripheral Interface) LPC (Low Pin Count)
Legacy slots and ports	PCI
Audio	HD audio (High Definition audio)
Ethernet	PCI Express GLCI (Gigabit LAN Connect Interface)
WiFi	PCI Express
Bluetooth	USB 2.0

1.4.1.5 I/O ports and jacks

A computer's Input and Output (I/O) ports and jacks might include the following.

Port / Jack	Application	Port / Jack	Application
USB	Connects computer to peripheral devices such as printers.	VGA	Connects computer to CRT monitor. VGA stands for Video Graphics Adapter.
RJ45	Connects computer to Ethernet LAN.	S-Video	Connects computer to TV, or camcorder to computer.
DVI	Connects computer to LCD monitor. DVI stands for Digital Video Interface. DVI is being replaced by DisplayPort.	Composite in / RCA (red, white, yellow)	Connects camcorder to computer.
HDMI	Connects computer to LCD monitor. HDMI stands for High Definition Multimedia Interface. HDMI cable supports both video and audio.	Component Video Out (red, blue, green)	Connects computer to TV or High Definition TV (HDTV).
Firewire	Connects video camera (camcorder) to computer.	75 ohm	Connects TV to computer.
Audio	Connect computer to microphone, headphone and audio line.		

1.4.1.6 Wireless connectivity

A trend for computers to go wireless has been picking up speed the last few years. Today's computers come equipped with many different wireless technologies such as Infrared (IrDA), Bluetooth, WiFi, Wireless USB and soon Worldwide Interoperability for Microwave Access (WiMAX). The following table summarizes these wireless technologies.

Wireless technology	Characteristics
IrDA	IrDA was the earliest of these technologies to be integrated into the computer. It uses line of sight and is used for short distances of about a meter. IrDA can be used for example to connect a printer or PDA to a computer.
Bluetooth	Bluetooth works over short distances of about ten meters, but unlike IrDA, it doesn't require line of sight. It is gradually replacing IrDA. Bluetooth connections are referred to as Wireless Personal Area Networks (WPAN) or Wireless Desk Area Networks (WDAN). Bluetooth is used for example to connect a cell phone or camera to a computer.
WiFi	WiFi is presently the hottest of these wireless technologies. Its integration inside computers has already gone through a few iterations of 802.11 a / b / g, and now 802.11n. This latest version, 802.11n, uses many antennas in a technique called Multiple Input Multiple Output (MIMO) to offer very fast connection speeds. It covers distances of about one hundred meters and delivers speeds in the tens of megabits per second. It is used to set up Wireless LANs (WLAN). One example of WiFi is a WLAN at home connecting multiple computers and printers.
Wireless USB	Wireless USB is becoming available on some computers as of early 2008. It covers distances of about ten meters and supports high speeds of about one hundred megabits per second. Since it works over the same distances as Bluetooth, it may replace Bluetooth in some applications.
WiMAX	WiMAX can be used in Wireless Metropolitan Area Networks (WMAN) since it supports high speeds like WiFi but over distances of miles.

1.4.1.7 Slots

Slots allow for the connection of devices to the motherboard through buses. Since the latest and fastest bus is Peripheral Component Interconnect Express (PCI Express), new computers come with PCI Express slots although some computers also provide slots to support older buses such as PCI. PCI Express slots for desktop computers come in different sizes as shown in the figure below. The bigger the size of the slot, the higher the speed it delivers.

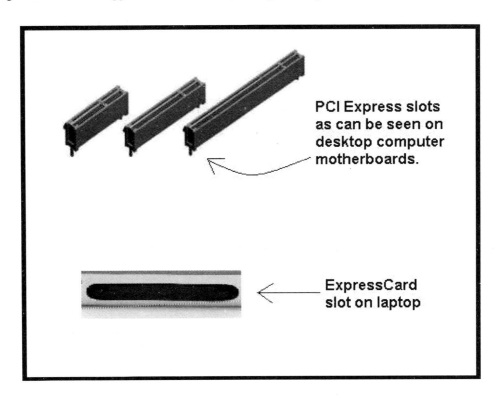

On laptops, ExpressCard slots have become common. Note that there are two ExpressCard sizes: ExpressCard/54 and ExpressCard/34. ExpressCard/34 is smaller than ExpressCard/54; however, ExpressCard/54 is more versatile since it not only accepts ExpressCard/34 but also supports more applications such as SmartCard and Compact Flash readers.

1.4.1.8 BIOS

Basic Input/Output System (BIOS), which is pronounced "bye-oss", is a chip on the motherboard and is essential when booting or starting a computer. Its operation is detailed in the software section.

1.4.1.9 Hard disk

A hard disk is used to store huge amounts of data ranging from the computer operating system to our personal data such as photos and music. The hard disk comes in different physical sizes, called form factors, such as 3.5 inches (3.5") and 2.5". The bigger form factor (3.5") is used in desktop computers whereas the smaller form factors (2.5" and smaller) are used in laptops.

A hard disk is made of a stack of platters, called disks, which are concentrically mounted on the same axis called a spindle. The disks hold data on both sides. These disks spin at very high rates, currently at 5400 revolutions per minute (rpm) and 7200 rpm. Each disk is logically divided into tracks, which are concentric paths on the surface of the disk, and each track is divided into segments called sectors. In order to read the data from the disks, a special mechanical head hovers over the disk and moves over the tracks as illustrated in the figure below.

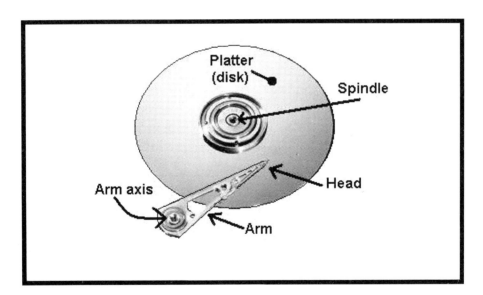

Hard disks could be internal or external to the computer. Some computers may be equipped with more than one hard disk. Capacities of hard disks keep rising to meet the users' insatiable storage needs. As of early 2008, available capacities for laptop computers range from 120 gigabytes (GB) to 500 GB. For desktop computers, the capacity reaches the terabyte (TB) level.

The hard disk interface with the motherboard and the CPU is important since most of a computer user's data resides on the hard disk. The latest hard disk interface is called Serial Advanced Technology Attachment (SATA) and allows for high data transfer rates.

A recent competition to the Hard Disk Drive (HDD) has been the Solid State Drive (SSD), which is made of flash memory and does not contain any moving mechanical parts. SSDs are much more expensive than HDDs. In early 2008, some SSD capacities reached 120 GB.

1.4.1.10 Optical drive

The optical drive serves to read and write various types of optical discs in various types of formats. Optical discs could be single sided, double sided, one-layered, and multi-layered. A double-sided disc has twice the capacity of a single-sided disc. A multi-layered disc holds much more capacity than a single-layered disc. Obviously, a double-sided, multi-layered disc has the highest capacity.

Optical discs hold data in a variety of formats, from the early Compact Disc – Read Only Memory (CD-ROM) to the latest Blu-ray Digital Versatile Disc (DVD). The following table shows these disc formats.

Format	Characteristics
CD-ROM CD-R CD-RW	CD-ROM (pronounced c-d-rom) was the earliest form of pre-recorded optical disc media. CD-R (pronounced c-d-r) stands for Compact Disc Recordable and was the first format of blank optical discs that the user could record on. A CD-R can only be burned, or recorded on, once. CD-RW (pronounced c-d-r-w) stands for Compact Disc ReWritable and can be recorded on time and time again. The capacity of these discs is about 700 MB.
DVD-ROM DVD-RAM DVD-R DVD-RW DVD+R DVD+RW	DVD-ROM (pronounced d-v-d-rom) is used for pre-recorded media, such as software from vendors. DVD-RAM (pronounced d-v-d-ram) can be used for multiple recordings just like a hard disk, but is not a popular format. DVD-R (pronounced d-v-d-dash-r) was the first popular format for blank DVDs. DVD-RW (pronounced d-v-d-dash-r-w) can be burned multiple times. DVD+R (pronounced d-v-d-plus-r) and DVD+RW (pronounced d-v-d-plus-r-w) are more efficient than their predecessors DVD-R and DVD-RW. The capacity of these DVD discs is about 4.7 GB for single-sided, one-layered discs.
Blu-ray DVD	Blu-ray is the latest DVD format. Its capacity is about 50 GB for a dual-layer disc.

As of early 2008, many computers come equipped with a "SuperMulti" optical drive that supports all the optical disc formats up to Blu-ray, that is DVD+R/RW, DVD-R/RW, DVD-RAM, DVD-ROM, CD-R/RW and CD-ROM. Some optical drives support all formats, including Blu-ray.

1.4.1.11 Keyboard, touchpad and mouse

The keyboard and mouse serve as the computer user's input interface. Laptops use a touchpad (also called trackpad) to replace the mouse. The figure below shows a typical keyboard and touchpad layout for a laptop computer. The keyboard consists of typewriter keys, cursor control or arrow keys, functions keys and other keys. These other keys may represent an operating system or some applications. The touchpad comes with two buttons, a left one and a right one.

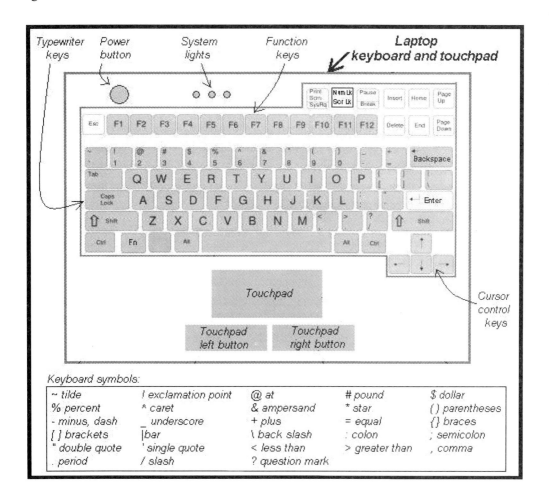

Some keyboards use an ergonomic design that is different from the traditionally rectangular design in order to comfortably conform to the user's hands. Also, many keyboards have gone wireless by using Bluetooth.

The mouse design has changed radically as the mouse has gone wireless too, using Bluetooth, and adopted ergonomic designs such as touch-sensitive technology under a uniform shell that responds to the user's finger pressure. In some designs, a mouse can also serve as a remote control or laser pointer.

1.4.1.12 Monitor, screen and webcam

The desktop monitor and laptop screen sizes have moved from the old standard aspect ratio of 4 to 3 (4:3) to the wide-screen ratio of 16:9 or 16:10. The wide-screen ratio makes for better viewing of movies since the whole screen is filled. The screens are available in sizes ranging from 11" to 20" and even higher.

The resolution has also gone up, now reaching up to 1920 by 1200 (1920 x 1200) and higher. The computer user can use the operating system to change the resolution of the display; however, for best viewing results the resolution should be set to the native resolution of the screen. Note that resolution sizes are referred to with different names. For example, 1920 x 1200 is called Wide-screen Ultra eXtended Graphics Array (WUXGA), and 1280 x 800 is referred to as WXGA.

For desktop computers, both the case and the monitor should be equipped with DVI, DisplayPort or HDMI ports for best results. DVI, DisplayPort and HDMI pass the digital signal from the graphics processor to the screen without any conversion to analog as with the old VGA. This all-digital process results in crisper and better displays on the screen. Also, for better viewing, some LCD screens come equipped with LED backlighting.

Webcams, short for web cameras, have become an essential part of the computer in this web age. These tiny cameras come either as separate units or as integrated parts of the computer. For example, some laptops have a webcam mounted above the screen. The capabilities of the webcams now allow them to not only take still photos but also generate good-quality video. As an example, a webcam may have a still-picture resolution of about two megapixels, and can capture high-definition video at 960 x 720 and 30 frames per second. Adding to the convenience and practicality of webcams, some of them are wireless.

1.4.1.13 Power supply

Desktop and laptop computers come equipped with integrated power supplies. In addition, laptops include lithium-ion batteries that allow them to be portable and run without an Alternating Current (AC) power supply for a few hours.

The AC power supply varies around the world and is mainly available as about 220 volts (V) at 50 Hertz (Hz) or 110V at 60 Hz. For convenience, computers are equipped with universal power adapters that can work with either AC power supply.

1.4.1.14 Computer hardware trends

The computer hardware keeps changing and improving over time. Some of the trends that are emerging or expected to happen are outlined in the following table.

Hardware	Future developments
CPU GPU Chipset	■ Using Moore's Law as a guide, the CPU will be able to incorporate more cores than the presently available two and four. ■ Intel is planning to follow AMD's lead and move the memory controller from the North Bridge to the CPU, thus managing the memory directly from the CPU. ■ Intel and AMD are planning to integrate the GPU inside the CPU by 2009. In this case, the North Bridge would disappear and the CPU will connect directly to the South Bridge.
Memory	DDR2 will be replaced by the much faster DDR3.
HDD	The HDD will still be the king of storage for some time to come as new multimedia applications require tremendous amounts of storage, but SSD is starting to be adopted. Given the steep price decline trends of flash memory, SSD will become commonly adopted at the end of this decade.
Wireless	The computer is going wireless. With Bluetooth, Wireless USB, WiFi-n and WiMAX, computer cables will become history. Even recharging laptops will become wireless.
Laptop Battery	The search is on to replace lithium-ion batteries. The holy grail is for a laptop to run for a whole workday on a single battery charge.
LCD	LCD is king of the hill now, but newer display technologies are being developed. The technology with the most promise is OLED (Organic LED), which allows for thinner and more energy-efficient displays.

1.4.1.15 Computer hardware example

The following table shows the hardware configuration of a top-of-the-line laptop in early 2008.

\multicolumn{3}{c}{COMPUTER HARDWARE CONFIGURATION}		
Component	**Configuration**	**Remarks**
CPU	Intel Core 2 Duo, T9300	AMD and others also make CPUs
Chipset and bus	Intel 965 chipset	AMD and others also make chipsets
Memory	2 Gigabytes DDR II RAM	DDR III is available but expensive
GPU	Nvidia GeForce 8600 with 512 MB	AMD (former ATI) also makes GPUs
Ports	USB, Firewire, HDMI, DVI	Wireless USB is available
Slots	PCI Express card	Some slots accept flash cards such as SD
LAN connectivity	WiFi abgn, Ethernet jack	WiFi-n standard will be ratified in 2008
Audio jacks	Headphone, line in , line out	Microphone is also provided
Hard disk	250 GB SATA HDD	SSD is available in up to 160 GB
Optical drive	Super Multi	Blu-ray drives are available
Screen	Wide screen 15.4″	Wide screen is now the popular format
Power supply	Universal power adapter, Battery	Supports 110V at 60Hz to about 220V at 50Hz. Battery lasts for about three hours

1.4.2 Computer software

The computer software can be diagrammed as shown in the following figure.

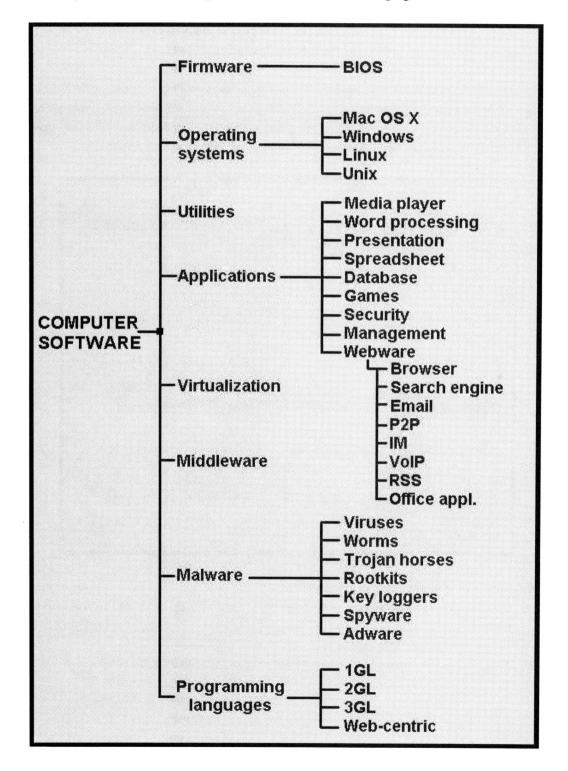

1.4.2.1 BIOS

The BIOS firmware serves to boot up, i.e. start, a computer correctly. After the power button is pressed to turn on the computer, the following tasks happen in sequence.

- The BIOS performs a Power-On Self Test (POST) to ascertain that the computer's crucial components such as the CPU and memory are functioning properly.

- The BIOS displays a startup screen. At this stage, the computer user can, if necessary, access the system configuration by quickly depressing one of the function keys, such as F1, or the Escape (ESC) key. The BIOS system configuration includes many features that can be edited such as the following list of features from a BIOS made by Award:

Standard CMOS Features	Power BIOS Features
Advanced BIOS Features	Load Fail-Safe Defaults
Advanced Chipset Features	Load Optimized Defaults
Integrated Peripherals	Set Supervisor Password
Power Management Setup	Set User Password
PnP/PCI/PCI-E Configurations	Save and Exit Setup
PC Health Status	Exit Without Saving

- The BIOS identifies the boot drive, such as the hard disk, and finds the first piece of the Operating System, the bootstrap loader program. The BIOS then hands over control to this program.

- The Operating System loads up into memory and takes over control of the computer.

1.4.2.2 Operating system

The Operating System (OS) is the computer software that makes it possible for the user to use the computer hardware. Without an Operating System to bring it to life, the hardware of a computer would be a mere and useless assembly of electronic parts. The Operating System controls and manages all the hardware in the computer and makes it available to the user. In addition, the Operating System serves as the foundation for all the other software that is added to a computer to give it more functionality. The figure below shows the Operating System's position relative to the user, other software and the computer hardware.

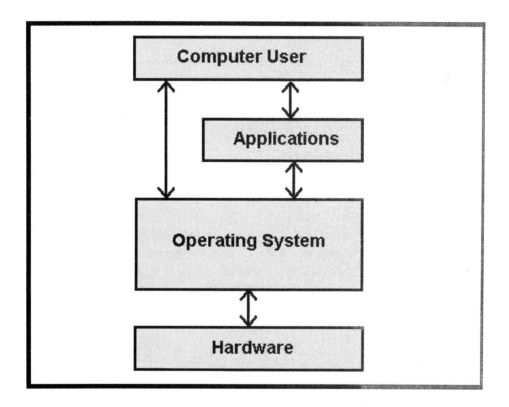

Operating Systems are divided into the following four categories.

- *Real-Time OS*. Examples of this type of OS are found in scientific devices and mobile phones. This OS typically has a specific and limited functionality.
- *Single-user, single-task OS*. Examples of this OS can be found in most mobile phones, although some smartphones allow for multitasking.
- *Single-user, multitask OS*. This is the mainstream OS for personal computers. Examples include Apple OS X and Windows.
- *Multi-user OS*. This OS can be found in servers, mainframes and supercomputers. Unix is one such OS.

Operating Systems have evolved, so as to improve their computing power, by incorporating new technologies such as:

- *Multi-threading.* This technology allows an OS to process a program's different parts simultaneously and not sequentially.
- *Multitasking.* This technology allows an OS to run multiple programs simultaneously.
- *Multiprocessing.* This technology allows an OS to run using multiple CPUs or multiple cores within a CPU.

An OS for today's personal computers is a complex and huge bundle of software that can reach into the millions of lines of code. An OS has many components, the main three being the following.

- *Kernel.* This is the heart of the OS and performs such functions as managing the hardware.
- *File system.* This is the part that specifies the storage-media formatting.
- *Device drivers.* This is the part that allows the OS to control the computer hardware.
- *Graphical User Interface (GUI).* This is the part that provides an interface to the user.

An OS mainly performs the following tasks.

- Provide a Graphical User Interface (GUI) to the user to facilitate the user's navigation through all the computer functions.
- Manage the usage of computer resources, such as the CPU and memory, among the different software programs or processes that may request these resources.
- Perform file services such as keeping track of file locations in directories and doing file backups if so programmed.
- Act as a platform for any additional software that is installed on the computer.
- Allow access to and use of peripheral devices.
- Allow networking.

The competition for the personal computer OS has long been dominated by Microsoft. Starting with Disk Operating System (DOS), Microsoft used its business acumen, fierce competitive tactics, and marketing to dominate the field. After it vanquished PC-DOS and IBM's OS/2 in the early years of competition, it established a dominating market share that bordered on monopoly. This situation continued until recent years when new challenges started posing tremendous threats to Microsoft's dominance. These threats manifested themselves in three forms. First, viable or even better alternatives, such as Apple OS X and Linux, started attracting more users. Second, virtualization broke the one-OS monopoly on a computer and allowed users more choices. Third, the need for a computer OS was put into question by the emergence of the Internet cloud computing.

As of early 2008, the popular OS choices included Apple OS X, Windows XP and Vista, and the many varieties of Linux such as Ubuntu.

1.4.2.3 Utilities

Software utilities are programs that add to the functionality or efficiency of an OS. Since no OS, whether newly created or updated, is perfect, utilities will always continue to be invented. Usually, existing utilities are integrated into the OS and become part of it in its following iteration. Since utilities are usually created by many entities other than the OS developer, they help the OS developer with new ideas and technologies that make the OS better with each OS update.

1.4.2.4 Applications

Next to the OS, applications constitute the next most important part of the computer software. Software applications make the computer an essential tool in our daily lives. Some of the most important applications are listed below.

Application	Description
Media Player	A media player, such as Windows Media Player, allows the user to listen to music, and watch movies and videos.
Word processing	One such application is Microsoft Word, which allows the user to create, edit and print documents.
Presentation	One such application is Microsoft Powerpoint, which allows the user to create, edit and print slides.
Spreadsheet	One such application is Microsoft Excel, which allows the user to create, edit and print spreadsheets, such as accounting spreadsheets.
Database	This application allows for the structured storage and efficient retrieval of all kinds of data such as customer information.
Games	This is a very popular application, especially among younger users. This application can be either standalone or online.
Security	This application is essential in protecting the computer from outside risks such as viruses.
Management	This application can be useful in managing groups of computers.

In recent years, as the Web became popular, Web applications started becoming an alternative to desktop standalone applications. For example, instead of buying and using Microsoft Word on one's personal computer, a user could go online and use one of the many online word-processing applications. Many such online word-processing applications come free of charge. A list of online applications, or Webware, follows below.

Webware	Description
Browser	This application, such as Firefox or IE Explorer, allows the user to surf the Internet and use all of the Webware listed below.
Search engine	This application allows the user to find any kind of information online by simply entering a search string. Examples of search engines are Google and Yahoo. In China, Baidu is the leading search engine.
Email	This application allows the user to keep in touch with friends, relatives, colleagues, customers and so on.
P2P	This application, which stands for Peer-to-Peer, allows users to efficiently share and download online content such as music and movies.
IM	This application, which stands for Instant Messaging, allows users to contact each other in real time. Examples of IM applications include QQ and MSN messenger.
VoIP	This application, which stands for Voice-Over-IP, has revolutionized the way users make phone calls by routing the calls to the Internet instead of the traditional telephone system. Using VoIP applications, such as Skype, users can talk freely to friends around the world, simply by using their computer microphone and speakers.
RSS	This application, which stands for Really Simple Syndication, provides the user with an automatic and summary update of a website's changes.
Office Applications	These are the traditional word processing, presentation and spreadsheet applications which have been ported online. Google provides such online applications. Realizing the threat to its traditional model of standalone applications on the desktop, Microsoft has also moved to offer some versions of its applications online.

1.4.2.5   Virtualization

Virtualization software allows a computer to run more than one OS. For example, a computer could run Linux and Windows, or Apple Mac OS and Windows. This is possible because the virtualization software, which is functionally located between the hardware and the Operating Systems, provides a platform called a Virtual Machine on top of which different Operating Systems can run, as illustrated in the figure below.

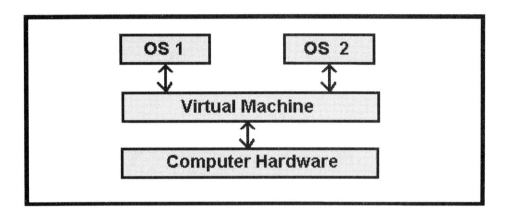

1.4.2.6 Middleware

Middleware is software that allows different applications on separate computer systems to communicate and work with each other. Such systems could be using different hardware and running different Operating Systems. On each system, Middleware lies between the application and the OS. Middleware integrates such systems by presenting a uniform set of Application Programming Interfaces (API) that applications can be written to.

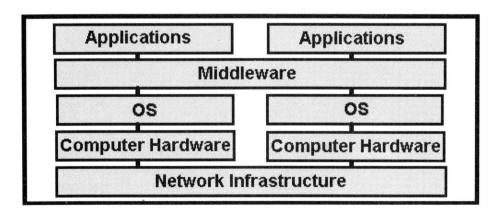

1.4.2.7 Malware

Malware, which stands for malicious software, is harmful software that negatively affects the functioning of a computer, destroys or corrupts data, steals personal information, or subjects the user to unsolicited advertisements. The different types of Malware are listed in the table below.

Malware	Description
Virus	A virus is a software program that spreads from computer to computer via the Internet (email, IM, downloads) or some other methods such as USB disks. It can corrupt or destroy data when a user runs or opens it.
Worm	A worm is a special type of virus that can replicate itself on a user's computer and infect many files. In addition, a worm takes advantage of networks to automatically spread to and infect other networked computers.
Trojan Horse	A Trojan Horse, as its name applies, is a harmful program that is hidden inside a seemingly useful program. Once the seemingly useful program is open, the Trojan Horse can cause damage to the computer such as by deleting data or opening a backdoor to hackers.
Rootkit	A Rootkit is malicious software that runs whenever a computer is booted up. Since it becomes active before the computer has fully booted up, it is hard to detect.
Key logger	A Key Logger is a program that logs, or copies, all the keystrokes of a computer user.
Spyware	Spyware is malicious software that steals the user's information and secretly transmits it to some entity on the Internet. It usually comes disguised inside what seem to be useful software downloads.
Adware	Adware is a type of Spyware that does some annoying things such as change a person's default webpage and display unwanted advertisements.

1.4.2.8 Programming languages

Programming languages are used to write all kinds of software programs, such as applications and Operating Systems. There is a multitude of programming languages, but not all are popular. As can be expected, programming languages have evolved over time. There is not a single-standard way to classify them, but one such way could be as follows.

Programming Language	Description
First-Generation Language (1GL)	The first programming language was the Machine Language. This type of language was used, for example, to manually program the early Intel 8088 microprocessor. Machine Language uses numeric notation, such as hexadecimal notation. Obviously, this kind of programming is very tedious and not practical. But Machine Language is always required, even now, because it is the language that the processor uses and understands.
Second-Generation Language (2GL)	In order to make programming easier, a second-generation programming language was invented. It is called Assembly Language. Assembly Language uses mnemonic instructions instead of numeric notations. Some examples of Assembly Language instructions include MOV, which stands for "move", ADD, which is self-explanatory, STA for "store" and so on.
Third-Generation Languages (3GL)	Machine Language and Assembly Language are both considered low-level languages, and are machine-dependent. They are not user-friendly to the programmer. Thus, third-generation or high-level languages were invented. These 3GLs use a syntax that makes it relatively easier to build larger programs that can run on different machines. The most popular 3GL languages include Fortran, Basic, Pascal, C, C++, and C#. Fortran is suitable for writing scientific and engineering applications. Pascal is more structured than Fortran and thus suitable for more types of applications. C++ and C# are called Object-Oriented Programming (OOP) languages.
Web-centric Languages	With the advent of the Internet, new application paradigms surfaced and there was a need for newer programming ideas. The Internet, or rather Web, led to the invention of Hyper-Text Markup Language (HTML), eXtensible Markup Language (XML), Java and Javascript. HTML and XML are used to program Web pages. Java and Javascript are used to program the interactions between the user's computer and Internet servers.

Before a program written in a high-level or Assembly language is executed on a CPU, the program needs to be translated into the Machine Language that the CPU understands. This process is illustrated in the following figure.

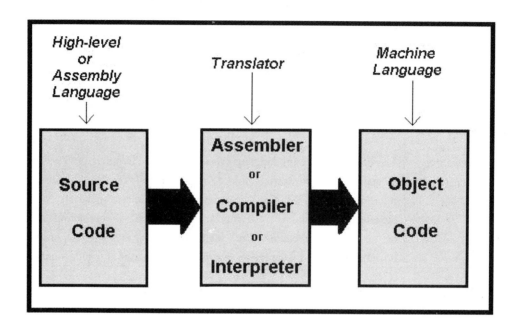

Assembly Language is translated into Machine Language using an Assembler. High-level languages can be translated using either a Compiler or an Interpreter, or sometimes both. A Compiler translates the whole program into Machine Language binary code. An Interpreter, on the other hand, translates the program one statement at a time. Note that in the case of Java, the translation process consists of two steps: first, the source program is compiled into an intermediate code called "byte-code", second, this "byte-code" is converted into Machine Language by the Java Virtual Machine.

When using a high-level language to develop a program, especially a large one, a programmer needs to consider how to approach the task and carry it out. The figure below illustrates one such approach. Note that an algorithm is a logical step-by-step plan of how to write a program.

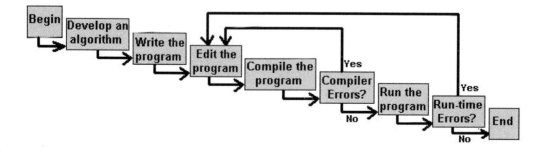

1.5 Computer scenarios

1.5.1 Selecting a new computer

When selecting a new computer, the user should consider many factors. A list of such factors and their explanations follow below.

Computer type. Computers come in mainly two form factors, desktops and laptops. Recently, laptops have become the most popular form factor because of their portability, small space requirement and improved processing power. Some laptops can even serve as desktop computer replacements. There are still some niches where the desktop computer remains king as in the extreme computer gaming area where the heat dissipation requires big fans and heat sinks. Still, for most users, as in the education field, a laptop is a perfect choice.

Processing power. The processing power of a computer is a main consideration when selecting a new computer. It used to be that a computer's processing power referred to the speed of the CPU. Since the CPU speeds have reached some upper limit of around 4 GHz, nowadays a computer's processing power refers to the CPU speed, other CPU technologies such as the number of cores, and the chipset architecture. All of these three elements contribute to the raw power of a computer. As an example, in early 2008, a laptop computer with excellent processing power and using an Intel design would have a dual-core CPU running at about 2.6GHz and a 965 chipset.

Memory. The more memory a computer has, the faster it can operate. A good choice of memory capacity to run today's Operating Systems is about 1 to 4GB, with 2GB being average.

Graphics. Given the switch in information processing from pure text to today's rich multimedia, the graphics processing power of a computer has become very important. For usual computer usage such as word processing, spreadsheet tabulating, slide presentation, Internet surfing, basic picture editing, and simple game playing, an Integrated Graphics Processor (IGP) is sufficient. However, for intensive computer game playing, a Graphics Processing Unit (GPU) is necessary. A GPU needs fast memory such as GDDR3, and the more the better. As an example, in early 2008, a laptop with excellent graphics processing power would have an Nvidia GeForce 8600 GPU with 512 MB of GDDR3 memory.

Storage. The storage needs of the computer user have risen exponentially as the user needs to store all kinds of information such as documents, music and video. The hard disk is the main storage place. As of early 2008, the highest hard disk capacity for laptops reached 500GB, while that for desktops reached into the terabyte level of 1TB, i.e. 1000GB. A recent storage alternative is the Solid-State Drive (SSD), which uses flash memory for storage instead of the magnetic platters used in hard disks. The SSD is very expensive when compared to the hard disk drive, but it has found a niche in the ultra-light laptops. As the price of flash memory tumbles, the SSD will become a more viable and common storage option. As of early 2008, the highest SSD capacity reached about 120GB.

Optical drive. Optical disc formats have changed from the early CD-ROM to today's Blu-ray, and allow for both reading and burning discs. A good optical drive, for example the SuperMulti, must accommodate all the formats such as CD-ROM, CD-R/RW, DVD-ROM, DVD-RAM, DVD-R/RW, and DVD+R/RW. Since Blu-ray is the newest high-definition format, more and more optical drives will support it also.

Connectivity. A computer needs to connect to all kinds of peripherals. Traditionally, ports served such a purpose. Today's most common port is the USB port. A computer should have at least two USB ports. In addition, a computer must have a DVI or HDMI port to connect to a monitor. Another high-speed port available mainly on Apple computers is Firewire. A recent trend in connectivity has been to go wireless so as to do away with all those messy connecting cables. A computer should support WiFi-n and Bluetooth connectivity. Wireless USB has become available and may become more common in the future. An additional wireless connectivity that is expected to be added to computers is WiMAX, which works over longer distances than and will complement WiFi-n. Besides ports, a computer needs to offer slot connectivity. A desktop computer may offer a few PCI-Express slots to add cards such as video cards. On laptops, a slot such as an ExpressCard/34 or ExpressCard/54 must be provided.

Usage. When selecting a computer, a user needs to consider what applications the computer will be used for. For usual applications such as word processing, Internet surfing and movie watching, an average-priced computer is adequate. However, for computer users who want the latest in advanced gadgetry, nothing can satisfy their appetite but a top-of-the-line computer.

Operating System. Microsoft Windows dominated this area for a long time. For a variety of reasons, more and more users have started switching to Apple Mac OS X and Linux. For users in the education, publication and art fields, Apple offers a superior choice. In addition, since adopting the Intel hardware for its computer architecture, Apple has become an equal or better choice to Windows in any area, except in the gaming area. Linux usually offers the cheapest alternative but still lags behind in adoption among common users. As the Linux GUI becomes more standardized, and more applications are ported to it, Linux will command a bigger share of the market.

Screen size. A computer screen should be wide-screen. The old standard aspect ratio of 4:3 has been dropped. A wide-screen allows for better viewing of movies since the whole screen is used in this case. Screens come in different sizes. The average size is about 15 inches. Bigger sizes reach up to 22 inches. Some ultra-portable laptops have screens of about 11, 12 or 13 inches.

Weight. When selecting a laptop, weight is a major consideration. No one wants to lug around a heavy piece of hardware. Some recent laptops, such as the Apple MacBook Air, are very light and so thin that they can fit into an office vanilla envelope.

Style. The computer industry has become more and more of a commodity business, especially in the low-end market. However, in the high-end market, good design can still command high prices. Apple and Sony excel in computer styling and some users are willing to pay higher prices to acquire such computers. A good design doesn't necessarily mean adding lots of buttons, ports, lights and color to a computer box. For example, Apple offers what may be characterized as minimalist designs, but very stylish ones.

After-sale service. A user should consider the after-sale service of a brand. In general, top brands offer good but not cheap service. For example, computer companies offer to extend the warranty service period, but at a price. Also, computer companies offer call-center service, but the user is required to pay.

Price. The good thing about computer technology is the constantly declining price trend. New technology, such as the latest CPU, may sell at a premium when first introduced. However, after about a few months, it will experience steep price declines. As long as the user is not chasing after the latest and greatest in gadgetry, the user can find not only affordable but great computer deals. Spending about $1,000 should get a user a laptop computer that can satisfactorily handle any task. Users, for whom price is not a primary concern, can shell out about $3,000 for the latest in laptops.

1.5.2 Selecting a gaming computer

Avid computer game users need to properly select their computers because computer games are power-intensive applications and need the most powerful of computer platforms. One of the first requirements of a good computer for playing games is a fast graphics-processing engine. This means a fast Graphics Processing Unit (GPU). The Integrated Graphics Processor (IGP) that comes with some chipsets is inadequate and can only handle simple games. For real rendering and enjoyment of computer games, a GPU is necessary. Some computer systems employ two GPUs and make them work in tandem for even better performance. A fast GPU generates a lot of heat that without dissipation can burn the computer. Thus, cooling is of the essence. Video cards come with all kinds of cooling systems such as fans and elaborate heat sinks. A GPU also needs access to the fastest of memory. As of early 2008, the best of video memory is GDDR3. This kind of computer setup is usually provided in desktops since most laptops at the present are too small to accommodate so much heat dissipation equipment. Still, some computer manufacturers have provided laptops that are especially designed for playing computer games.

In addition to the GPU and related equipment, the best of gaming computers use the latest and most powerful of CPUs. In early 2008, these gaming computers use CPUs that are clocked at the highest speeds, or CPUs that combine high speed and multi-cores, such as two or four cores.

Some game players are not satisfied even with the most powerful of CPUs and always find ways to over-clock them to get more performance.

As far as software platforms for playing computer games, Windows is presently recognized as the best platform because of its huge library of computer games and its support for the latest in graphics interfaces such as DirectX11.

1.5.3 Computer usage

Computers allow users to do many things and some of the most common computer applications include the following:

- Generating, editing, printing and storing all kinds of data. Examples include word processing and graphics editing.
- Surfing the Internet. Examples of online activities include browsing web pages, emailing, chatting, searching for information and downloading content.
- Playing computer games. Examples include standalone computer games or online computer games.
- Downloading and watching movies.
- Downloading and listening to music.
- Storing all kinds of information, such as work data or personal photos and videos.
- Connecting to and sharing information with peripherals such as USB disks, digital cameras, video cameras and mobile phones.

1.5.4 Computer maintenance

Users should regularly maintain their computers to keep them functioning properly and efficiently. Some of the maintenance activities include the following:

- Backing up important data from the computer to such external media as optical discs, USB disks and external hard disks.
- Downloading and installing the latest Operating System (OS) updates. Some Operating Systems allow this updating to be done automatically via the Internet.
- Updating to the latest BIOS firmware.
- Updating to the latest device drivers from hardware manufacturers.
- Updating the anti-malware software to guard against the ever-changing malware.
- Deleting unnecessary files to free up disk space.
- Running the disk de-fragmenting software to recover disk space and for better efficiency.
- Cleaning dust from the monitor screen for clearer viewing.
- Cleaning dust from the computer's fan area to maintain good cooling air flow.

1.5.5 Setting up a wireless home network

The availability of wireless technology allows users to clear their desks from all the cable clutter and to move the computer, such as a laptop, freely around the house. Computers come available with wireless technologies like Infrared (IrDA), Bluetooth, WiFi-n and Wireless USB. These wireless technologies allow the computer to connect wirelessly to such peripherals as printers, scanners, digital cameras and mobile phones (if these peripherals support the wireless technology of course). In addition, a user could connect multiple computers at home in a wireless LAN using WiFi. By adding a wireless router to the wireless LAN and connecting this router to an ADSL modem, the user will be able to surf the Internet from any of the computers anywhere at home.

1.5.6 Printing a document

In order to print a document on a printer, a user could for instance open a word processor such as MS Word and then open the document in question. The user could then simply click on the print button in the toolbar. In order to control the printing process in detail, the user could instead click on the file menu and choose the print option from the drop-down menu. A dialog box will open and allow the user to control such things as what printer to use, what pages to print, how many copies to print and so on.

There is a much simpler alternative where the user does not need to open a word processor to print a document. The user simply drags the icon of the document to be printed onto the icon of the printer.

1.5.7 Going online

If a user wants to go online to access the Internet, the following steps could be used:

- ◆ Turn on the computer and wait for it to boot up.
- ◆ Make sure there is a network connection. If it is a dial-up connection, the computer needs to be connected to a dial-up modem. If it is a broadband connection, the computer needs to be connected to broadband modem such as an ADSL modem. If it is a wireless connection, the computer needs to be connected via WiFi to a wireless router that is connected to a broadband modem.
- ◆ Double click on the browser icon, such as the Firefox or IE icon. The browser will open to the default web page. The user can then start surfing the Internet.

1.5.8 Scanning

If a user needs to digitize and store inside the computer some old paper copies of documents or photos, the user could use a scanner as follows:

- Turn on the scanner and the computer and ascertain that the two are connected.
- Put the paper copy in the scanner and close the scanner's lid.
- Open a graphics application, such as Photoshop, that allows for importing from peripherals such as scanners.
- In the graphics application file menu, select the option of importing from the scanner.
- In the dialog box that opens, select the desired options such as the color and size of the scanning.
- Preview the scan, then scan and save the scanned image in the computer.

1.5.9 Writing a computer program

If a user needs to write a computer program using a high-level language such as Java, the user could follow the following steps:

- Come up with an algorithm of how to write the program. The algorithm is a logical-flow diagram summarizing the computer code steps.
- Use an Integrated Development Environment (IDE) software package such as JCreator to write the program code.
- Edit the program code for any errors.
- Compile the program. If there are compiler errors, then go back to the editing step above. If there are no errors, then proceed to the following step.
- Run the program. If there are run-time errors, then go back to the editing step above. If there are no run-time errors, then proceed to the following step.
- Add documentation to the program, as needed, in order to facilitate any future revisions or enhancements to the program.

1.5.10 Comparing computer companies

The computer landscape keeps changing rapidly through technology and corporate developments. As of early 2008, the top four computer companies in the world by volume of sales were in order: HP, Dell, Acer and Lenovo. Some achieved their ranking mainly based on their in-house developments, and some did it through acquisitions. For example, HP acquired Compaq, Acer acquired Gateway and Packard Bell, and Lenovo acquired IBM's personal computer business.

However, being bigger does not mean been the best in technological innovation or style. This fact is illustrated by Apple, which commands a smaller market share but offers the most technologically advanced and best-styled computers. Some of the highlights of these computer companies follow below.

HP. HP took over as world market leader in recent years using both solid technological designs and acquisitions. Their biggest acquisition was of the Compaq computer company. HP offers a wide variety of computers that satisfy the demands of all market sectors, and is reputed for its quality designs. As of early 2008, HP became the biggest IT company in the world, supplanting IBM.

Dell. Dell used to be the high-flyer in the computer business. It used a direct marketing and sales approach and a build-on-demand manufacturing process that minimized its costs and afforded it high-margin profits. However, Dell stumbled in recent years through some missteps such as poor after-sale service and lack of retail channel sales. Dell is trying to get back to its leading position and is entering previously ignored niches; for example, it now offers tablet laptops and some of the best gaming computers.

Acer. Acer vaulted to its number three position in the world by acquiring Gateway and Packard Bell.

Lenovo. Lenovo became a world player in the computer industry when it acquired IBM's personal computer business. Lenovo is the leader in the China computer market. It offers computers that cater to all sectors, not only the usually affordable desktops but also some of the most expensive laptops.

Apple. Apple is the darling of the computer purists. Its CEO, Steve Jobs, is undoubtedly the most visionary of all computer CEOs. He established his reputation based on constant and pioneering innovations throughout the history of the personal computer. Over the years, Apple has maintained a loyal following in the education, publishing and art fields. Recently, after Apple adopted the Intel architecture for its computers, its market share increased tremendously. Apple computers can run not only their own Operating System, the Apple Mac OS X, but also Windows. Apple computers are recognized as the most technologically advanced and most stylish of all computers, albeit at a higher cost to the consumer.

1.5.11 Peripherals

Some of the peripherals that a computer could be connected to are as follows:

- Printers.
- Scanners.
- Digital cameras.
- Video cameras.
- Disks such as USB disks or external hard disks.
- Mobile phones.

1.6 Computer exercises

1.6.1 Reading comprehension

1. Enumerate all the types of computers and their main purposes.
2. What are the main hardware components of a personal computer?
3. What is the basic three-step processing cycle of a CPU?
4. Name some of the main parts of a CPU?
5. What does Moore's Law state about the number of transistors inside a CPU?
6. What measurement unit is used to describe the speed of a CPU?
7. What do the terms "Duo" and "Quad" mean when used in conjunction with a CPU?
8. What acronyms are used to refer to the amount of memory inside a computer?
9. Which memory can the CPU access faster, the CPU cache or the hard disk virtual memory?
10. A gaming computer should come equipped with a GPU or an IGP?
11. What is the function of the chipset?
12. What is the latest bus technology that is presently used in new computers?
13. Presently, where is the memory controller located in the Intel and AMD designs?
14. What is another name for the chipset South Bridge?
15. Enumerate all the ports that a computer might have?
16. What is an RJ45 port/jack used for?
17. What is a DVI port used for?
18. Enumerate all the wireless capabilities of a computer.
19. What are some differences between IrDA and Bluetooth? Between Bluetooth and WiFi?
20. What is the BIOS essentially used for?
21. What are some common form factors for today's Hard Disk Drives?
22. What is the difference between an HDD and an SSD?
23. What is the difference between a DVD-ROM and a DVD-R discs?
24. What part of a laptop functions as the mouse?
25. What is the advantage of a wide-screen over the old 4:3 standard screen?
26. What screen parameter is used to refer to numerical designations such as 1920 x 1200?
27. What are the world's two available AC power supplies?
28. Enumerate all the types of computer software.
29. What are the four categories of Operating Systems?
30. What does multitasking mean? Multithreading? Multiprocessing?
31. Name some popular Operating Systems.
32. Name some popular software applications.
33. What is the purpose of Virtualization software?
34. Name all the Malware that might infect a computer.

(The answers to these questions are at the end of the book)

1.6.2 Reading and pronouncing acronyms

Complete the following table by showing how these computer acronyms are pronounced and what they stand for.

Acronym	Pronunciation	Acronym expansion
CPU		
BIOS		
RAM		
GPU		
DVD-RW		
DVD+RW		
HDD		
SSD		
LAN		
DRAM		
GB		
MB		
GHz		
nm		
RJ45		
DVI		
WiFi		
ESC		
GUI		
C#		
C++		
P2P		
VoIP		
I/O		
rpm		
DOS		
PCB		
FSB		
USB		

(The answers to these questions are at the end of the book)

1.6.3 Decoding computer jargon

The following text is a computer advertisement. It uses cryptic computer jargon that laymen would not understand. Translate this computer advertisement into plain English.

- Intel Core 2 Duo T9300
- Windows Vista Home Premium
- 1GB - 4GB DDRII
- 15.4" WXGA screen
- NVIDEA GeForce 8600, 256MB
- 160/200GB Hard Disk
- SuperMulti
- 802.11 abgn
- 3MPixel webcam
- 2.7 Kg

(The answer is at the end of the book)

1.6.4 Computer essays

1. Write a detailed description of your own computer's hardware and software.
2. Describe what you use your computer for.
3. Assume you had to design the perfect computer. What would it be?
4. Describe the future and possible trends of the computer industry.
5. Do some research and write a compact summary of the history of the computer industry.

1.6.5 Speaking exercises

1. Do a role play about a customer asking a sales person some questions at a computer shop.
2. Do a role play about a customer calling a service center and asking for technical help.
3. Do a role play about two gamers talking about their favorite computer games.
4. Debate which computer games are the most exciting.
5. Debate which Operating System is the best among Apple Mac OS X, Windows and Linux.
6. Debate which company makes the best computers.
7. Debate whether the PC will become obsolete with the advent of cloud computing.
8. Debate which chip is more important: the CPU or the GPU. Talk about their future trends.
9. Debate whether online downloading and storage will make DVDs obsolete.
10. Debate whether spammers should be prosecuted.
11. Debate the problems and benefits that hackers bring to the software industry and users.
12. Debate which portable computer form factor will prevail,e.g. notebooks,netbooks and so on.
13. Debate whether tablets, i.e. notebooks with touch-screens, will become popular.
14. Debate whether the notebook will make the desktop computer obsolete.
15. Debate whether voice recognition will make the keyboard obsolete.
16. Debate whether computers will some day become powerful enough to control us.
17. Give a speech about the computer market in your home country.
18. Describe how the computer booting process works.
19. Describe the many functions of the CPU.
20. Describe the functions of the chipset.
21. Describe the various types of memory inside a computer and their uses.
22. Describe the advantages and disadvantages of Solid State Drives.
23. Describe the progression of the chip manufacturing technology.
24. Describe the different ports on a computer, their functions and trends.
25. Describe the differences between the various display ports, such as VGA, DVI, and so on.
26. Describe the configuration of the optimum gaming computer.
27. Describe some of the problems you encounter with using a computer.
28. Describe the regular maintenance chores you perform to keep your computer working.
29. Describe any bad experiences you had with malware.
30. Enumerate the various word-processing actions such as copy, paste and so on.

1.6.6 Identifying computer parts

Match the words in the following table to the correct computer parts in the figure below.

1. Webcam	10. Bezel
2. Icons	11. Windows
3. Power button	12. Screen
4. Touchpad	13. Touchpad buttons
5. Ports	14. Speakers
6. Hinges	15. Security slot
7. Bay	16. Power adapter
8. Optical drive	17. Keyboard
9. Slot	18. Cursor

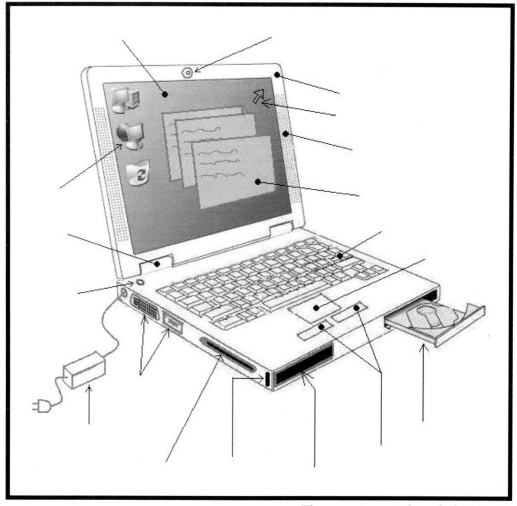

(The answers are at the end of the book)

1.6.7 Cloze

Fill in the blanks in the following statements with the correct computer words.

1. The main chip on the motherboard is called a _____.
2. The piece of software that serves to boot up a computer is called the _____.
3. The CPU is connected to the rest of the chips on the motherboard via a _____.
4. A laptop's cooling system is made of heat sinks and a _____.
5. The main storage in a computer is provided by a _____.
6. The fast memory provided on a CPU is called _____ memory.
7. In addition to a fast CPU, a good gaming computer should have one or more _____.
8. The chipset's _____ Bridge connects all the I/O devices.
9. A Solid-State Drive uses _____ memory and has no moving mechanical parts.
10. On a laptop, the _____ take the place of a mouse.
11. After the BIOS boots up, it hands over the computer control to the _____.
12. DVI and USB are examples of _____ on a computer.
13. The small pictures representing different programs on the screen are called _____.
14. Double clicking on an icon on the screen will open a _____.
15. For a C++ program to be understood by the CPU, it has to be translated into _____.
16. Viruses and Trojan Horses are examples of _____.
17. If an AC power supply is not available, a laptop can still operate using a _____.
18. The heart or core of an Operating System is called the _____.
19. An Operating System relies on _____ to control and manage the hardware.
20. Software programs that add to the functionality of an Operating System are called _____.
21. If a computer is to run two Operating Systems, it needs to have _____ software.
22. A programming language translator could be an Assembler, Interpreter or _____.
23. If a computer is to be used for a video chat, it needs to have a _____.
24. In some airports and cafés, a user could wirelessly surf the Internet using _____.
25. A screen that has a 16:9 or 16:10 aspect ratio is called a _____.
26. Desktops provide a few PCI Express _____ for adding cards such as video cards.
27. A Hard-Disk Drive spins at high speeds, such as 7200 _____.
28. A DVD-RW disc allows the user to both read and _____ data.
29. The software application that allows a user to surf the Internet is called a _____.
30. An Operating System's ability to run on multiple-core CPUs is called _____.
31. An Operating System's ability to run multiple programs simultaneously is called _____.
32. The software application that allows for making slides is called _____ software.
33. When looking for information online, a user could use a _____.
34. A CPU is mounted on a motherboard using a _____.
35. Devices, such as printers, that can be used with a computer are called _____.

(The answers to these questions are at the end of the book)

1.6.8 Computer action words

Match the following verbs in the table to the computer words below. Note that each verb may match more than one computer word.

Add	Assemble	Back up	Boot up	Buy
Change	Choose	Click on	Close	Code
Compile	Compress	Configure	Connect	Connect to
Copy	Cut	Debug	Decompress	Defragment
Delete	Decrypt	Design	Develop	Disconnect
Disconnect from	Double click	Download	Drag	Edit
Eject	Encrypt	Format	Hide	Highlight
Hold down	Increase	Insert	Install	Interpret
Left click	Maximize	Minimize	Move	Name
Open	Overclock	Paste	Point	Power on
Press	Print	Push	Recycle	Refresh
Remove	Rename	Right click	Run	Save
Select	Sell	Set	Scroll up	Scroll down
Select	Translate	Turn off	Turn on	Type
Upgrade	Use	Write		

_____ a window

_____ an icon

_____ a cursor

_____ a display

_____ a file

_____ a port

_____ software

_____ text

_____ a program

_____ memory

_____ a computer

_____ a key/button

_____ a mouse

_____ a resolution

_____ a card

_____ a hard disk

_____ a monitor

_____ a webcam

_____ a chip

(The answers to these questions are at the end of the book)

1.7 Computer glossary

API	Application Programming Interface. Software interface used by third-party developers	**CPU register**	A temporary storage element inside a CPU used to load and process data units
Battery	Power storage and delivery device	**CPU cache**	A temporary storage area within a CPU used for fast data access
Bay	Opening in a computer that can accommodate a hard disk, optical drive, battery and so on	**Cursor**	Pointing symbol on the screen that moves in tandem with the mouse
BIOS	Basic Input Output System. Firmware used to start a computer	**Desktop computer**	A computer that has separate monitor/case, keyboard and mouse
Bluetooth	Short distance wireless connection technology	**Device driver**	Software part of the Operating System that supports the hardware
Browser	Software program used to surf the Internet	**Firmware**	Software that comes integrated within a chip
Bus	Set of wire circuits that connect chips	**FSB**	Front Side Bus. Bus that connects the CPU to the Chipset
Chip	A small, thin, flat piece of semiconductor material on which are etched electronic circuits	**GPU**	Graphics Processing Unit. A chip for processing graphics
Chipset	A set of chips for controlling the bus. The chipset may provide other functions such as graphics	**GUI**	Graphical User Interface. The Operating System interface that uses a graphical screen and a mouse for navigation
Chip socket	A mechanical, hollow part on a board that is used to mount a chip	**Hard disk**	Data storage device
Computer	A device for processing data	**Hardware**	All physical parts of a computer
Case	The main box of a desktop computer	**Icon**	Small picture used to represent a program
Core	A processing unit inside a CPU. Old CPUs had only one core, but today's CPUs can have many	**IGP**	Integrated Graphics Processor. A Chipset part that processes graphics
CPU	Central Processing Unit. The main chip or heart of a computer. It processes the computer's inputs and outputs	**Interface**	Physical or logical layout that allows separate elements to connect to each other

I/O	Input Output	**Power adapter**	An electrical device for connecting a computer to an AC power supply
Kernel	Core of an Operating System	**Power supply**	The AC power that is either 220V or 110V
Keyboard	Computer input device	**Programming language**	Software tool that can be used to write software programs
LAN	Local Area Network. Connects computers in a small area such as an office, building or school	**Scanner**	A peripheral for converting paper content into digital content
Laptop computer	A portable computer such as a notebook	**Screen**	The display of a monitor
LCD monitor	Liquid Crystal Display monitor. Flat display device	**Server**	Computer used in data centers
Mainframe	A powerful, data center computer	**Slot**	A long, narrow opening for cards
Malware	Malicious software. Harmful software	**Software**	Code inside a computer
Memory	Data storage made of chips	**Software application**	A program that satisfies a user's need such as data processing
Middleware	Software to allow different applications on separate computer systems to work with each other	**Software utility**	A program that adds to the functionality of an Operating System
Motherboard	Main board inside a computer	**SSD**	Solid State Drive. A storage device made of flash memory
Mouse	A point-and-click I/O device	**Supercomputer**	The most powerful computer
Notebook computer	A portable computer. A laptop	**Tablet notebook**	A portable computer that uses touch-screen input
Operating system	Foundation software of a computer	**Touchpad**	A small area on a laptop computer near the keyboard that functions as a mouse
Optical drive	CD, VCD, DVD read/write device	**Touchpad button**	One of two buttons that are part of a touchpad
Palmtop computer	Small computer that fits in the hand's palm	**USB disk**	A storage device that uses flash memory and has a USB interface
Peripheral	Outside device that works with a computer	**USB port**	USB interface on a computer
Port	Physical or logical interface	**Video card**	A computer card that includes a GPU and fast memory

Virtual memory	Memory created by the Operating System on the hard disk to complement the RAM memory	**WiFi**	Wireless Fidelity. A wireless LAN technology used for wireless Internet access
Virtualization software	Software that allows a computer to run more than one Operating System	**Wireless**	Using space instead of wires
Virus	A type of malicious software that can destroy data	**Workstation**	A computer used in engineering applications
Webcam	Web camera		

UNIT 2

INTERNET

INTERNET KEYWORDS

Access	存取 / 接入	Modem	调制解调器
ADSL	不对称数字用户环线	Net bar	网吧
Adware	促销件 / 促销软件	Netiquette	网上礼仪
Attachment	附件	Netizen	网民
Avatar	化身	Piracy	盗版
Blog	博客	Plug-in	插件
Bookmark	书签	Pornography	色情
Browser	浏览器	Portal	网口
Chat	交谈 / 聊天	Protocol layer	协议层
Cloud computing	云计算	P2P	对等体到对等体
Cookie	甜块 / 酷奇程序	Router	路由器
Cyberspace	虚拟空间	Search engine	搜索机 / 搜索引擎
Dial-up	拨号	Server	服务器
DNS	域名系统	Shareware	共享软件
Domain name	域名	Snail mail	慢速邮递 / 蜗牛邮件
Download	下载	Social networking	社交
Email	电子邮件	Spam	广告垃圾邮件
Emoticon	情感符号	Spyware	间谍软件
Filter	过滤程序	Surf	网上浏览
Firewall	防火墙	TCP	传输控制协议
Flame	激怒	Trojan horse	特洛伊木马 （程序）
Freeware	免费软件	Upload	上载
FTP	文件传送协议	URL	网址
Hacker	黑客	Virus	病毒
Instant messaging	即时消息	Virus scan	病毒扫描
Intranet	内联网	VoIP	IP 语音通信
IP	网际协议	Webcam	摄像头
IP address	IP 地址	Website	网站
ISP	因特网服务提供方	Webware	万维网件 / Web 件
Key-logger	键盘记录软件	WiFi	无线网络
Link	链接	WiMAX	微波存取全球互通
Mailbox	邮筒	Worm	蠕虫
Malware	恶意软件		

2.1 Introduction

The Internet is a worldwide collection of networks that are connected together and that provide access to all kinds of information for users. Indeed, the Internet was once known as "The Information Superhighway". While the Internet was not the harbinger of the Information Revolution, it has arguably become its main locomotive and has completely permeated our daily lives. Using the Internet has become a daily necessity. So big has been its impact that not accessing it for one day would leave a person feeling disconnected and left behind the rest of the world. Most of us are now netizens of this Internet virtual world known as cyberspace.

2.2 Internet history

The Internet originated in the late 1960s as a research project of the US Department of Defense. The agency responsible for it was the Defense Advanced Research Projects Agency (DARPA). The purpose of DARPA was to create a network that could survive an enemy attack. This nascent Internet started in California with only a couple of nodes. Over the following decades, it rapidly expanded to connect the rest of the United States and the world.

Some of the most important factors in the rapid development of the early Internet were the close cooperation between DARPA and some leading US universities in network R&D, the adoption of TCP/IP as the protocol stack for the Internet, the addition of corporate connections to the Internet, and finally the transition of the Internet to the private sector.

Applications also played a key factor in the adoption of the Internet. The first killer application on the Internet was email, which radically transformed the communications field. The second and blockbuster application was the Web, which revolutionized the Internet and made it easily accessible to every user.

With the development of the Web and the popularization of personal computers, Internet access exploded exponentially. It reached the farthest corners of the world and connected all countries. It facilitated communications and truly made our world one global village.

An interesting note about the development of the Internet is that both early on and after the invention of the Web, pornography was a big factor in the popularization of the Internet, just as it was with the popularization of the VCR and DVD players. More recently, online games and social networking have taken over and have kept the Internet growth momentum unabated.

Today, the Internet has become an all-encompassing tool. It serves as a communication tool. It serves as a repository for all sorts of data. It has begun to displace the personal computer and may someday eliminate the need for it. The Internet has drawn us into a new world, cyberspace.

2.3 Internet architecture

The Internet is a global collection and interconnection of networks of all sizes throughout the world. These networks could be small Local Area Networks (LAN) with just a few users, Metropolitan Area Networks (MAN) with thousands of users, Wide Area Networks (WAN) with tens of thousands of users, or any in-between-size networks. Attached to these networks are all types of computers such as personal computers, servers, mainframes and supercomputers. In addition to computers, the Internet may connect to other electronic products such as mobile phones, surveillance cameras, GPS devices and TV sets. *(The Internet network architecture is further expanded in section 2.3.1).*

In order to allow all the Internet disparate products to properly interface and communicate with each other, the Internet uses a set of communication protocols called the Transmission Control Protocol / Internet Protocol (TCP/IP) protocol suite. The TCP/IP protocol suite is a stack of layered protocols with different functions at each layer. This layered approach handles Internet communication in a logical way from the bits at the network physical level to the data packets at the application level. In fact, one of the key reasons for the early success of the Internet was its adoption of TCP/IP as the standard protocol suite. *(The TCP/IP protocol suite is further described in section 2.3.2).*

TCP/IP assigns unique addresses, called IP addresses, to connected equipment so as to unambiguously identify any entity that communicates over the Internet. This is one way to manage the immense number of connected equipment. At the time of its inception, the Internet included a look up file that mapped the IP addresses to their corresponding equipment. The file consisted of entries where each entry showed the name of a host and its IP address. Host names are used in addition to IP addresses because they are easier to remember. However, the Internet expanded so rapidly that such a simple and centralized look up system soon became inadequate. Thus, a distributed and scalable look up system called the Domain Name System (DNS) was invented. DNS divides the Internet into a hierarchical design as follows. First, the Internet is divided into parts called top-level domains. Second, these domains are divided into smaller domains, which are further divided into even smaller domains, and so on to many levels. Having such a hierarchical division of the Internet allows for easier management when performing tasks such as adding connections, assigning addresses and routing traffic. Domains are named using a textual and logical nomenclature. One example of a domain name is "techsupport.china-telecom.com". In this example, "com" is the first or top-level domain; "china-telecom" is the second-level domain; "techsupport" is the third-level domain. This type of domain designation is logical and easily understood by humans. DNS tables include such domain names and their corresponding IP addresses. For example, the domain name "techsupport.china-telecom.com" could have an IP address of 10.5.248.3. *(DNS is further described in section 2.3.3).*

2.3.1 Internet network architecture

The overall Internet architecture can be summarized as shown in the following figure.

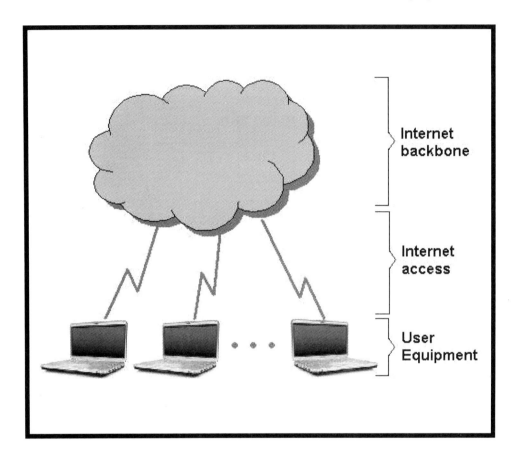

As can be seen in the above figure, there are three main parts to the architecture of the Internet:

- User equipment.
- Internet access.
- Internet backbone.

2.3.1.1 User equipment

User equipment usually means computers such as laptops, desktops, workstations and so on. However, nowadays many electronic devices can also connect to the Internet. Such devices include mobile phones, game consoles, TVs, and so on. Note that since modems may belong to and be provided by an Internet Service Provider (ISP), they are not included as part of the user equipment but rather as part of the Internet access.

2.3.1.2 Internet access

The Internet access can be summarized as shown in the following figure.

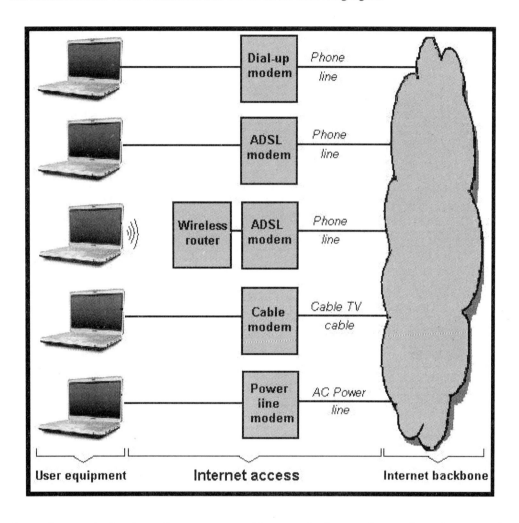

As can be seen in the above figure, a user could access the Internet in a variety of ways. The oldest and slowest way used the dial-up modem with provided a speed of 56 Kilobits per second (Kbps). Nowadays more and more users use broadband connections which are much faster than dial-up. The most popular broadband connection is Asynchronous Digital Subscriber Line (ADSL). In order to use this type of connection, the user needs an ADSL modem. The user's computer can be connected to the ADSL modem either through the computer's RJ45 LAN port or wirelessly such as via WiFi.

Another type of broadband connection is provided by Cable TV companies. In this case, the user's computer is connected to a Cable modem. Finally, a new type of broadband connection is provided by electric power companies. In this case, the user's computer is connected to a Power line modem.

2.3.1.3 Internet backbone

The Internet backbone is the collection of networks, such as those of the Internet Service Providers (ISP). These networks connect to each other as shown in the following figure.

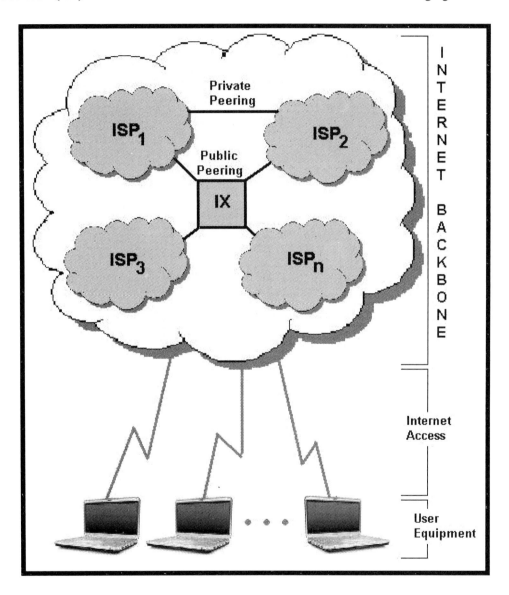

As can be seen in the above figure, the ISPs in the Internet backbone connect to each other via one of two ways. The first way is called Private Peering, and means a one-to-one connection between only two ISPs. The second way is called Public Peering and means that many ISPs connect together at one physical point called an Internet eXchange (IX). Note that this connection point is sometimes referred to as an Internet eXchange Point (IXP) or a Network Access Point (NAP).

2.3.1.4 Internet example

An example of an Internet end-to-end connection is shown in the following figure.

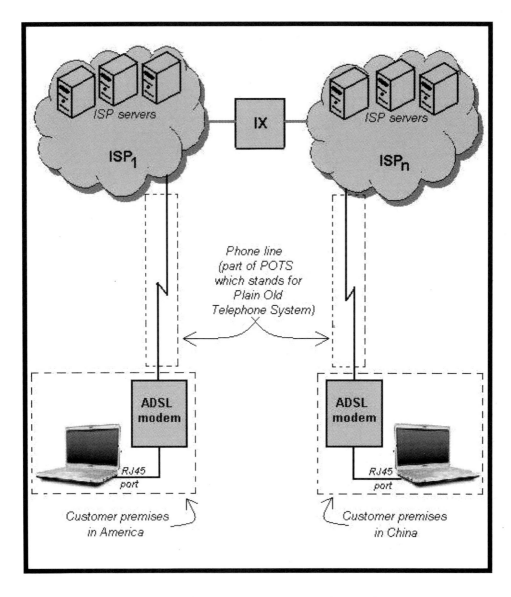

The above picture shows an example of an Internet customer in America connected through the Internet to another Internet customer in China. The end-to-end connection is as follows: The American customer's computer connects through an RJ45 port to an ADSL modem, which connects through POTS to ISP_1, which connects through an IX to ISP_2, which connects through POTS to the Chinese customer's ADSL modem, which connects through an RJ45 port to the Chinese customer's computer.

2.3.2 Internet protocols

2.3.2.1 TCP/IP introduction

Communication on the Internet is based on the Transmission Control Protocol / Internet Protocol (TCP/IP) protocol stack as illustrated in the following figure.

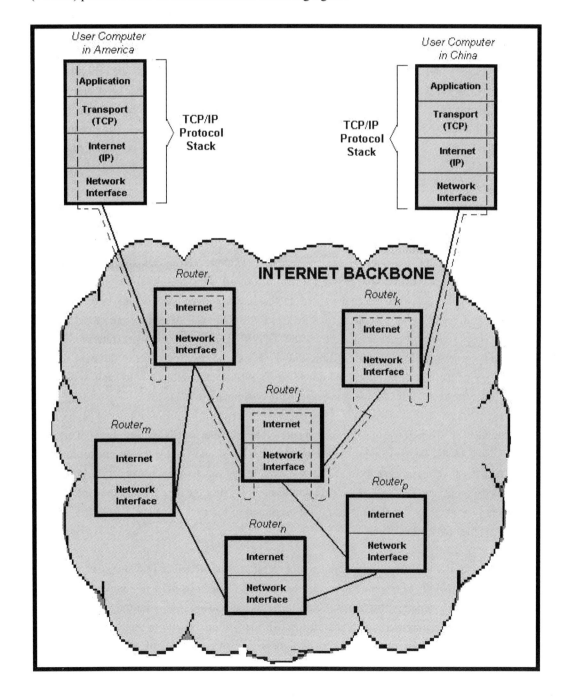

As can be seen in the previous figure, the TCP/IP protocol stack from top to bottom consists of the following layers: Application, Transport, Internet, and Network Interface. Each layer performs specific functions.

In order to understand the basic concept of how the TCP/IP stack works, let us consider the example in the previous figure where a user in America is chatting with a user in China. Also, in order to simplify the description, let us only consider the general flow of the data through the layers. The details of each layer's functions will be presented later. Using these assumptions then, the flow of data from the computer in America to the computer in China is shown as a dotted line in the figure. The chat program on the computer in America uses the Application layer to package the data to be sent into Application-layer data. This data is then sent down the TCP/IP protocol stack in the computer to the Transport layer, then the Internet layer and finally the Network Interface layer. Each layer, as it receives data from the above layer, adds its own packaging information to this data and sends the resulting data down the stack. After the data reaches and is processed by the Network Interface layer, it is sent out of the computer on to the Internet.

Inside the Internet, the data is routed to the computer in China via network devices called routers. As shown in the above figure, the data is forwarded through routers "$router_i$", "$router_j$", and then "$router_k$". Only the bottom two layers of the TCP/IP protocol stack are present in routers. A router receives the data on its Network Interface layer. Upon receiving data, this layer strips out its own packaging information and passes the rest of the data up to the Internet layer. The data goes up the TCP/IP stack in the router to reach the Internet layer because this layer needs to analyze it and decide how to route it forward to its destination. After it is processed by the router Internet layer, the data is sent down the TCP/IP stack to the Network Interface layer, which adds its own packaging information and sends out the resulting data to the next router. This process of the data flowing up and down the TCP/IP stack continues with each router that the data goes through. Finally, the data reaches the computer in China.

The computer in China receives the data on its Network Interface layer and sends it up the TCP/IP stack to the Internet layer, then the Transport layer, and finally the Application layer. Each layer, as it receives data from the lower layer, strips out its own packaging information from this data and sends the rest of the data up the stack. After the data reaches the Application layer, it is processed by the chat program and presented to the user in China. And that is how the data reaches the user in China!

Note that along the way from the computer in America to the computer in China, the data may flow through some other network equipment than routers. Such equipment could be repeaters, hubs, switches, modems, multiplexers, demultiplexers and so on. In addition, the data may traverse various transmission media and go through many transformations such as from digital signals to analog signals, or from electrical signals to airwaves. All of this equipment and transformations operate at the TCP/IP Network Interface layer level.

2.3.2.2 TCP/IP layer functions

As shown in the previous section, the TCP/IP protocol stack consists of four layers: Application, Transport, Internet and Network Interface. The question arises as to the reason for such a layered design. In fact, not only TCP/IP but also other protocol stacks use a layered design. The answer is that a layered design is a logical approach to handling communication across a network or networks. Indeed, such communication is quite complex and involves many different aspects. For example, communication has to deal with such issues as the physical topology of the networks, the manner of connecting to such networks, the data packaging, the data delivery, the communication reliability and so on. A layered design divides these tasks among different modules, or layers, in a logical way. In a layered stack, such as TCP/IP, a layer does not need to know the intricacies and details of other layers. A layer only needs to know how to interface with adjacent layers, i.e. how to exchange data with the layers above and below it. A layered design has another benefit in that software programs only need to interface with the top layer, the Application layer. Thus, software programs can run unchanged on different networks.

The functions of the TCP/IP layers are summarized in the following table.

TCP/IP Application layer

The Application layer exchanges data with software programs and the Transport layer.

When the Application layer is exchanging data with software programs, e.g. Microsoft Internet Explorer (IE), the software programs make use of the many application protocols of this layer such as the HyperText Transfer Protocol (HTTP), which is used for browsing, and the File Transfer Protocol (FTP), which is used to transfer files. After the Application layer gets the data from the software programs, it packages it and sends it to the Transport layer below.

When data is received from the Transport layer below, the data is directed to the right application protocol (e.g. HTTP), which strips its packaging and sends the data to the right software program.

TCP/IP Transport layer

The Transport layer exchanges data with the Application and Internet layers.

When receiving data from the Application layer above, the Transport layer packages that data by adding a Transport-layer header before sending the data to the Internet layer below. This package of data including the Transport-layer header is called a packet.

When receiving data from the Internet layer below, the Transport layer strips off the Transport-layer header before sending the data to the Application layer above. The Transport layer uses an identifier called "Port Number" to relay data to the proper application protocol. For example, the Port Number for HTTP is 80.

The transport layer consists of two main protocols, the Transmission Control Protocol (TCP) and the User Datagram Protocol (UDP). Their specific functions are as follows.

TCP is a connection-oriented protocol, i.e. it establishes an end-to-end, peer-to-peer connection before data exchange begins. TCP uses a procedure called a handshake to establish such a connection. At the end of the data exchange, TCP terminates the connection. TCP can set up multiple, simultaneous, full-duplex such connections.

TCP is a reliable protocol, i.e. it guarantees correct delivery of data. TCP achieves data integrity via a checksum, and delivery guarantee via retransmission and acknowledgements.

TCP also provides peer-to-peer data flow control. It accomplishes this flow control via a mechanism called the "Sliding Window."

UDP, on the other hand, is connectionless, i.e. it does not establish an end-to-end, peer-to-peer connection before data exchange begins. UDP is also unreliable, i.e. it does not guarantee data delivery. UDP relies on other layers to provide reliability.

TCP/IP Internet layer

The Internet layer exchanges data with the Transport and Network Interface layers.

When receiving data from the Transport layer above, the Internet layer packages that data by adding a Internet-layer header before sending the data to the Network Interface layer below. This package of data including the Internet-layer header is called a packet or datagram.

When receiving data from the Network Interface layer below, the Internet layer strips off the Internet-layer header before sending the data to the Transport layer above.

The Internet layer's central function is to route traffic through networks. The Internet layer uses a variety of routing protocols to efficiently accomplish this task.

The main protocol in this layer is the Internet Protocol (IP). Similar to the UDP protocol above, IP is also connectionless and unreliable. IP relies on other layers to provide reliability.

IP provides an addressing scheme that allocates IP addresses to network entities. These IP addresses are logical, not physical. The physical or hardware addresses of equipment are described in the Network Interface layer below.

IP also provides fragmentation and reassembly of packets. When data received from the Transport layer above is too large, IP breaks it into fragments before sending it to the Network Interface layer below. At the destination, IP reassembles these fragments.

TCP/IP Network Interface layer

The Network Interface layer (also called Network Access layer) exchanges data with the Internet layer, and interfaces with the physical communication medium such as an Ethernet, a dial-up connection, or a Wide Area Network (WAN).

When receiving data from the Internet layer above, the Network Interface layer packages that data by adding a Network Interface header and trailer. This packaging is called encapsulation, and the resulting data is called a frame. The Network Interface layer, then, uses its Physical sub-layer to send out the data on the physical communication medium.

When receiving data from the physical communication medium via its Physical sub-layer, the Network Interface layer strips off the Network-Interface-layer header and trailer before sending the data to the Internet layer above.

The structure of the Network Interface layer is related to the physical media of the network. For example, in the case of Ethernet, the Network Interface layer could be divided into three sub-layers: the Logic Link Control (LLC) sub-layer, the Media Access Control (MAC) sub-layer, and the Physical sub-layer as shown below. LLC is used to deliver data from the Network Interface layer to the proper Internet layer protocol. This is necessary since the Internet layer has more protocols than just IP. The MAC sub-layer is responsible for packaging the frames and uses a system of addressing called physical, hardware or MAC addressing. The Physical sub-layer is responsible for sending out or receiving the signals that represent the frame data.

```
┌─────────────────────────┐
│   Logic Link Control    │
│         (LLC)           │
├─────────────────────────┤
│  Media Access Control   │
│         (MAC)           │
├─────────────────────────┤
│        Physical         │
└─────────────────────────┘
```

2.3.2.3 TCP/IP data packaging

Each TCP/IP layer packages data, as it passes through it, as illustrated in the following figure.

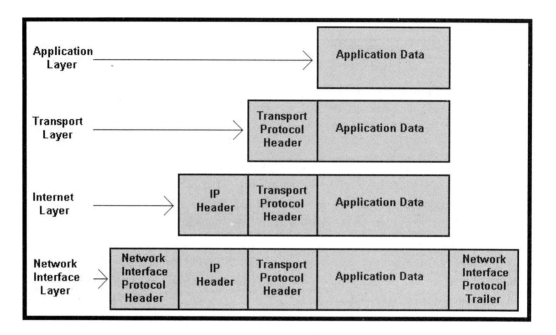

As can be seen in the above figure, the Transport layer adds a Transport Protocol Header to the Application Data, the Internet layer tacks on an additional IP Header, and the Network Interface layer adds a Network Interface Protocol Header and Trailer. In the case where the transport protocol is TCP and the physical network is Ethernet, the above figure becomes as follows.

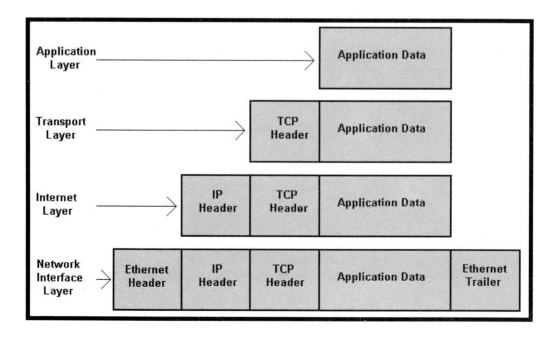

2.3.2.4 TCP/IP data flow

A summary illustration of the data flow up or down the TCP/IP stack is shown in the table below.

When the local host or computer is transmitting data to a peer, the data *flows down* the TCP/IP protocol stack and is acted on by the layers as follows:	When the local host or computer is receiving data from a peer, the data *flows up* the TCP/IP protocol stack and is acted on by the layers as follows:
The Application layer 1. Gets data from the program that requests the services of one of its protocols, 2. Uses DNS to find the IP address of the destination address, 3. Adds the socket (IP address and protocol port number) information to the data, 4. Passes the data down to the Transport layer	The Application layer 14. Delivers data to the program 13. Delivers data to the correct protocol using the socket port, 12. Gets data from the Transport layer,
The Transport layer 5. Gets data from the Application layer, 6. Uses the proper Transport layer protocol (TCP or UDP) based on the socket port number, 7. Adds a Transport layer header, 8. Passes the data down to the Internet layer	The Transport layer 11. Passes the data up to the Application layer's correct protocol 10. Strips the Transport layer header, 9. Checks the Application layer protocol number or port in the Transport layer header, 8. Gets data from the Internet layer,
The Internet layer 9. Gets data from the Transport layer, 10. Adds an Internet layer header, 11. Passes the data down to the Network Interface layer	The Internet layer 7. Passes the data up to the Transport layer's correct protocol 6. Strips out the Internet layer header, 5. Checks the Transport layer protocol number or port in the Internet layer header, 4. Gets data from the Network Interface layer,
The Network Interface layer 12. Gets data from the Internet layer, 13. Appends a Network Interface header and trailer, 14. Sends the data out as signals on the network communication medium	The Network Interface layer 3. Passes the data up to the Internet layer 2. Strips out the header and trailer, 1. Gets data, as signals from the network communication medium, and reconstructs it as Network Interface frames,

2.3.2.5 TCP/IP protocol suite

The TCP/IP protocol suite includes the protocols shown in the following figure.

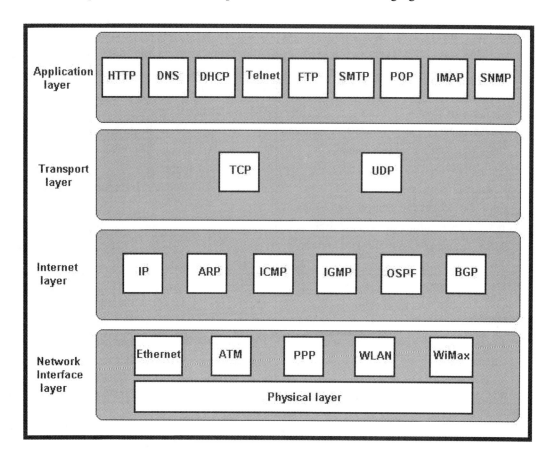

The definitions and functions of the above TCP/IP protocols are summarized in the following table, starting from the Application layer protocols and down to the Network Interface layer protocols.

TCP/IP Protocol	Definitions and functions
HTTP	HTTP stands for HyperText Transfer Protocol. It is a protocol used by browsers to communicate with websites and transmit web pages.
DNS	DNS stands for Domain Name System. It allows for the lookup of the IP addresses of hostnames or websites.

DHCP	DHCP stands for Dynamic Host Configuration Protocol: A DHCP server is used to automatically configure the TCP/IP information, such as computer IP addresses and DNS addresses, of computers on its network.
Telnet	Telnet stands for TErminaL NETwork. It is a remote terminal application that allows a user to log in a remote server.
FTP	FTP stands for File Transfer Protocol. It is a file transfer protocol.
SMTP	SMTP stands for Simple Mail Transfer Protocol. It is a protocol used to send email.
POP	POP stands for Post Office Protocol. It allows users to access their email that is in a mailbox on a remote server.
IMAP	IMAP stands for Internet Message Access Protocol. If functions as POP above, but is more powerful.
SNMP	SNMP stands for Simple Network Management Protocol. It is used for managing network equipment.
TCP	TCP stands for Transmission Control Protocol. It is the most commonly used Transport protocol. TCP is connection-oriented, i.e. it establishes a peer-to-peer handshake session when communication starts and terminates the session when communication ends. It can support multiple peer-to-peer sessions, and performs data flow control using a sliding-window mechanism. TCP is also reliable, i.e. it provides a method for correctly delivering data.
UDP	UDP stands for User Datagram Protocol. It is a Transport protocol. UDP is connectionless, i.e. it does not establish a peer-to-peer session. UDP is unreliable, i.e. it does not guarantee data delivery.

IP	IP stands for Internet Protocol. It is an Internet protocol that defines IP addressing which is used for routing through networks. IP is connectionless, i.e. it does not provide an end-to-end peer-to-peer session. It is unreliable, i.e. it relies on other layers to provide error detection and correction. IP also performs other functions such as the fragmentation and reassembly of IP packets, and supports multicasting, i.e. sending a single IP packet to multiple destinations.
ARP	ARP stands for Address Resolution Protocol. It is used to find the physical address (also called Media Access Control or MAC address) of a computer given its IP address.
ICMP	ICMP stands for Internet Control Message Protocol. It is a protocol used by routers to exchange control messages, such as diagnostics and data flow control, between themselves.
IGMP	IGMP stands for Internet Group Management Protocol. It is used to manage computers that are part of an IP multicast group (IP multicast means one IP packet is sent to several computers simultaneously).
OSPF	OSPF stands for Open Shortest Path First. It is a routing protocol that is more powerful than the older Routing Information Protocol (RIP).
BGP	BGP stands for Border Gateway Protocol. It is a powerful routing protocol used in and between large networks.
Ethernet	Ethernet is the most popular Local Area Network (LAN).
ATM	ATM stands for Asynchronous Transfer Mode. It is a packet-switching protocol that uses fixed-size cells for communication.
PPP	PPP stands for Point-to-Point Protocol. It is a protocol for setting up point-to-point direct connections.

WLAN	WLAN stands for Wireless Local Area Network. It is a protocol that is sometimes referred to as WiFi, and is used to establish wireless LANs.
WiMAX	WiMAX stands for Worldwide Interoperability for Microwave Access. It is a protocol that can be used to set up broadband wireless Metropolitan Area Networks (MAN).

Finally, the Physical layer encompasses the transmission media channels and related equipment that the data passes through. The transmission media could be twisted-pair wires, coaxial cables, fiber cables, and space. The equipment could be computer ports, LAN repeaters, antenna dishes and so on.

2.3.2.6 TCP/IP implementation

TCP/IP is implemented in hosts such as computers as illustrated in the following table.

TCP/IP layer	**Implementation**
Application	The TCP/IP Application layer is implemented as part of the host Operating System (e.g. Windows, Linux), or can be a third-party application.
Transport	The TCP/IP Transport layer is implemented as part of the host Operating System (e.g. Windows, Linux).
Internet	The TCP/IP Internet layer is implemented as part of the host Operating System (e.g. Windows, Linux).
Network Interface	The TCP/IP Network Interface layer is implemented as a combination of Operating System (e.g. Windows, Linux) device drivers, firmware (as in a network adapter), and hardware.

2.3.2.7 TCP/IP configuration

Configuring a computer with TCP/IP is straightforward and sometimes automatically done. When a user connects to a network such as an ISP, the network's DHCP server automatically configures the user's computer with the following information:

- IP Address,
- Net Mask,
- Default Gateway,
- Primary DNS server,
- Secondary DNS server.

A sample TCP/IP configuration of a computer using Microsoft Windows XP is as shown in the following figure.

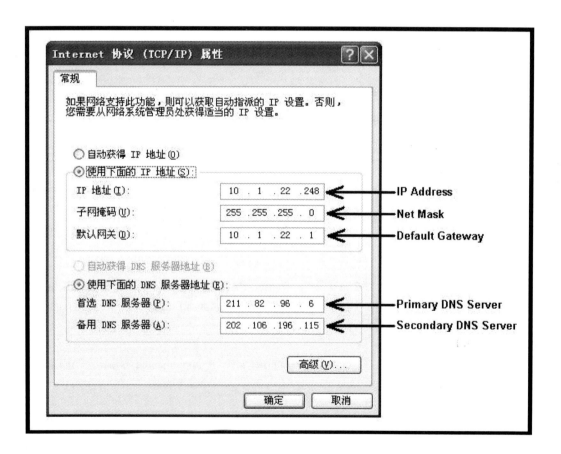

Note that such a TCP/IP configuration can either be done automatically via DHCP or input manually. Also, there are two DNS servers, a primary and a secondary. DNS queries are essential for the proper functioning of the Internet, and thus, a secondary DNS server is configured as a backup.

2.3.2.8 TCP/IP future

TCP/IP was a key contributor to the early success of the Internet, and continues to evolve to meet present and future demands. One important development in TCP/IP is the new version, called IP version 6 (IPv6), which is gradually replacing the old IP version 4 (IPv4). The advantages of IPv6 are summarized in the following table.

Advantages of IPv6	
Addressing	The most significant feature of IPv6 is the address scheme, which has been expanded to meet any foreseeable future demand. Whereas IPv4 addresses are 32-bit long, IPv6 addresses are 128-bit long. Such a large amount of addresses (2^{128}) is so large that if it were divided among all the people in the world, each person would have billions and billions of IP addresses!!!
Provisioning	When customers switch service providers, the renumbering of their IP addresses is more simplified and automated than before. This ease of provisioning is the result of the huge number of available addresses.
Security	IPv6 is inherently more secure since it includes, as an integral part, IPsec, which is a feature that provides security.
Efficiency	IPv6 provides a more efficient flow of data through the networks since IPv6 packets have no checksum that requires routers to do error checking at every hop along the route.

The future looks bright for TCP/IP. The porting of applications to TCP/IP continues unabated. For example, mass media has been migrating to the Internet. Newspapers, then radio, and now television use the Internet medium for delivery. In the communication field, a similar trend has developed. Fixed-phone communications have been switching en-masse to an IP-based environment. Mobile-phone communications will follow a similar road in the future.

The notion of IP everywhere is becoming a reality. In the future, it is possible that every gadget will be connected to the Internet, from the television set to the toaster oven. Even people may someday be connected to the Internet using body-implanted Radio Frequency ID (RFID) chips.

2.3.3 Internet domain name system

The Internet uses a system of logical addresses, called IP addresses, to identify connected equipment. Such equipment could be computers, routers, mobile phones and so on. The IP addresses are numeric in nature and too long for users to remember. An IPv4 address has 28 bits, and an IPv6 address has 128 bits. Such long strings of numbers are impossible for users to recall. Humans are more adept at remembering words than numbers. Thus, a system was invented to assign word strings, or names, to IP addresses. This system is called the Domain Name System (DNS). DNS is basically a table of entries, where each entry includes an IP address and its corresponding equipment name.

As its name implies, DNS consists of domains. Domains are logical partitions of the Internet cyberspace. DNS organizes these Internet domains in a hierarchical, distributed database that resembles a tree and that facilitates the look-up of DNS entries. Thus, there are domains, which have sub-domains, which have sub-domains and so on to many levels. The DNS domain structure is shown in the following figure.

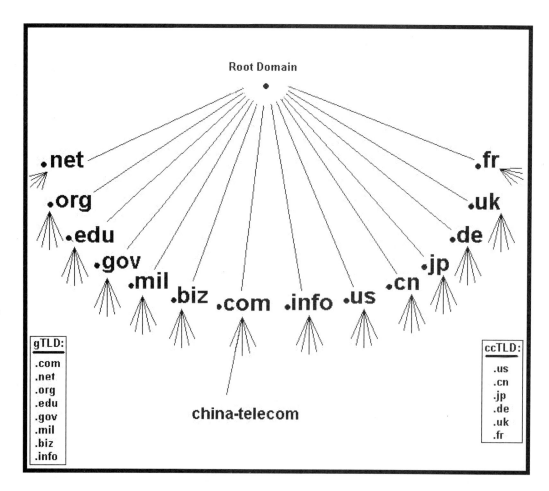

In the previous figure, the "." is called the root domain. Below the root domain are the Top-Level Domains (TLD). The TLDs could be Global Top-Level Domains (gTLD), such as ".com" and ".net", or Country Code Top-Level Domains (ccTLD), such as ".us" for America and ".cn" for China. The TLDs are divided into sub-domains, which are divided into sub-domains, and so on to many levels.

The previous figure shows the domain name "china-telecom.com." as an example. This domain naming method follows a convention that states that the syntax of the domain name from right to left, i.e. "." ".com" "china-telecom", gives the exact location of the domain in the DNS domain structure. Note that there is a dot at the end of the domain name. When a domain name has a dot at the end, it indicates the absolute location of the domain in the DNS structure. Such a domain name with a trailing dot is called a Fully Qualified Domain Name (FQDN). The trailing dot is usually omitted when writing domain names, but the browser software automatically appends it.

A list of gTLDs and ccTLDs with their meanings are shown in the following two tables.

Global Top-Level Domains (gTLD)	
gTLD	Entities that use the gTLD
.com	Commercial
.net	Network-related
.org	Non-commercial
.edu	Educational
.gov	Government
.mil	Military
.biz	Business
.info	Information

Country Code Top-Level Domains (ccTLD)			
Country	ccTLD	Country	ccTLD
USA	.us	China	.cn
Japan	.jp	UK	.uk
Germany	.de	France	.fr

The DNS structure information is held in DNS name servers. Each DNS name server maintains information about an assigned portion of the DNS space called zone. A DNS name server that serves a zone is said to have authority over that zone. Thus, a DNS name server, that has authority over a certain zone, would have a list of that zone's domain names and corresponding IP addresses. For reliability purposes, a zone is usually served by more than one DNS name server.

An example of the way that DNS servers are used is illustrated in the figure on the following page. As can be seen in that figure, the operating system of the user's computer includes a program called a Resolver. The Resolver, as its name indicates, is used to resolve domain names into their IP addresses. For example, when a user needs to view a website, the browser will request the Resolver to find the IP address of that website.

The computer Resolver contacts the ISP DNS name servers that are configured on the computer. The way that the computer Resolver queries the ISP DNS name server is called recursive querying. This means that the ISP DNS name server responds to the computer Resolver's query with the IP address of the queried domain, not with a referral to another DNS server.

The ISP DNS name server uses a different type of querying to find the IP address of the queried domain. This type of querying is called iterative querying. As can be seen in the figure, iterative querying means that the ISP DNS name server may query a few DNS servers in turn, and some of them may return referrals to other DNS servers, rather than the IP address of the queried domain.

A final note about DNS Resolvers and servers is that they cache answers to queries so as to provide a quicker response to future similar queries. However, in order to maintain the accuracy of the cached data, this data is assigned a Time-to-Live value after which it becomes invalid.

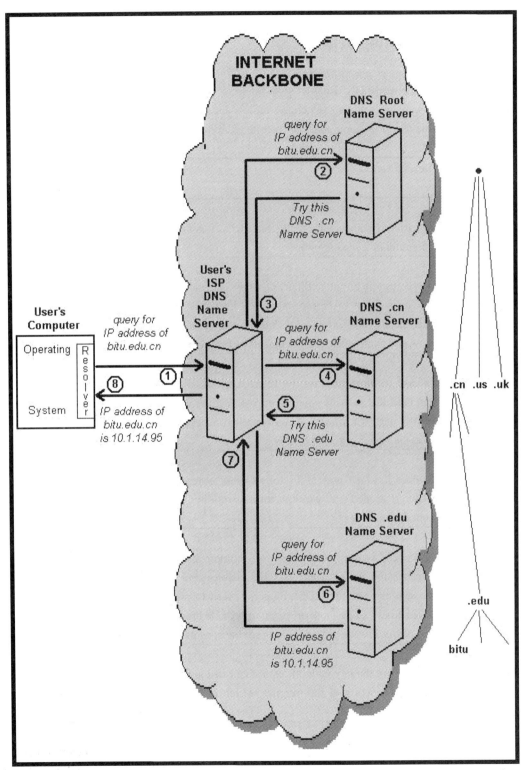

2.3.4 Internet equipment

As a collection of networks, the Internet uses all kinds of network equipment such as hosts, modems, repeaters, hubs, bridges, switches, routers, multiplexers, demultiplexers and so on. The following table describes some of these Internet equipment items.

Network Equipment	Description
Host	A variety of hosts access the Internet. For example, a host could be a laptop computer or a mobile phone.
Network Interface Card (NIC)	A NIC can be an integral part of a host or a card that is inserted inside a host. A NIC provides a LAN port called RJ-45 that is used for broadband access (in the past, a NIC also provided a dial-up port called RJ-11, but dial-up access is too slow and is now fast being replaced by broadband access).
Radio antennas	In case the host accesses the Internet wirelessly, the host is equipped with radio antennas that provide wireless access. If the wireless access uses WiFi, then the host is part of a wireless LAN (wireless access may also use WiMAX, in which case the host is part of a MAN).
Wireless router	In case the host uses WiFi for wireless access to the Internet, then a wireless router is needed. A wireless router can allow many hosts to share one Internet connection.
Modulator Demodulator (Modem)	A modem is used to transmit the computer's digital signals over the analog transmission media, such as wires, cables and space. The different types of modern modems are ADSL modems (used to provide broadband access through phone lines), cable modems (used to provide broadband access through TV cable), and power line modems (used to provide broadband access through power lines).
Network routers	Routers are the key network equipment inside the Internet. Routers provide the essential function of the Internet, which is to route traffic between sources and destinations.
Network servers	Servers provide many functions such as configuring users' computers (DHCP servers), providing IP addresses of domain names (DNS servers), and providing Web pages (Web servers).

The following figure illustrates the different types of Internet equipment. Inside the Internet backbone and ISPs are the routers and servers. At the customer premises are the hosts (computers) and modems. In the case of the old dial-up access method, computers may be equipped with an internal dial-up modem. In the case of wired broadband access, computers are connected to ADSL, Cable or Power line modems. In the case of wireless broadband access, computers are equipped with WiFi or WiMAX antennas.

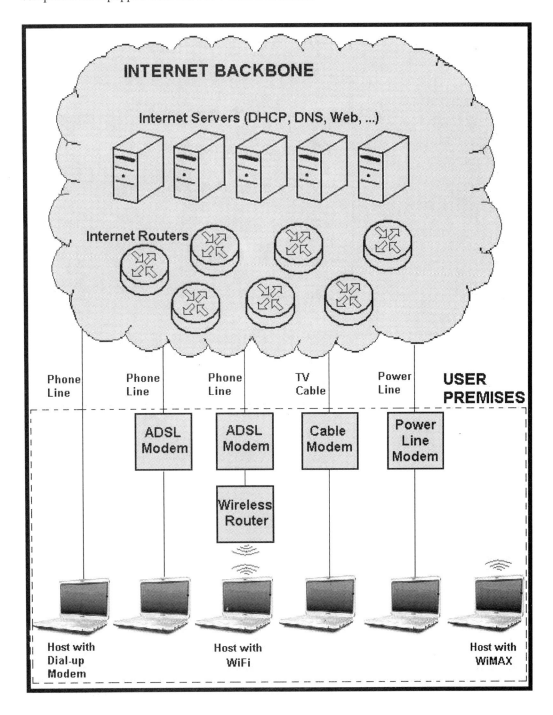

2.4 Internet services and applications

The following figure shows the services and applications offered on the Internet.

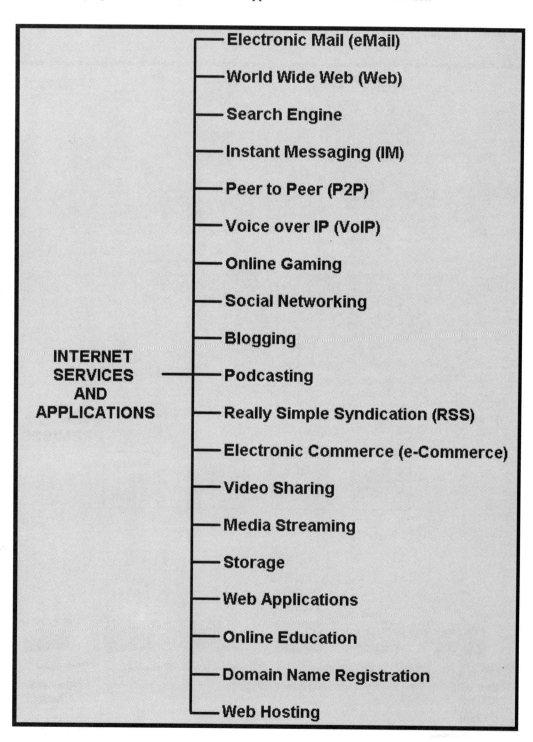

2.4.1 Email

The first killer application on the Internet was email. Email replaced and considerably reduced the need for post office mail since it had so many advantages such as: no need for paper or postage stamps, almost instant delivery, ease of editing, ease of archiving, and ease of reaching multiple recipients.

Email uses the Simple Mail Transfer Protocol (SMTP) of the TCP/IP protocol suite to exchange messages between Internet users. Email uses Mail Exchange Servers to keep track of the location of users so that whatever domain the users might be on, they can be reached. Note that SMTP is used for sending email to a recipient's mailbox, which may reside on an ISP's mail server and not on the recipient's personal computer. In order for email to be retrieved from this mailbox on the mail server to the recipient's personal computer, a different protocol other than SMTP is used. The most popular protocols for accomplishing this retrieval of email are the Post Office Protocol version 3 (POP3) and the Internet Message Access Protocol version 4 (IMAP4). The figure below shows how email is sent from a user in America to a user in China.

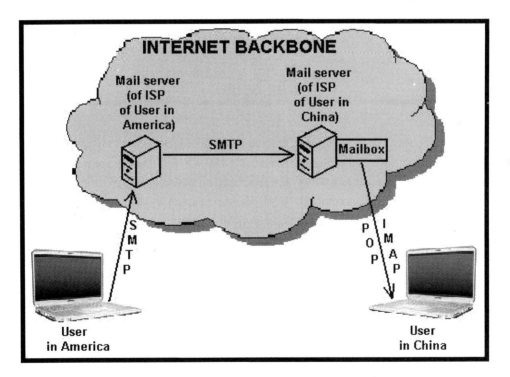

Since email predates the invention of the Web and the browser, it has always been available as a separate software module from the browser. However, with the invention and ease of use of the Web, email has become integrated with browsers in what is called Webmail. Presently, the most popular Webmail packages are Yahoo Mail from Yahoo, GMail from Google, and Hotmail from Microsoft.

2.4.2 Web

The second killer application, which revolutionized the Internet, is the World Wide Web, also known as the Web. The Web has so radically transformed the Internet that the two are sometimes used interchangeably. However, the Web is just a part of the Internet. The Web is the huge interlinked collection of information that can be accessed using a browser such as Mozilla Firefox, Apple Safari or Microsoft IE. The Web information is indexed via pointers called the Uniform Resource Locators (URL) or Uniform Resource Identifiers (URI), which are represented by links on web pages. A user can access any information resource by clicking on its URL or URI using a browser. The following figure shows the syntax of a URL or URI.

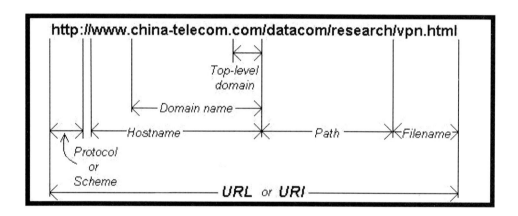

Web pages are constructed using special programming languages such as HyperText Markup Language (HTML) or eXtensible Markup Language (XML). Web pages have become livelier in their presentation by adding dynamic features such as flashing text, moving pictures and videos. These web page enhancements have become possible by using new programming languages such as Java and Javascript. Some popular software packages that can be used to build web pages are Dreamweaver and Frontpage.

Web pages make up a website. A website could have one or more web pages. A website resides on a Web server. The two most popular Web server software packages are Apache from the Apache Software Foundation and Internet Information Services (IIS) from Microsoft.

The Web uses the HyperText Transfer Protocol (HTTP) of the TCP/IP protocol suite for communication. For example, when one uses a browser and clicks on the URL of a web page, the browser uses HTTP to send a request to the server on which the web page resides, and then that server uses HTTP to send the web page to the browser. For secure communications that use encryption such as email or bank accounts, a more secure version of HTTP called HyperText Transfer Protocol Secure (HTTPS) is used.

2.4.3 Other Internet services and applications

In addition to email and the Web, there are many other important Internet services and applications as listed below.

Search engine. As the world becomes digitized and more information is ported online, the need for cataloguing such information becomes essential. Search engines fill such a role. Search engines have built up a huge indexed catalog or database of the Internet by using automated browsing that follows all possible links and then processing the information at those links by indexing and ranking it. Using such an inventory approach, search engines have in essence built an Internet directory. When a user enters a search string in a search engine, the search engine looks up its database and returns a list of possible matches. As of early 2008, the most popular search engines in America were Google, Yahoo and MSN. Other countries may have their own search engines; for example, in China the leading search engine has been Baidu.

Instant messaging (IM). Instant messaging refers to online chatting applications such as QQ and MSN Messenger. The application is called instant in contrast to email since in chatting the correspondence takes place in real time, i.e. instantly. Today's IM tools offer text, voice and video chatting capabilities. They allow for conferencing of multiple participants and the exchange of data such as documents and graphics. Textual chatting is also enhanced via such add-ons as emoticons and avatars. Emoticons are small facial pictures that convey a person's emotions such as happiness, sadness, excitement and so on. Avatars are digital images used by IM users to represent themselves in IM chat rooms and cyberspace.

Peer to peer (P2P). A P2P application allows a community of users to exchange data that resides on their personal computers. For example, one user could directly access another user's computer and download data such as music, e-books or movies. The index of such data and the location of the data are either maintained in one central server or distributed among several network nodes. The users are supposed to be equal partners and not only download others' data, but also allow others the same privilege. Napster was the P2P pioneer and was wildly popular. However, because of copyright issues, it had to cease functioning under the old free-data-exchange model. Since Napster, other P2P services have sprouted, but many were forced to shut down for the same reasons. Some P2P services have adapted to the copyright issues by pursuing such functioning models as advertising and paid subscriptions.

Voice over IP (VoIP). As the Internet reached into the farthest corners of the world and more people became netizens, it was only a matter of time before the Internet became a conduit for voice communication. VoIP is the application that allows for conducting such communication. Using VoIP, the Internet is slowly replacing the old telephone switched network. With VoIP, netizens all over the world can talk free of charge when using their computers' microphones and speakers. Some companies also extend this service to regular home phones by charging low fees. An example of a company that offers VoIP service is Skype.

Online gaming. Online gaming has become one of the hottest online activities, to the point of even becoming addictive in some cases. One major difference between online games and standalone computer or video games is that online games allow netizens from all over the world to compete against each other. Adding to the popularity of online gaming is the fact that the major video game consoles such the Nintendo Revolution, Sony Playstation and Microsoft Xbox now offer online gaming.

Social networking. Social networking is basically an amalgamation of previously separate online applications such as chatting, building personal web pages, uploading one's photos and so on. Social network services now offer all these features and more in one neatly integrated environment. However, many social networks developed over time without any standardization or peering between them. This development has resulted in cases where users have to input and maintain the same personal information in different social networks. Obviously, this situation is not efficient if a user decides to join various social networks. Fortunately, a standardization process has been set up to remedy this duplication problem and many social networks have signed up for this process. As of early 2008, the major social networks in America included Facebook and MySpace.

Blogging. Blogging began as a sort of keeping an online diary. Many web portals give users space to maintain blogs. Blogs include not only text but also pictures. Over time blogging has evolved from simply being a personal diary to also become part of the journalistic landscape covering all sorts of topics such as technology, entertainment, politics and sports.

Podcasting. Podcasting is similar to maintaining a personal radio or television station online. Podcasts can be sound (voice) recordings, video recordings or both. In some sense, podcasting is a multimedia form of blogging and has evolved in a similar way to become part of the reporting landscape.

Really Simple Syndication (RSS). RSS is a useful tool to keep Web users abreast of changes in their favorite websites. For example, if a user subscribes to a website's RSS service, then whenever the website is updated with new information, that information is sent or fed to the subscribing user as an RSS feed. A user can subscribe to feeds from all kinds of websites by using a special program called RSS Reader.

Electronic commerce (e-Commerce). The Internet, and subsequently the Web, has provided an almost-ideal platform for conducting business. This platform allows for conducting business between companies, consumers and governments. While e-Business designates the use of the Internet or Web platform to conduct or enhance any business facet, e-Commerce refers to the use of this platform to conduct trade services such as Business-to-Business (B2B), Business-to-Consumer (B2C), Business-to-Government (B2G), and Consumer-to-Consumer (C2C). Examples of C2C include online auctions and individual retail shops, such as provided by eBay. e-Commerce also includes other trade supporting services like payment services, such as provided by PayPal.

Video sharing. The exchange of online information since the early days of the Internet has evolved from text to pictures to video. Today's broadband connections to the Internet allow netizens to share such bandwidth-hogging applications as videos. Netizens make videos about all sorts of topics and upload them to video-sharing sites such as YouTube.

Media streaming. It used to be that in order to view a multimedia file, such as a video, a netizen had to first completely download the file and then open it. Media streaming is different in that it allows for viewing the file while it is being downloaded. One example of media streaming is receiving online radio or TV broadcasts.

Storage. Netizens generate all kinds of information that needs to be stored. For example, netizens create documents, photos, pictures, music and videos. Traditionally, the personal computer served as the storage place. However, nowadays the Internet has become a viable storage alternative. Some Internet sites offer gigabyte or even unlimited storage capacities. Not only is online storage virtually free of charge, but it also offers the advantages of being accessed from anywhere and easily shared with other netizens.

Web applications. Some speculate that the age of the personal computer in its present form will be changing and its functions will be transferred to the Internet cloud. Some of these functions, such as storage, have already become available on the Internet. The critical function of computer applications is now also becoming available online. For example, some websites offer online word processing, graphics editing and spreadsheet tabulating.

Online education. Online education refers to using the Internet to provide teaching material and classes. Online education can be offered on a wide-scale to reach multiple and distant locations. One particular advantage of online education is that netizens from all over the world can have access to lectures by world-famous authorities. Some online education programs offer college degrees that are becoming accepted by academic institutions.

Domain name registration. The Internet or Web is a virtual real estate landscape, and netizens are its residents. Just as in real estate people own residences, netizens own online spaces or domains. There are many Internet organizations that provide registration services that allow netizens to choose domain names and register them. Netizens have to pay annual fees to keep their domain names. Just as real estate can be viewed as an investment tool, domain names have also become investment tools. Some domain names with catchy spelling can be sold for millions of dollars.

Web hosting. After a netizen registers a domain name, the netizen could opt to make it a website. In this case, the netizen would need to find a web hosting company to host the website. Web hosting companies charge fees for this service and offer all kinds of website enhancement features such as email and advertising.

2.5 Internet issues

2.5.1 Advantages and disadvantages

The Internet's advantages far outweigh its disadvantages. The biggest advantage of the Internet is the fact that the Internet is a pillar of the Information age, which has positively transformed our world. The global reach and communication-facilitating power of the Internet have brought the world closer like never before. The Internet has really made our world a "global village" where everyone and everything is within easy access. Such unprecedented transformation of the world has brought both economic and social benefits. The economic benefits are exemplified by the myriad of previously described technical applications and services that increase work productivity and business opportunities. The social benefits include bridging culture gaps and building more channels for communication and understanding in the world.

The Internet's disadvantages include both technical and social problems. On the technical side, malware is a serious issue that threatens the security of the Internet. There is an ongoing cat-and-mouse battle between the malware side and the software industry. Since it can be assumed that no software code can ever be hacker-proof, it is reasonable to assume that such a battle will go on. However, with proper software code evolution and legal measures, malware can be contained to a manageable level. On the social side, the Internet has some problems such as addiction, pornography, and lack of real human interaction. Another problem, which is more of a political nature, is cyber terrorism. Some terrorist organizations, and some contend maybe even countries, have resorted to the Internet to conduct terrorist training, spying and hacking. Terrorists have found ingenious ways to conceal their Internet communications. For example, they chat using encrypted messages or hide their messages inside graphics.

2.5.2 Internet administration

The Internet was an American invention and was first deployed in America. However, the Web was not an American invention, and today's Internet is a worldwide infrastructure shared by countries all around the world. This evolution of the Internet has led many countries to question the American control of the Internet, such as the American control of the root domain name servers. These countries argue that the United Nations (UN) should be in charge of the administration of the Internet. The US counters that such a UN bureaucratic leadership would stifle the future development of the Internet. Both sides have valid points, and it can be assumed that a mutually acceptable arrangement will be found.

2.6 Internet future

The Internet has evolved into an essential part of our lives. If has forever changed our lives for the better and will continue to evolve to provide more capabilities and benefits to users worldwide. Some of the properties that the Internet is evolving to are outlined below.

2.6.1 Faster access

The Internet used to be very slow. In fact, "www" used to be referred to jokingly as "world wide wait". Nowadays, gone are the days of dial-up. Broadband access is upon us and is providing for a more enjoyable surfing experience. However, the nature of Internet access is that nothing seems to satiate users' appetite. Today's broadband access is still not fast enough when shared with other users, or when downloading huge videos files. In the future, Internet access will be bumped up much higher in order to approach the instant response feel of personal computers.

2.6.2 Internet ubiquity

It used to be that when one wanted to access the Internet, one had to either do it from home or a net bar, unless one paid for expensive cellular access. Nowadays, the wireless technology WiFi offers more location choices such as cafes and airports, either free of charge or at small fees. This trend toward ubiquity of Internet access will continue as longer-range wireless technologies such as WiMAX are deployed. In the future, ubiquitous Internet wireless access will be offered anywhere, anytime, at low or no charges.

2.6.3 Internet connectivity

Originally, only computers could connect to the Internet. Nowadays, mobile phones also can be used to surf the Internet. In the future, anything could be connected to the Internet. At home, Internet connections could be provided to control security lights and alarms, lighting, kitchen appliances such as refrigerators and ovens, living room entertainment equipment such as video recorders, and home environment equipment such as air conditioners and furnaces. In a car, Internet connections could be needed to download travel information, download music or movies, provide vehicle-location information, and provide vehicle diagnostics such as engine status.

People and animals, especially pets, also could be connected to the Internet. One example is GPS-embedded collars for tracking lost dogs. Another example is the use of Radio Frequency ID (RFID) chips implanted under the skin to provide a person's location or maybe a person's health diagnostics.

2.6.4 Internet computing

In the early days of computing, when mainframes were popular, IBM advocated a centric, resource-sharing computing model where the mainframe provided all the raw computing power, and users only needed simple terminals for input and output. Then, came Microsoft, which advocated a decentralization of this model because it wanted to sell software to personal computers. In Microsoft's plan, a user could have all the computer power he/she needs right in the personal computer. Microsoft, of course, succeeded in implementing its vision. Now, however, there is a movement toward going back to the old model with the Internet functioning as the central computer. This model of an Internet cloud that provides computing power to individuals and companies is quite reasonable since it relieves customers from all the hassles of software buying, downloading, installing, upgrading, configuring, and maintaining.

2.6.5 Internet storage

With the advent of video, users' storage needs have soared to stratospheric levels. Gone are the days when a hundred gigabytes of storage were sufficient. Today, even terabyte hard disks are not enough for the storage-hungry files such as high-definition videos and movies. Users need storage space not only for new content, but also for archiving. The Internet has risen to this challenge and now offers free storage in the gigabytes. In the future, the Internet could offer even higher storage capacities, free of charge.

2.6.6 Internet telephony

The Internet has changed the fixed-phone industry, both local and long distance, by offering satisfactory voice quality at much cheaper rates. The Internet will in the future change the mobile phone industry as well. Mobile phones will use wireless technologies, such as WiFi and WiMAX, to make calls through the Internet.

2.6.7 Politics

Political systems in democracies are based on people representation through elected officials such as congressmen. This system of representation is old and antiquated. It has served democracy well but has not kept up with social and technological changes. Indeed, the question could be asked as to why have such political middlemen decide the affairs of a country when people can use the Internet as a platform to directly debate and decide any issues. The Internet will not entirely eliminate a government but will make it much smaller, effective, responsive, and representative.

2.7 Internet scenarios

2.7.1 Searching for information

The Internet has become the world's largest public library. It is the repository of all kinds of information, which is available in text, graphics and video formats. Helping users to find and access such information are search engines such as Google and Yahoo. The process of using search engines to find information is very simple. Users type in the search strings that indicate the information they are looking for, and instantaneously the search engines return lists of web pages that may contain that information. Search engines offer users the ability to customize their searches by specifying some search parameters. Still, search engines nowadays are nowhere close to perfect and most often return lists of useless web pages. Users need to spend time browsing the list of returned web pages in order to determine their appropriateness.

2.7.2 Downloading content

The Internet is full of downloadable material, such as e-books, software, music, pictures, videos, and movies. Some material can be downloaded free of charge, while other material requires payment. Since the downloadable content can sometimes be huge files that may require a long time to download, special downloading software has been invented to speed up the downloading process. A big issue related to downloading is piracy. In America, tough Intellectual Property Rights (IPR) regulations and prosecutions have basically stamped out piracy. However, in other countries, piracy is still an issue.

2.7.3 Designing web pages

Web page proper design is important because viewers are influenced by the look of web pages. If a web page is too cluttered, it sends a message of disorganization and may make viewers unwilling to browse it. If a web page contains grammatical mistakes such as spelling errors, it conveys an image of inferior quality and makes viewers skip it. If a web page uses the wrong colors, it may be hard for viewers to read it. In fact, there is a whole assortment of web page factors that web page designers should pay attention to if they want to generate page hits. Helping web page designers produce professional designs are many web page design software programs. These programs simplify the design steps, help make web pages more dynamic and interactive such as with applets, and also include templates to match different design requirements.

2.7.4 Getting a domain name

Both companies and individuals can get domain names. The process is as follows. The registrant, i.e. the company or individual user, decides on a name for a domain and the Top-Level Domain (TLD) under which to register. Next, the registrant needs to do a search to ascertain that such a domain name has not already been registered by someone else. Then, the registrant needs to contact a registrar, i.e. a company that specializes in registering and selling domain names to users, and sign a contract with the registrar. The domain name now becomes the property of the registrant for the duration of the contract. The registrant can either just hold the domain name as property (cyber squatters do this) or use it to open a website. In this latter case, the registrant needs to contract with a website hosting company.

2.7.5 Wireless surfing

As of early 2008, if a user wanted to access the Internet wirelessly, then the user had two choices: WiFi or cellular. WiFi is quite popular since most new computers come equipped with it. WiFi, also known by its different versions of 802.11 a/b/g/n, allows wireless access at homes, cafés, airports and anywhere there is a WiFi hotspot. Cellular access to the Internet is through the mobile phone network. Thus, a computer using this method of wireless access needs to be equipped with a cellular card.

2.7.6 Communicating online

Communicating online has become so easy and convenient. There are so many choices to make oneself heard in cyberspace. There is email such as Hotmail, Instant Messaging (IM) such as QQ, blogging from many websites, VoIP such as Skype, and social networking such as Facebook. IM offers text, voice and video chatting capabilities. Some websites also allow the sending of messages to mobile phones.

2.7.7 Personal online shopping

Personal online shopping has become a viable method of shopping. For example, shopping for books, music, and movies is best done online. Not only is the search for such items easier online, but also users usually get better prices online. Of course the list of items that can be bought online is now unlimited. For example, some supermarkets offer online shopping. Customers go to these supermarkets' websites, select goods, have these goods delivered to their homes, and pay either online with a credit card or with cash on delivery.

2.8 Internet exercises

2.8.1 Reading comprehension

1. Which country deployed the original Internet?
2. What is the difference between the Internet and the Web?
3. What was the first Internet killer application?
4. What are the ways that netizens can chat with each other?
5. What is the name of the protocol suite on which the Internet is based?
6. The Internet architecture is usually divided into what three parts?
7. What are the two ways that ISPs can peer with each other?
8. Name the different types of Internet access.
9. Name the four layers of the TCP/IP protocol stack.
10. Name some of the TCP/IP Application layer protocols.
11. Name the two main TCP/IP Transport layer protocols.
12. Name some of the TCP/IP Internet layer protocols.
13. Name some of the TCP/IP Network Interface layer protocols.
14. How is the TCP/IP protocol stack implemented on a computer?
15. What TCP/IP information is usually configured on an Internet user's computer?
16. What is the most common type of LAN nowadays?
17. How do the Transport and Internet layers package the data that they receive?
18. Which Application layer protocol is used to download web pages?
19. Which Application layer protocol is used to send email?
20. Which Application layer protocol is used to look up IP addresses of domains?
21. Which Application layer protocol is used to automatically configure networked computers?
22. What are the two versions of the Internet that are currently deployed?
23. What was the main reason for deploying IPv6?
24. Name some of the main Top-Level Domains.
25. What network equipment device is used to route Internet traffic?
26. What equipment device connects a user's computer to a phone line for Internet access?
27. What Internet application is used to find information on the Internet?
28. What Internet application is used to get web page updates?
29. What Internet application allows for making free or cheap phone calls on the Internet?
30. What are some of the Internet disadvantages?

(The answers to these questions are at the end of the book)

2.8.2 Reading and pronouncing acronyms

Complete the following table by showing how these Internet acronyms are pronounced and what they stand for.

Acronym	Pronunciation	Acronym expansion
DNS		
HTTP		
POP		
IMAP		
ARP		
WiFi		
WiMAX		
WAN		
MAN		
POTS		
MAC		
PPP		
IPv6		
IM		
TCP/IP		
B2B		
B2C		
B2G		
C2C		
NIC		
.com		
.org		
.edu		
.us		
.cn		
.biz		
.mil		
.gov		
.net		

(The answers to these questions are at the end of the book)

2.8.3 Cloze

Fill in the blanks in the following statements with the correct words.

1. The Internet is a worldwide collection of interconnected _____.
2. The Internet was originally deployed in the _____.
3. Slow dial-up connections have been replaced by _____ connections.
4. In order to surf the Internet, a user needs to use a software program called a _____.
5. The company installed a _____ on its network to keep hackers away.
6. When looking for information online, a user can try one of the many _____.
7. My mailbox is full of unwanted _____ from advertisers.
8. A website can be reached by clicking on its _____.
9. Today's chat software is comprehensive and allows for text, voice and _____ chatting.
10. Internet users should protect their computers by installing anti-_____ software.
11. In order to test their systems, some companies hire _____ to try to break into them.
12. WiFi and WiMAX provide _____ access to the Internet.
13. An ADSL modem is used to provide broadband access over a _____ line.
14. A layered-model of a communication protocol suite such as TCP/IP is called a _____.
15. DNS is used to find the corresponding _____ of domain names.
16. An ISP uses a _____ server to automatically configure the users' computers.
17. _____ allows an Internet connection to be used for making free or cheap telephone calls.
18. A browser uses a protocol called _____ to get web pages.
19. Using _____, an Internet user can stay updated with his/her favorite web pages.
20. Some Internet users write _____ as a sort of diary to be shared with other netizens.
21. _____ use the packets' IP addresses to send them to the proper destination.
22. Because it is much slower than email, post office mail is referred to as _____.
23. Very popular applications such as email and the Web are called _____ applications.
24. A website's full domain name is called its _____ or _____.
25. One of the major advantages of IPv6 over IPv4 is that it provides many more _____.
26. An IPv4 address has 32 _____, whereas an IPv6 address has 128.
27. A computer that is connected to the Internet needs to be configured with a unique _____.
28. A website that provides a comprehensive set of Internet services is called a _____.
29. B2B and B2C are examples of _____.
30. Top-Level Domains can be Global, such as ".com", and _____, such as ".us".
31. On a computer, TCP/IP is mainly implemented as part of the _____.
32. The most common type of LAN nowadays is _____.
33. Online sex-related material such as pictures and videos is called _____.
34. The illegal online posting and free downloading of copyrighted material is called _____.

(The answers to these questions are at the end of the book)

2.8.4 Internet action words

Match the following verbs in the table to the Internet words below. Note that each verb may match more than one Internet word.

Access	Assign	Attach	Bookmark	Browse
Buy	Change	Chat	Check	Click on
Code in	Compile	Compose	Configure	Connect
Connect to	Create	Decrypt	Delete	Design
Download	Draw	Encrypt	Execute	Forward
Get	Go	Infected by	Link to	Log on
Meet	Open	Point to	Program in	Read
Receive	Register	Reply to	Run	Save
Select	Send	Set up	Shop	Store
Study	Surf	Transfer	Type	Use

_____ email _____ a domain name

_____ a browser _____ a router

_____ Java _____ online

_____ the Internet _____ an IP address

_____ a web page _____ a link

_____ a virus

(The answers to these questions are at the end of the book)

2.8.5 Identifying internet elements

Match the words in the following table to the correct Internet elements in the figure below.

Browser icon
Browser window
Chat window
Emoticon
IM icon
Link
URL or URI

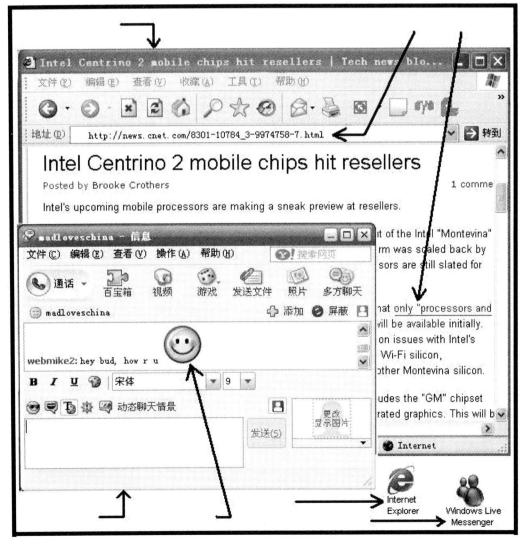

(The answers are at the end of the book)

2.8.6 Internet essays

1. Write an essay about how the Internet has changed the world.
2. Write an essay about the future development of the Internet.
3. Write an essay about how to design an excellent web page.
4. Write an essay about the Internet's effects on education.
5. Write an essay about the Internet's effects on entertainment and media.
6. Write an essay about doing business on the Internet.
7. Write an essay about the dangers Internet users encounter.
8. Write an essay about how the Internet could be used to save endangered cultures.
9. Write an essay about how the Internet could be used as an efficient advertising tool.
10. Write an essay summarizing some of the highlights in your blog.

2.8.7 Speaking exercises

1. Debate the advantages and disadvantages of the Internet.
2. Debate whether the United States or the United Nations should administer the Internet.
3. Debate whether teenagers' access to the Internet should be restricted or limited.
4. Debate whether countries should censor Internet content.
5. Debate whether hackers should be prosecuted.
6. Debate whether the Internet will make personal computers obsolete.
7. Give a talk about how you use the Internet.
8. Brainstorm about future Internet killer applications.
9. Debate whether online pornography should be legalized.
10. Give a talk about the abbreviations used in chat rooms.
11. Describe how to configure a computer for Internet access.
12. Summarize in your own words the advantages of IPv6 over IPv4.
13. Debate which search engine is best.
14. Debate which portal is best.
15. Describe some examples of good netiquette.
16. Brainstorm some new catchy domain names that could be sold for large profits.
17. Describe the functions of the layers of the TCP/IP stack.
18. Describe the differences between TCP and UDP.
19. Debate the advantages and disadvantages of English being the Internet lingua franca.
20. Debate whether excessive P2P data flows through the Internet should be restricted by ISPs.

2.9 Internet glossary

ADSL	Technology that allows a regular phone line to be used for broadband access	**Cybercafé**	A public establishment where users can surf the Internet
Adware	Type of Malware that tracks a user's online activity and displays unwanted ads	**Cyber crime**	Crime committed in cyberspace
Attachment	Extra material, such as pictures, added to an email message	**Cyberspace**	The whole virtual realm or space that users are part of when they surf the Internet
Avatar	A cyberspace user's virtual image, such as a cartoon picture	**Dial-up**	Slow method of Internet access via a phone line and modem
Blog	Online diaries and other records written by online users	**DNS**	Domain Name System. A system used to look up the IP addresses of domain names
Bookmark	Add a web page to one's list of favorite web pages	**Domain name**	Name of a cyberspace site, e.g. www.lebaishi.com
Browser	Software application that allows surfing of the Internet	**Download**	To get some material from the Internet to one's computer
Chat	Communicating online and in real time with other netizens using text, voice or video	**Email**	Internet communication tool that replaced the old post office mail
Cookie	Small file put on a user's computer by a website to keep track of the user	**Emoticon**	Small, cartoon face that shows various emotions, such as smiling, and that is used in chatting
Cursor	The arrow or bar symbol that moves on the screen in step with the mouse's movement	**Filter**	A software program used to block inappropriate Internet material

Firewall	An implementation, hardware and/or software, used to protect networks from unwanted access	**Link**	A highlighted website domain name that users click on to visit the website
Flame	Online verbal attack by one netizen on another	**Mailbox**	An online resource for email storage, retrieval and so on
Freeware	Software that is free to use	**Malware**	Malicious Software. All types of software that can harm users
FTP	File Transfer Protocol. Protocol used to download or upload large files	**Modem**	Modulator Demodulator. A device to connect a computer to an analog transmission medium
Hacker	Someone who breaks into others' computer systems	**Net bar**	A public establishment where users can surf the Internet
Icon	Small picture representing a software program	**Netiquette**	A set of recommended behavior rules when surfing the Internet
Instant messaging	IM. Real-time communication tool, such as MSN Messenger and QQ	**Netizen**	Network Citizen. An Internet user
Intranet	An organization's internal network	**Operating system**	The foundation software that controls the functioning of a computer. One example is Linux
IP address	A numeric, logical address that identifies an Internet resource. One example is 10.1.2.99	**Piracy**	The online illegal trafficking of copyrighted material
ISP	Internet Service Provider. A network entity that provides Internet access service	**Plug-in**	A software program that can be added to a browser to enhance it
LAN	Local Area Network. A network to connect computers in a local area such an office, building or campus	**Pornography**	Sexually related content

Protocol	A set of rules that govern how an interface functions	Surf	Use the Internet
P2P	Peer to Peer. An application for user-to-user file sharing	Trojan horse	Harmful program hidden inside a seemingly safe program
Router	A networking device that connects networks and routes traffic	Upload	To move content from a computer to the Internet
RSS	Really Simple Syndication. An application that provides website updates to subscribed users	URL	Uniform Resource Locator. Text-form address of website
Search engine	A software tool for finding information online	Virus	Malicious software that can harm a computer when it is run
Server	A special computer used for data processing applications	VoIP	Voice over IP. Technology for making phone calls on the Internet
Shareware	Software that requires payment after a short trial period	Webcam	Web camera
Snail mail	Post office mail	Web page hit	A click on a web page by a user
Software	All the code that resides inside a computer or host	Website	A cyberspace address. It consists of one or more web pages
Software application	A software program that handles a specific need such as browsing	Webware	Web Software
Software utility	A software program that can enhance an operating system	WiFi	Wireless Fidelity. Wireless technology for Internet access
Spam	Unsollicited email from advertisers	WiMAX	Worldwide Interoperability for Microwave access. Broadband wireless technology
Spyware	Malware that spies on users	Worm	A replicating virus

UNIT 3

MOBILE PHONES

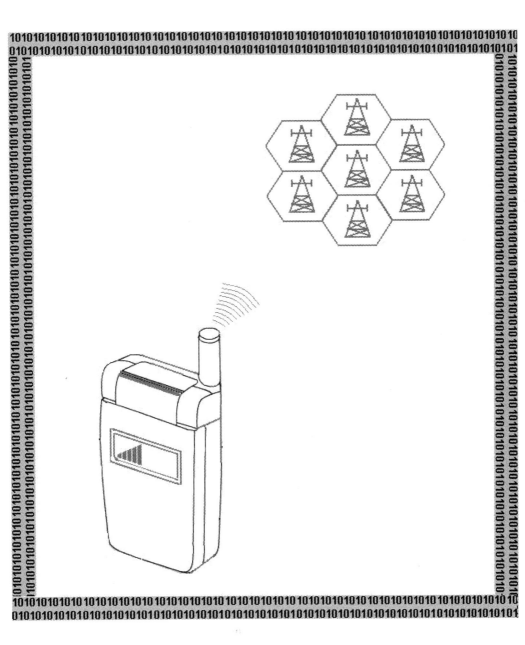

MOBILE PHONE KEYWORDS

ADC	模数转换器	Latency	延迟时间
Antenna	天线	LTE	长期演进
AuC	鉴别中心	Main board	主板
Bluetooth	蓝牙	MIMO	多输入多输出
BSC	基站控制器	MMS	多媒体信息服务
BSS	基站（子）系统	Mobile phone	手机
BTS	无线电收发机基站	MSC	移动交换中心
Case	外壳	Navigation key	导航键
CDMA	码分多路存取	Node B	结点 B
Cell	小区	OLED	有机发光二级管
Cell cluster	小区群集	Pixel	像素
Cell phone	手机	Projector	投影仪
Channel	信（通）道	Recharge	充电
Codec	编译码器	RAN	无线接入网
DAC	数模转换器	RNC	无线网络控制器
Display	屏幕 / 显示	RNS	无线网络（子）系统
Downlink	下行链路	Roam	漫步 / 漫游
DSP	数字信号处理器	RTOS	实时操作系统
EDGE	GSM 演进的增强数据速率	Sensor	传感器
		SGSN	服务 GPRS 支持节点
FDD	频分双工	SIM card	用户身份模块卡
FDMA	频分多路存取	Smartphone	智能手机
Flash	闪光灯	SMS	短消息服务
Form factor	形状因子	Speaker	扬声器
Frequency spectrum	频谱	Stylus	触控笔
GMSC	网关移动业务交换中心	TDD	时分双工
		TDMA	时分多路存取
GGSN	网关 GPRS 支持节点	3G	第三代移动通信系统
GSM	全球移动通信系统	Touch-screen	触摸屏
GPRS	通用分组无线业务	UE	用户设备
Handoff	移交 / 越区切换	UMTS	通用移动通信系统
Handset	手机	Uplink	上行链路
HLR	本网地址登记	VLR	来访者地址登记
HSPA	高速分组存取	Zoom	变焦
Keypad	小键盘		

3.1 Introduction

Nowadays, if there were one high-tech device we could not live without, that device would have to be the mobile phone. The mobile phone has surpassed the computer and other high-tech gadgets in popularity to become our most essential tool. The mobile phone reached this central role by allowing us to be in touch with the world anytime and anywhere. The mobile phone also keeps enhancing its importance by incorporating functions of other high-tech devices such as computers, radios, televisions, cameras and so on.

3.2 Mobile phone history

Mobile phones have been around for about two decades. During this time, they have evolved through a few generations in order to keep up with users' requirements. The first-generation (1G) mobile phone systems came about to address the users' mobility by unshackling the users from the fixed phones. The 1G mobile phones were bulky (sometimes likened to bricks), and analog, i.e. they used analog signals to connect to the mobile phone networks.

The second-generation (2G) mobile phone systems came about to allow more users to use the limited frequency spectrum. The 2G mobile phones achieved this spectrum efficiency by using digital signals to communicate with the mobile phone networks. Indeed, digital signals can be compressed and multiplexed to give the phone system a bigger capacity. As of 2008, the 2G mobile phones are still widely used and come in two types. The most popular type is called Global System for Mobile communications (GSM) and uses Time Division Multiple Access (TDMA). The other type is called Code Division Multiple Access (CDMA).

The 2G mobile phone systems mainly address voice communication, and their data capability is quite paltry. While waiting for the third-generation (3G) mobile communications systems to fully address this data transfer need, sub-generations called 2.5G and 2.75G have been deployed. The 2.5G and 2.75G mobile phone systems support such data services as Short Messaging Service (SMS), Multimedia Messaging Service (MMS), Wireless Application Protocol (WAP), and video games. In the case of GSM, the 2.5G technology is referred to as the General Packet Radio Service (GPRS), and the 2.75G technology is referred to as the Enhanced Data rates for GSM Evolution (EDGE).

The 3G mobile phone systems, which are currently being deployed, provide faster data transfer rates. They are broadband systems and support simple voice calls, video calls, and all kinds of Internet services such as web browsing, email, instant messaging, online searching and so on. There are three 3G technologies. The first one is called the Universal Mobile Telecommunications System (UMTS) and uses wideband CDMA; thus, it is also referred to as WCDMA. UMTS is the 3G evolution of GSM. The second 3G technology is called

CDMA2000 and is the 3G evolution of CDMA. The third 3G technology, mainly developed and supported by China, is called the Time Division Synchronous CDMA (TD-SCDMA).

As with the evolution from 2G to 3G, the evolution from 3G to 4G is also going through sub-generations. Namely, UMTS has evolved to a 3.5G technology called the High Speed Packet Access (HSPA), which delivers higher data transfer rates.

The fourth-generation (4G) mobile phone systems are needed to provide real broadband (such as speeds of tens of megabits per second) wireless access to accommodate the huge data traffic that has eclipsed the traditional voice traffic. UMTS is evolving to a 4G technology called the Long Term Evolution (LTE). CDMA2000 may evolve to a 4G technology called the Ultra Mobile Broadband (UMB). Finally, there is a very promising 4G technology that has already started being deployed and is called the Worldwide Interoperability for Microwave Access (WiMAX).

The following figure shows the evolution of the mobile phone technology.

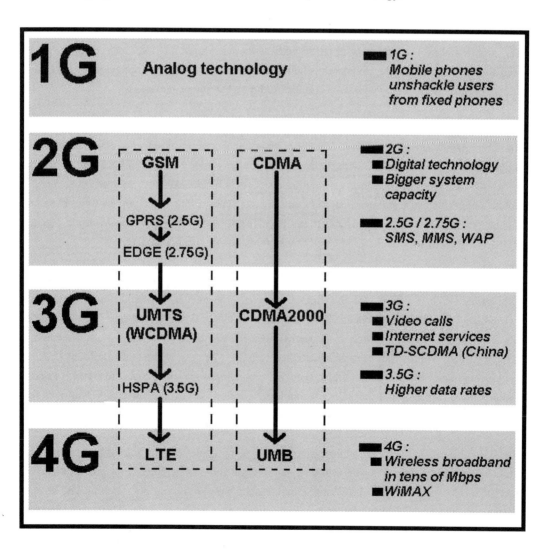

UNIT 3   MOBILE PHONES

3.3   Mobile phone handsets

The overall mobile phone system could be regarded as consisting of two main entities, the mobile phone handsets and the mobile phone network.   The mobile phone handsets are highly integrated electronic devices that consist of hardware and software.   They are also available in a variety of form factors and perform many functions.

3.3.1   Mobile phone form factors

Mobile phones have come a long way, from the early days when they were referred to as bricks because of their bulky shape, to the modern slick designs such as the iPhone from Apple.   This evolution in design was necessary to cater to the various consumer tastes.   Today's mobile phones come in various form factors that consumers can choose from.   These form factors include the following designs: candy bar, clamshell, flip, slider, swivel, and twist.   These form factors are illustrated in the following figure.

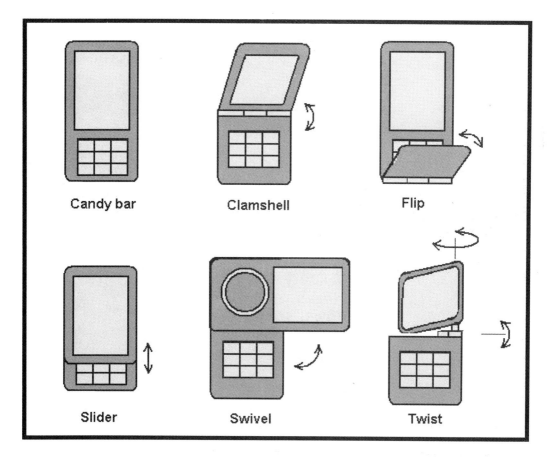

3.3.2 Mobile phone hardware

The mobile phone handset hardware includes the elements shown in the following figure.

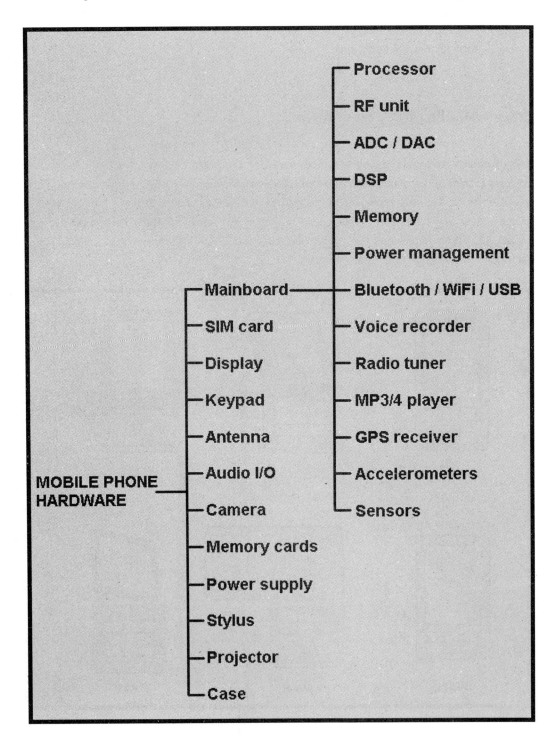

3.3.2.1 Main board

The main board, also called the motherboard, is a multi-layer Printed Circuit Board (PCB) on which is mounted most of the electronic circuitry inside a mobile phone. The main board electronics include the following components.

- *Processor*. The processors in today's mobile phones, especially smartphones, which are basically small computers, manage both the voice and data interfaces. For the voice interface, the processors manage the interaction of the mobile phone with the mobile phone network during such phases as registration, authentication, call setup, call termination, call handoff and so on. For the data interface, the processors manage such data flows as the keyboard input, display output and so on.

  The mobile phone processors are designed to have a very low power consumption so as to meet the users' demand for a long battery life. As a comparison, whereas laptop computers' processors may have power envelopes of about 25 to 45W, mobile phones' processors are limited to power envelopes of less than about 1W.

- *RF unit*. Mobile phones are wireless devices that need to communicate with the mobile phone networks. This wireless communication is possible via antennas: the antennas on the mobile phones on one hand, and the antennas on the mobile phone networks' towers on the other. Inside the mobile phone, the Radio Frequency (RF) unit on the main board transmits and receives antenna signals.

- *ADC / DAC*. Voice input into a mobile phone is an analog signal and thus needs to be digitized so that it can be processed by the mobile phone. This digital conversion is done by the Analog to Digital Converter (ADC). Conversely, digital signals from the mobile phone that are output as voice or audio signals are converted into analog signals using the Digital to Analog Converter (DAC). The ADC and DAC inside a mobile phone are parts of a unit called the coder/decoder or codec.

- *DSP*. Signal processing and manipulation inside a mobile phone is a critical function that is accomplished by a high-speed Digital Signal Processor (DSP). Indeed, voice communication does not tolerate any significant delays, and thus the voice signal needs to be processed in real time. The DSP accomplishes this real-time task using its incredibly powerful signal processing capability. The DSP processes both incoming and outgoing voice signals to make phone conversations sound normal, without any annoying delays or echoes. The DSP signal processing tasks include modulation/demodulation, coding/decoding and equalization.

- *Memory*. The main board contains memory in the form of ROM, flash, and sometimes RAM. ROM memory is used to store the operating system. Since ROM memory is read only and cannot be overwritten, the operating system of the mobile phone is safely stored even when turning off the phone, and deleting or formatting the internal memory. Flash memory is used to store the application programs and the data. Finally, RAM memory is used when running programs. Sometimes flash memory is used to replace RAM.

- *Power management*. Power management inside a mobile phone accomplishes multiple tasks such as conserving power, displaying the battery charge status, and recharging the battery.

- *Bluetooth / WiFi / USB*. A mobile phone may use Bluetooth to wirelessly connect with other mobile phones or peripherals such as headsets. For surfing the Internet, a mobile phone may use WiFi to wirelessly connect to the Internet. A mobile phone may also have a USB port for connecting to USB enabled devices.

- *Voice recorder*. A voice recorder is used to record voice and audio. It is useful when taking voice notes.

- *Radio tuner*. An FM radio tuner allows a user to listen to FM radio programs.

- *MP3/4 player*. An MP3 player is used to play music while an MP4 player can be used to play video and movie clips.

- *GPS receiver*. A Global Positioning System (GPS) receiver can provide location services such as emergency and navigation services. Mobile phones use a variation of GPS called Assisted GPS (A-GPS), which means that the mobile phones use information from the mobile phone network in order to quickly home in on the GPS satellites.

- *Accelerometers*. Accelerometers can sense movement and are used to automatically change the display view between portrait and landscape modes by simply rotating the mobile phone. While portrait viewing is the most commonly used mode, sometimes landscape viewing is more appropriate such as when viewing video or movie clips.

- *Sensors*. Sensors are designed into mobile phones to make them more user and environment friendly. For example, a proximity sensor is used to turn off the mobile phone display when the handset is held close to the ear, thus conserving power. In another example, an ambient light sensor is used to adjust the display brightness to the surrounding environment, thus making the display clear whether in bright or dark areas.

3.3.2.2 SIM card

A mobile phone Subscriber Identity Module (SIM) card is a small card, about the size of a postage stamp or small coin, which contains the identification and connection information needed to register a mobile phone with a mobile phone network and to make calls. Specifically, a SIM card holds the user's phone number. So a user can keep the same phone number when switching phones simply by using the same SIM card in the new phone. In addition to the user's phone number, a SIM card holds a number called the International Mobile Subscriber Identity (IMSI), which uniquely identifies the user. The IMSI is used because there are many mobile networks around the world. In order to keep the anonymity of the user, the IMSI is usually not transmitted by the mobile phone to the network. Instead, a randomly generated number called the Temporary IMSI (TIMSI) is sent. Besides these numbers, a SIM card can also store data such as the list of phone numbers of a user's contacts.

Since a mobile phone's SIM card holds sensitive information, it can be password protected with a Personal Identification Number (PIN) that the user chooses. As an additional security feature, if the PIN code is incorrectly entered three times in a row, the SIM card is locked. In this case, the user needs another number, the Personal Unblocking Key (PUK), to unlock it. The PUK code is furnished to the user when the user purchases a SIM card.

The SIM card is removable, fits into a socket or tray in the mobile phone, and is usually held in place by some type of mechanical spring latch. Since each SIM card is unique, it is identified by a unique International Circuit Card ID (ICCID) number. Finally, in UMTS (3G), this card is referred to as a Universal Subscriber Identity Module (USIM).

3.3.2.3 Display

When it comes to mobile phone displays, Organic Light Emitting Diodes (OLED) displays have displaced LCD displays because of the following important factors. First, OLEDs emit their own light and thus OLED displays do not need backlighting whereas LCD displays do. Second, OLED displays use less power since they do not require backlighting. Third, they have a high contrast ratio and display rich colors with large viewing angles.

Mobile phone displays come in different sizes. However, since mobile phones are designed to be small enough to fit into pockets, they cannot have very large displays. Perhaps the best current display size is the 3.5" display chosen by Apple Inc. on its stylishly and ergonomically well-designed iPhone. On such a display, even web pages look impressive.

Traditionally, the displays of mobile phones functioned simply as information output displays. However, nowadays some displays are touch-screens and used for information input. Such touch-screens may display virtual keyboards in many languages. A user may use fingers or a stylus to interface with the touch-screen. A recent development in this area is the Apple Multi-touch, which detects multiple-finger input. For example, a pinch using the thumb and index fingers is used to minimize a picture, whereas a spreading of the two fingers is used to enlarge a picture.

In addition to a mobile phone's main display, another small display is sometimes used such as on some clamshell phones. This small display, also referred to as an indicator window or an external display, is used to display such data as the time, date, network signal strength, and battery charge status.

3.3.2.4 Keypad

Mobile phones come with different keypads. The most traditional of keypads is the alphanumeric one in which the numbers 0 to 9 and the alphabet are arranged in four rows of three keys or buttons each. The keypad also includes some special function keys or buttons such as for power. Keypads may also have a navigation key that allows for up, down, left and right navigation on the display.

Keypads have evolved to other designs as well. For example, some mobile phones use virtual keypads on touch-screen displays. The user interacts with the buttons of these virtual keypads via fingers or a stylus.

Another keypad design that has arisen to meet the need for email input on mobile phones is the QWERTY keypad. This is a tiny replica of the computer keyboard.

3.3.2.5 Antenna

Mobile phone antennas are used to transmit signals to and receive signals from the mobile phone networks. They accomplish this task by transforming the mobile phone outgoing signals from electric signals to electromagnetic waves, and transforming the incoming signals from electromagnetic waves to electric signals. The length of an antenna is inversely proportional to the transmission frequency; thus, the higher the transmission frequency, the shorter the antenna.

Early mobile phones used external or retractable antennas that users needed to extend during calls. Then came small, fixed but protruding antennas called "stubbies" since they protruded out like stubs. In today's mobile phones, antennas are entirely internal, inside the cases of the mobile phones. These internal antennas are sometimes called invisible antennas or "intennas".

Today's mobile phones incorporate a variety of wireless technologies such as Bluetooth and WiFi.

Thus, mobile phone antennas need to handle more than just voice signals. A revolutionary new approach to antenna design called Multiple Input Multiple Output (MIMO) uses multiple antennas to provide very high data transfer rates. MIMO is used with the latest iteration of WiFi called WiFi-n, and 4G technologies such as WiMAX.

3.3.2.6 Audio I/O

Audio I/O on a mobile phone includes a microphone, a speaker, volume control buttons or dial, an earphone or headset jack, and an earphone or a headset. Mobile phones support many audio formats such as MP3 and WAV, and speakers can provide stereo sound. Some mobile phone speakers can be as loud as a typical FM radio set.

A convenient enhancement to mobile phones has been the adoption of Bluetooth headsets, which do away with encumbering wires. Bluetooth headsets can also provide stereo sound.

3.3.2.7 Camera

Just as they displaced radios and MP3 players, mobile phones are also taking on the functions of still and video cameras. Some camera mobile phones come equipped with up to 10 Megapixels, thus providing high-resolution images. These phone cameras sport such advanced features as autofocus, flash, and face recognition technology. Still images are usually stored in the popular JPEG format.

Mobile phones can also record video. CMOS image sensors, which are more economical for mass production, allowed this video function to be ported to mobile phones. Mobile phones can record video in many formats including MPEG4 and WMV.

3.3.2.8 Memory cards

Memory cards with higher and higher capacities that reach into the gigabytes have enabled mobile phones to run more applications and store more data. Some examples of capacities include 2, 4, 8, 16 and even more gigabytes.

These tiny, removable, flash-memory cards are available in many formats such as the Secure Digital (SD) format, e.g. miniSD and microSD, and the Multi Media Card (MMC) format, e.g. Reduced Size MMC (RS-MMC), and MMCmicro.

3.3.2.9 Power supply

Users expect mobile phone batteries to last for a long time on a single charge. Since these batteries are constrained by size and weight limits, their design is critically important. Nowadays, mobile phone batteries are made of Lithium-Ion (Li-Ion). Li-Ion batteries are efficient, i.e. they deliver a high power in a lightweight package, last a long time, and do not suffer from memory effect like older batteries.

Mobile phone batteries are rechargeable. In most mobile phones, these batteries are removable, thus allowing users to easily swap them. However, some mobile phones such as the iPhone from Apple come with their batteries soldered to the main board.

Mobile phones are sold with AC power adapters or chargers to recharge the batteries. Some mobile phones can also be powered via USB when they are connected to a computer.

3.3.2.10 Stylus

Some mobile phones include a stylus that could be used for handwriting and display navigation. For some languages such as Chinese, handwriting on the display using a stylus is an efficient input method. A stylus may also be a better tool than fingers when tapping on the display since it doesn't leave any smudges due to moisture. Finally, on some virtual keyboards on the display, the keys are too small and crowded together, and a stylus is needed for input.

3.3.2.11 Projector

Using mobile phones as projectors to display all kinds of information such as photos, videos, slides and documents is a promising future killer application. Soon mobile phones will be equipped with tiny projectors to make this feature become a reality. Coincidentally, mobile phones can already be used as remote controls and could potentially be used as laser pointers, and flashlights.

3.3.2.12 Case

Cases of mobile phones come in many form factors, colors, and materials. Some cases are inscribed or painted with the logos of famous fashion brands. Some expensive cases are even decked with precious stones.

3.3.3 Mobile phone functions

The mobile phone has tremendously enhanced its original voice-communication-only ability by integrating numerous useful functions that make it our most essential electronic device. These functions are outlined as follows.

Calling and messaging.
The mobile phone is a communication device that supports making and receiving phone calls, both voice and video ones. It can also be used for exchanging simple text SMS messages and multimedia MMS messages.

Multimedia.
The mobile phone is a multimedia device that can be used for taking pictures, recording videos, watching TV, watching videos and movies, listening to music, surfing the radio, and playing games.

Internet.
The mobile phone is an Internet device that can be used for surfing the Web, searching for information, downloading content, chatting via IM, exchanging email, and enjoying GPS-supported services.

Education.
The mobile phone is an education tool that can be used as an electronic dictionary and an e-book reader.

Personal Information Manager (PIM).
The mobile phone is a PIM that can be used for managing contacts, keeping a calendar, taking notes, managing tasks, and taking voice recordings.

Computer.
The mobile phone is a computer that can be used for performing office applications such as word processing, storing data, performing calculations, acting as a projector, and synching with other devices.

Wallet and watch.
The mobile phone is a device that is used as a watch, an alarm clock, an ID, and a credit card.

"Swiss army knife".
The mobile phone is a Swiss army knife in that it keeps adding more useful functions in a small package. Some of these functions include using the mobile phone as a remote control, a laser pointer, a flashlight, and so on.

The mobile phone functions are summarized in the following figure.

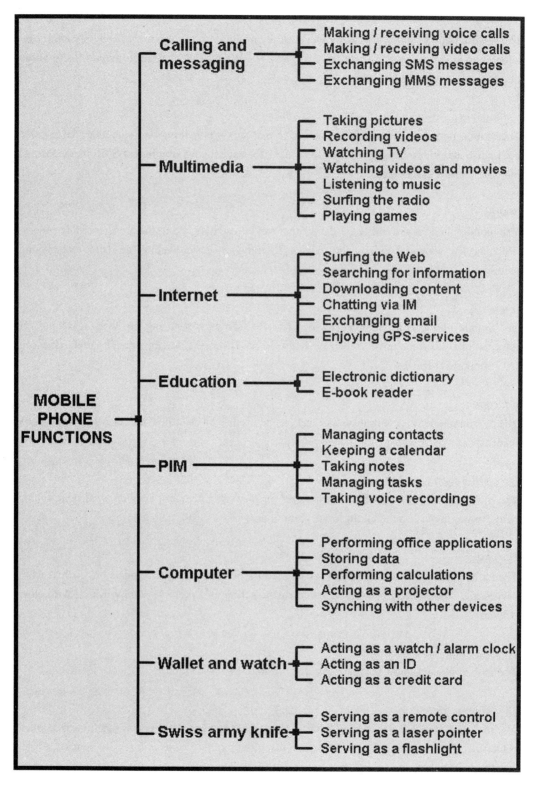

3.3.4 Mobile phone software

Mobile phone software consists of two main categories: communications software and applications software. Communications software is responsible for handling voice calls, thus, it is real time and needs to be up and running continuously. Traditionally, mobile phones use a Real Time Operating System (RTOS) to run the communications software.

Applications software includes all the end-user applications such as multimedia and graphics. Higher-end mobile phones such as smartphones include more applications than entry-level mobile phones. Smartphones usually use an Open Operating System (Open OS), such as Symbian or Linux, to run the applications software.

Smartphone software can be diagramed as a stack that consists of the following layers from bottom to top:

- Operating System (OS) kernel.
- Software libraries.
- Application Programming Interfaces (API) and Graphical User Interface (GUI).
- Applications.

3.3.5 Mobile phone processing power

The processing power of mobile phones has been evolving to meet their evolution from traditional voice-only to smartphone models. Depending on the model, a mobile phone may include the following processors.

- *A DSP for signal processing*. The DSP is used to process the physical layer (L1) of the communications software protocol stack.

- *A microcontroller running an RTOS*. The microcontroller is used to process the upper layers, Layers 2 and 3 (L2 and L3), of the communications software protocol stack. This microcontroller and the DSP may be integrated into a single ASIC called the Baseband Processor.

- *A processor running an Open OS*. This processor is used to run the user applications such as multimedia. This processor is called the Applications Processor. The Baseband and Applications Processors may be integrated into a single, multifunction processor.

3.4 Mobile phone networks

Mobile phone networks have evolved from the early analog-technology, limited-coverage 1G networks to today's 3G/4G digital, global networks. This evolution is driven and supported by huge numbers of customers who are shedding their fixed phones and signing up for the convenience of mobility. In many cases, the revenues of mobile phone network operators dwarf those of companies operating fixed phone networks as user migration toward phone mobility continues unabated. Mobile phone networks keep up with this surging user demand by designing efficient networks and upgrading them with the latest technologies.

3.4.1 Mobile phone network architecture

A basic diagram of the mobile phone system architecture is as shown in the following figure.

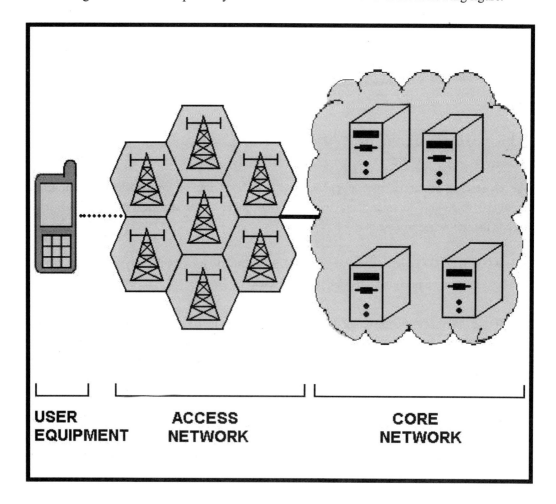

As can be seen in the previous figure, the mobile phone system architecture consists of three parts:

- The user equipment such as the mobile phone handsets,
- The access network made of transceiver towers and their related facilities,
- The core network.

3.4.1.1 User equipment

The user equipment could be mobile phones or devices equipped with cellular access. The user equipment is referred to differently depending on the technology. In 2G, the user equipment is labeled Mobile Station (MS), whereas in 3G it is called User Equipment (UE).

3.4.1.2 Access network

The access network is the most visible part of the mobile phone network because of its prominent radio towers and antennas. The access network is called the Radio Access Network (RAN) and is the bridge between the user equipment and the core network.

As the number of mobile phone users soared, the access network had to keep up with the demand. Since the frequency spectrum available for mobile phone communications is limited, mobile phone network operators design their access networks for an efficient use of this spectrum by dividing the access network coverage area into small parts, called cells. Cells are usually shown with hexagonal shapes that perfectly mesh in a honeycomb diagram. However, in reality such a layout is corrupted by such factors as the terrain and signal attenuation.

Each cell has its own transceiver (transmitter-receiver) tower, or base station. Adjacent base stations are grouped together and managed by a single network facility called the base station controller.

3.4.1.3 Core network

The core network performs the call-switching functions that allow mobile phone users to connect with other users, whether mobile or fixed-phone ones. The core network is comprised of switching facilities and supporting databases that are used for registration when mobile phones are activated, authentication when calls are made, handoff when users move among cells, billing and so forth. The core network technology is changing from the traditional circuit-switching model to a packet-switching model.

3.4.2 2G network architecture—GSM

A diagram of the GSM mobile phone network architecture is as shown in the following figure.

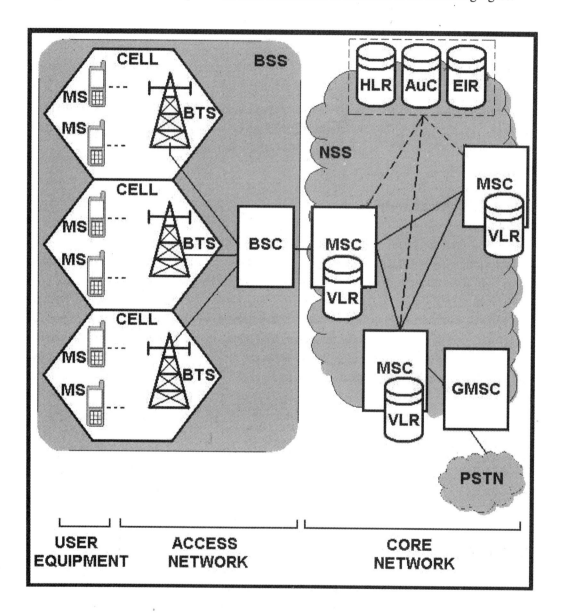

3.4.2.1 GSM user equipment

The user equipment could be mobile phones or devices equipped with cellular access. As can be seen in the above figure, in GSM terminology, the user equipment is referred to as Mobile Station (MS).

3.4.2.2 GSM access network

As can be seen in the previous figure, the GSM access network or RAN is structured as follows:

- The coverage area is divided into cells.
- Each cell has a base station or transceiver facility called the Base Transceiver Station (BTS). The BTS comprises all the equipment necessary to conduct radio communications with mobile phones. The BTS includes the tower, antennas, signal processors, and amplifiers.
- Adjacent base stations or BTSs are grouped together and managed by a single network facility called the Base Station Controller (BSC). The BSC handles the handoff between the BTSs as users roam among cells.
- A system of multiple BTSs and their corresponding BSC is called a Base Station Subsystem (BSS).

3.4.2.3 GSM core network

The GSM core network, also referred to as the Network and Switching Subsystem (NSS), is a circuit-switched network comprised of multiple Mobile Switching Centers (MSC). The MSC is the facility that performs the call switching process and allows mobile phone users to connect to other users.

Each MSC is connected to many BSCs and handles voice traffic from them. The MSC that is connected to the Public Switched Telephone Network (PSTN) is called the Gateway MSC (GMSC).

The MSC uses the following core network databases to accomplish its tasks:

- *Home Location Register (HLR)*. The HLR database stores the permanent data about mobile phone users. The HLR is a central and unique database inside the core network.
- *Visitor Location Register (VLR)*. The VLR database stores the temporary data about mobile phone users as they visit different cells. Each MSC has a co-located VLR.
- *Authentication Center (AuC)*. The AuC database is used for authenticating mobile phone users.
- *Equipment Identity Register (EIR)*. The EIR database is used to check the validation of mobile phones.

3.4.3 2.5G network architecture—GPRS

A diagram of the 2.5G mobile phone network architecture is as shown in the following figure.

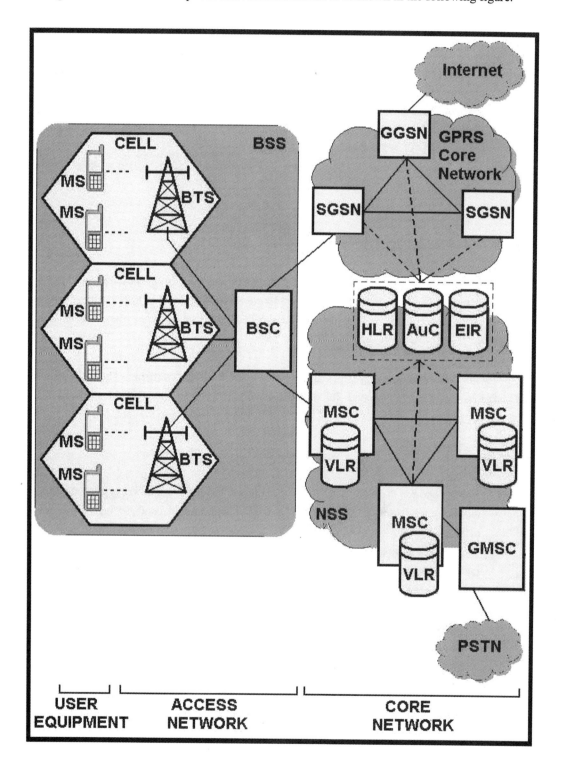

As can be seen in the previous figure, a major addition when transitioning from GSM (2G) to GPRS (2.5G) is the addition of a new data network in the core network. This new data network is called the GPRS core network.

3.4.3.1 GPRS user equipment

The GPRS user equipment is also referred to as Mobile Station (MS). Since GPRS offers a new air interface between the network radio towers and the MSs, GPRS users need to buy MSs that are GPRS capable. Note that these GPRS MSs are backward compatible with the traditional GSM networks.

3.4.3.2 GPRS access network

As can be seen in the previous figure, the BSC needs to interface with the new GPRS core network. Thus, the old GSM access network has to be upgraded to support the GPRS service. Namely, the BTS requires a software upgrade, while the BSC requires both a software upgrade and a hardware addition called the Packet Control Unit (PCU).

3.4.3.3 GPRS core network

When upgrading from a purely GSM network to GPRS, network operators need to expand the core network with a new packet switched network to support GPRS data. The GPRS network is an IP-based internal backbone that contains the following types of facilities:

- *Serving GPRS Support Node (SGSN)*. In a GPRS network, the BSC separates the traffic coming from mobile phones into voice and data. The BSC sends the voice traffic to the MSC as usual, but sends the data traffic to the SGSN. Thus, the SGSN acts as an MSC for the data traffic.
- *Gateway GPRS Support Node (GGSN)*. The GGSN acts as gateway to other data networks such as the Internet.

Since the GPRS network is IP-based but internal, the way it handles Internet data which is also IP-based is to tunnel it between the GGSN and the SGSN.

The GPRS IP network supports the transition from 2G to 3G and beyond. The ultimate goal of mobile phone network operators is to build all-IP networks that handle both voice and data.

3.4.4 3G network architecture—UMTS

A diagram of the UMTS mobile phone network architecture is as shown in the following figure.

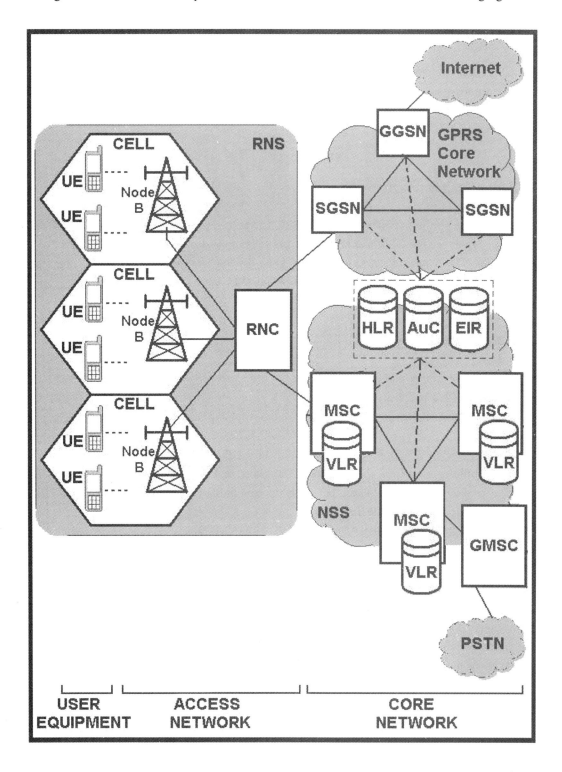

3.4.4.1 UMTS user equipment

The UMTS user equipment is referred to as User Equipment (UE). Since UMTS offers a new air interface between the network radio towers and the UEs, UMTS users need to buy UEs that are UMTS capable. Note that these UMTS UEs are backward compatible with the traditional GSM networks.

3.4.4.2 UMTS access network

The UMTS access network uses a similar topology to GSM/GPRS, but a different terminology as shown in the following table.

	GSM	UMTS
Base station	Base Transceiver Station (**BTS**)	**Node B**
Base station controller	Base Station Controller (**BSC**)	Radio Network Controller (**RNC**)
System of base stations controlled by one base station controller	Base Station Subsystem (**BSS**)	Radio Network Subsystem (**RNS**)
Access network	Radio Access Network (**RAN**)	UMTS Terrestrial Radio Access Network (**UTRAN**)

3.4.4.3 UMTS core network

The UMTS core network is based on the GSM/GPRS topology and continues the phased transition toward an all-IP network. The UMTS core network uses Asynchronous Transfer Mode (ATM) as the transmission technology to handle both voice and data traffic.

3.4.5 4G network architecture

Even as 3G systems are being deployed, 4G systems have been undergoing testing and sometimes deployment as in the case of WiMAX. WiMAX is the earliest 4G technology to be deployed. WiMAX came with a lot of hype and potential and was seen as the natural extension of the very popular WiFi. However, so far it has been adopted by only one major mobile phone network operator in America, Sprint. The other major operators in America, AT&T and Verizon, have chosen LTE.

The main objectives of 4G technology are twofold:

- All-IP infrastructure that supports both voice and data. This objective results in a consolidation and reduction in network elements, thus improving the overall network efficiency and reducing costs.
- High data rates and low latency. The low latency is necessary so as to support the stringent time requirements of voice and other traffic over IP with Quality of Service (QoS) guarantees.

LTE meets these objectives using such enhancements as more efficient signal-modulation techniques, multiple-antenna designs called Multiple Input Multiple Output (MIMO), and powerful network elements. The LTE system architecture is shown in the following figure.

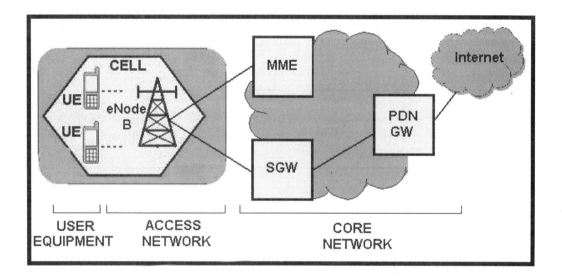

Note that the access network has been consolidated into one element, the evolved Node B (eNode B or eNB). The core network consists of two types of switching elements, the Serving Gateway (SGW) and the Packet Data Network Gateway (PDN GW), and a control element, the Mobility Management Entity (MME).

3.4.6 Mobile phone access technologies

The interface between mobile phones and a base station is called the air interface and is an important element in mobile communication. Communication over this interface takes place over a limited and valuable frequency spectrum that needs to be divided appropriately between users. Various multiple-access technologies are used to allow the interface to handle access by multiple users simultaneously. These multiple-access technologies are:

- *Frequency Division Multiple Access (FDMA)*. In FDMA, the available frequency spectrum is divided into frequency bands, or channels, that are allocated to users when they access the network.
- *Time Division Multiple Access (TDMA)*. In TDMA, the spectrum is divided into time slots that are allocated to users when they access the network.
- *Code Division Multiple Access (CDMA)*. In CDMA, the whole frequency spectrum is available to each user but each user's transmission is spread over the spectrum using unique spreading codes that distinguish each user from others.

These multiple-access technologies are illustrated in the following figure.

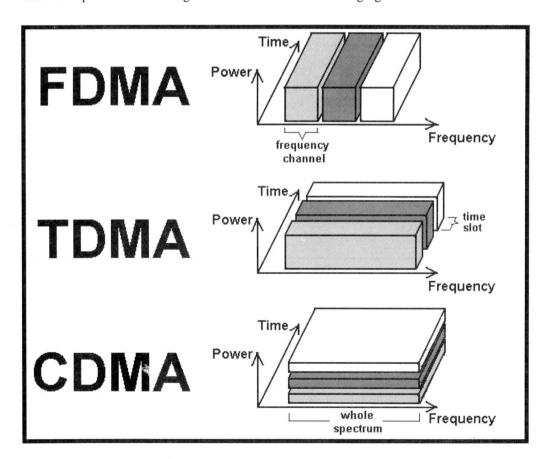

For 4G systems, a new type of multiple-access technology called Orthogonal Frequency Division Multiple Access (OFDMA) has been selected. OFDMA is similar to FDMA in concept but uses a huge number of carriers, each one carrying part of the data. OFDMA is spectrally efficient, and interference between the carrier data streams is eliminated by making them orthogonal.

The use of multiple-access technologies among the various mobile phone generations is illustrated in the following table.

Generation	Mobile phone system	Multiple-access technology
1G	All systems	FDMA
2G	GSM GPRS EDGE CDMA	TDMA CDMA
3G	UMTS (W-CDMA) HSPA CDMA2000	CDMA CDMA
4G	LTE WiMAX	OFDMA OFDMA

The data flow across the air interface is asymmetric, and a distinction is made when referring to the direction of the flow. The link from the mobile phone to the base station is called the "Uplink", and the link from the base station to the mobile phone is called the "Downlink".

The separation of these two sub-links is handled either in the frequency domain or the time domain. When the uplink and downlink are on different frequencies, this separation is called Frequency Division Duplex (FDD). When the uplink and downlink are separated time-wise, this separation is referred to as Time Division Duplex (TDD).

3.4.7 Mobile phone access cells

The coverage area of the mobile phone access network is divided into cells. Breaking the coverage area into cells makes for a flexible design that can be further partitioned, i.e. broken into more cells, to meet future rising demand. Traditionally cells were illustrated as perfect hexagons meshed together in a perfect honeycomb pattern. In reality such a pattern is affected by many factors such as the topology of the terrain.

The main reason for the division of the coverage area into cells is the limited frequency spectrum available for mobile communication. If the whole access network coverage area were only one cell, this spectrum would only accommodate a small number of simultaneous users and be impractical. Thus, the way to handle many users is to divide the coverage area into many cell clusters and reuse the spectrum among them. The challenge then is to minimize the frequency interference between the different cells.

One way to ascertain that adjacent cells do not interfere with each other is to assign them different frequency channels. The following figure shows some of the frequency-reuse designs that have been adopted.

Cluster size	Frequency reuse factor	Example of usage
7	$\frac{1}{7}$	FDMA
3	$\frac{1}{3}$	TDMA
1	1	CDMA

3.5 Future of mobile phones

The trend in mobile phones is toward the prevalence of smartphones. This trend has made today's mobile phones many folds more robust than the early voice-centric ones. Smartphones keep evolving by incorporating the functions previously available in separate devices. For example, smartphones can be used as substitutes for standalone radios, MP3/4 players, cameras, GPS receivers, gaming devices, computers and TV. This amazing integration of so many devices into one makes the smartphone the essential personal device.

Gazing into the future, what might the mobile phone systems of the future be like? In fact, today's smartphones are already very futuristic. Some additional developments or enhancements that might happen could be as follows.

Processing power. It is a certainty that the processing power of mobile phones will continue its upward trend. In the future, mobile phone processors will be clocking into the gigahertz range while still performing under the tight constraint of a small thermal envelope.

Memory. Mobile phones already come equipped with enough memory to run powerful operating systems similar to computers. They also offer storage capacities that reach into the gigabytes. In the future, mobile phones will offer capacities in the order of hundreds of gigabytes.

Display. The physical size of mobile phones is by definition constrained to a small footprint. However, the display size does not have to be. In the future, the display could be made of stretchable or foldable material that rolls out to the size of a small notebook. The display could even be a small lens on special eyeglasses that projects a 3D virtual screen as big as a TV.

Input. Input into a mobile phone is already multidimensional and can be carried out via voice, a keypad, a keyboard, a touchpad, a stylus, a foldable keyboard, and so on. In the future, holographic keyboards could also be a feature.

More functions. Mobile phones already serve in many capacities. In the future, some of the functions that will become more widespread include using the mobile phone as a projector, language interpreter, credit card, ID, electronic wallet, and so on.

Access to network. Mobile phones already can access the network via cellular and WiFi technologies. In the future, when 4G systems are deployed, the mobile phone access to the network will reach speeds of the order of a hundred megabits per second.

All-IP network. Mobile phone network operators are upgrading their assorted network facilities toward an all-IP network. In the future, this all-IP network will result in reduced costs of operation and maintenance for the network operators, and in rich applications for the users.

3.6 Mobile phone scenarios

3.6.1 Selecting a new mobile phone

When selecting a new mobile phone, one may feel overwhelmed by the plethora of choices. There are so many variables to consider such as usage, style, color, brand, features, price and so on.

Usage. The user needs to decide what the mobile phone will be used for. If the only usage requirement is for voice calls and SMS, then any low-end model would be satisfactory. For Internet access and multimedia features, a smartphone is the natural choice.

Style. Mobile phones come in various form factors such as the candy bar, clamshell, flip, slider, swivel and twist. In addition, some mobile phones may be designed for specific segments of consumers. For example, some mobile phones may be in the shape of animals, while some luxurious mobile phones come studded with precious stones.

Color. Mobile phone companies offer handsets in colors that vary from the classic to the outrageous. Colors range from solid to "cartoonish" with designs like Mickey Mouse. A classic look is the iPhone's metallic and black plastic combination.

Brand. Brand consideration is important since it reflects the quality of the product and the after-sale service. Top brands include Apple, Nokia, Samsung and LG.

Features. The amount of features on mobile phones can satisfy even the most demanding gadget geeks of the world. Mobile phones features include radio, voice recording, MP3/4 player, GPS receiver, TV, video games, and the list keeps growing.

Price. A mobile phone is no longer a luxury. The low-end segment of the mobile phone industry has become commoditized to a price point that is affordable even in poor countries. In some countries, the handset is included as part of the service contract with a network operator.

3.6.2 Mobile phone usage

We use our mobile phones in many different ways. Some people are just content to use their mobile phones for the basic functions of making phone calls and exchanging SMS messages. However, advanced mobile phones or smartphones are loaded with so many other practical features and functions that users can take advantage of.

Mobile phones are powerful multimedia devices. Snapping pictures or recording videos with mobile phones and sharing the results with friends and family is a fun and convenient way to share one's interests and joy. Watching TV, videos and movies allows users to enjoy their free or commuting time. Listening to music is very popular as mobile phones offer storage capacities for thousands of songs, and easy ways to download online music. Listening to music has become even more convenient with the advent of Bluetooth headsets that untangle the users from the encumbering earphone wires. Playing games on mobile phones is increasingly popular.

Mobile phones are computing devices. Surfing the Internet at 3G speeds and browsing information on screens, generously-sized and with vivid colors and clarity, is becoming more common. Online communication is available via email, SMS, MMS, and IM. Geo-tagging services combine the power of the Internet and GPS to allow mobile phone users to instantly find items of interest, such as the locations of their friends or favorite restaurants.

Mobile phones offer even more capabilities. They are educational devices that provide multi-lingual dictionaries. They are personal information management devices that allow for note taking, voice recording, calendar keeping, contact management and so on. They are watches, alarm clocks and calculators. Indeed, mobile phones are our essential companions in the information age.

3.6.3 Mobile phone maintenance

As a device that is used and operated on a continuous basis, the mobile phone requires regular maintenance to keep it functioning properly and efficiently. Some of the maintenance chores include recharging the battery, downloading software updates, cleaning the display, recharging the money balance and so on.

The battery, a lithium-ion one, usually lasts a few days before it needs to be recharged. On multimedia smartphones the battery may last much less in case of heavy usage of processing-intensive functions. Some users maintain a spare battery.

The software inside the mobile phone is a critical part of the device. It needs to be updated regularly so that the mobile phone can keep up with the latest technology improvements and stay secure. Indeed, malware has now permeated the mobile phone sphere, and mobile phone manufacturers continuously update their software to fix bugs and plug security holes.

The display screen of a mobile phone is a vital element that needs to be cleaned regularly. The screen is robust and long lasting, but smudges and scratches may reduce its efficiency; thus, regular cleaning and proper use are of the essential.

Finally, the money balance on some mobile phones can be recharged though buying a phone card. These phone cards come in many balance amounts.

UNIT 3   MOBILE PHONES

3.7   Mobile phone exercises

3.7.1   Reading comprehension

1. What was the main reason for the transition from 1G to 2G mobile phone systems?
2. What is the difference between the access technologies of 1G and 2G systems?
3. What was the main reason for the transition from 2G to 2.5/2.75/3G systems?
4. What is the most widely deployed 2G mobile communications system in the world?
5. Name the two most widely used 3G mobile communications systems in the world.
6. Enumerate the different form factors of mobile phones.
7. What are the main hardware components of a mobile phone?
8. What hardware element manages both the voice and data interfaces of a mobile phone?
9. What is the hardware unit that receives and transmits the antenna signals?
10. What hardware element changes analog signals to digital signals?
11. What hardware element changes digital signals to analog signals?
12. What hardware element processes signals in real time?
13. What type of memory is used for large-capacity storage inside a mobile phone?
14. What non-cellular wireless technologies may be present in a mobile phone?
15. Why do mobile phones use Assisted GPS instead of simply GPS?
16. What hardware element is used to rotate the display view when the phone is rotated?
17. What hardware element is used to adjust the display clarity to the surrounding environment?
18. What hardware element holds a user's phone number inside a GSM mobile phone?
19. Why did OLED displace LCD as the preferred display technology?
20. What are the various ways that information can be input into a mobile phone?
21. Name the possible uses of a mobile phone.
22. What type of operating system must run the communications software of a mobile phone?
23. Name some of the most popular Open Operating Systems in use today.
24. What are the three main parts of a mobile phone system architecture?
25. Name the different elements of a GSM Radio Access Network.
26. Name the different elements of a GSM core network.
27. What are the main objectives of 4G systems?
28. Which multiple-access technology allocates different frequency channels to different users?
29. Which multiple-access technology accommodates multiple users by using time slots?
30. If a cluster of cells contains three cells, what is the frequency reuse factor?
31. What are some of the factors that users consider when selecting a new mobile phone?
32. What are some of the maintenance chores required by a mobile phone?

(The answers to these questions are at the end of the book)

3.7.2 Reading and pronouncing acronyms

Complete the following table by showing how these mobile phone acronyms are pronounced and what they stand for.

Acronym	Pronunciation	Acronym expansion
IMSI		
DAC		
ADC		
SIM		
RAN		
3G		
WAP		
PIN		
MIMO		
GSM		
GPRS		
EDGE		
UMTS		
HSPA		
LTE		
WiMAX		
FDD		
TDD		
UE		
MS		
HLR		
VLR		
MSC		
FDMA		
DSP		
RTOS		

(The answers to these questions are at the end of the book)

3.7.3 Mobile phone essays

1. Write a detailed description of your own mobile phone.
2. Describe how you use your mobile phone.
3. If you were to design the perfect mobile phone, describe what it would be.
4. Describe the future possible trends of the mobile phone industry.
5. Compare the different brands of mobile phones and explain which one is the best.
6. Write an essay analyzing the mobile phone market in your home country.
7. Do some research and then write an essay on why GSM became the dominant 2G technology.
8. Write an essay about the convergence of the computer, the Internet and the mobile phone.
9. Write an essay about how mobile phones have affected society.

3.7.4 Speaking exercises

1. Enumerate all the different ways that you use your mobile phone.
2. Do a role play of a customer asking a sales person some questions at a mobile phone shop.
3. Do a role play about a customer calling a service center and asking for technical help.
4. Debate which mobile phone form factor is the best.
5. Debate which Open Operating System is the best for smartphones.
6. Debate which technology will emerge as the 4G winner among LTE, WiMAX, and UMB.
7. Debate whether the whole world should adopt one single 4G technology.
8. Debate which form of data input (keypad, touch-screen, etc) is best suited for mobile phones.
9. Debate which is the most important high-tech device, the mobile phone or the notebook.
10. Debate whether youngsters in primary school should own mobile phones.
11. Debate if mobile phone billing should be "only caller pays", as is the case with fixed phones.
12. Debate whether roaming fees should be abolished.
13. Debate whether the mobile phone has made the fixed phone obsolete or not.
14. Debate whether all mobile phones should use the same power adapter.
15. Talk about how to select a new mobile phone.
16. Talk about how to maintain one's mobile phone.
17. Talk about the etiquette of using a mobile phone.
18. Talk about some of the jargon or abbreviations used in SMS messages.
19. Describe how you use your mobile phone to surf the Internet.
20. Describe some new features you would like to see added to mobile phones.
21. Talk about some of the health hazards associated with using mobile phones.
22. Talk about the benefits of an all-IP mobile phone infrastructure.
23. Explain in your own words the reasons behind the evolution from 1G to 2G to 3G to 4G.

3.7.5 Identifying mobile phone parts

Match the words in the following table to the correct mobile phone parts in the figure below.

1. Battery charge icon	7. Network signal strength icon
2. Navigation key	8. Keypad
3. Case	9. Display
4. Antenna	10. Stylus
5. Bluetooth headset	11. Earphones
6. Power adapter / Charger	12. SIM card

(The answers are at the end of the book)

3.7.6 Cloze

Fill in the blanks in the following statements with the correct words.

1. The 2G systems came about to allow more users to use the limited _____.
2. Whereas 1G mobile phones used analog signals, 2G mobile phones used _____.
3. Whereas 1G systems used FDMA multiple-access, 2G ones introduced _____.
4. The most popular 2G mobile communications system in the world is _____.
5. The 3G mobile communications systems provide faster data _____.
6. _____ is the 3G evolution of GSM.
7. Mobile phone form factors include the candy bar, _____.
8. The processors in the smartphones manage both the voice and _____ interfaces.
9. Mobile phone processors are limited to _____ envelopes of less than 1W.
10. The RF unit on the main board transmits and receives _____ signals.
11. A user's voice is analog and is _____ using an Analog to Digital Converter (ADC).
12. _____ processing and manipulation inside a mobile phone is done by the DSP.
13. The type of memory used for large-capacity storage inside a mobile phone is ____ memory.
14. Mobile phone wireless headsets use the wireless technology _____.
15. Mobile phones use a variation of GPS called _____ GPS.
16. _____ are used to automatically rotate the display view as the phone is rotated.
17. An ambient light _____ is used to adjust the display brightness to different environments.
18. A _____ is used to keep the same phone number when switching GSM mobile phones.
19. A SIM card's sensitive information is password-protected with a _____.
20. Since they don't need _____, OLED displays are more power efficient than LCD ones.
21. Some displays are _____ and are used for information input into mobile phones.
22. 4G systems will use a revolutionary multiple _____ design known as MIMO.
23. Today's mobile phone _____ are made of Lithium-Ion.
24. Mobile phone software consists of _____ software and applications software.
25. Mobile phones use a _____ Operating System to run the communications software.
26. The _____ Access Network is the bridge between the user equipment and the core network.
27. Cells are usually diagrammed as a honeycomb of _____ shapes.
28. The core network technology is evolving from circuit switching to _____.
29. The VLR database stores the temporary data of _____ mobile phone users.
30. The AuC database is used for _____ mobile phone users.
31. The GPRS network is an IP-based _____ backbone.
32. The goals of 4G systems include an _____ infrastructure, and high _____ and low _____.
33. FDMA allocates different _____ channels to different users.
34. 4G systems will use a new _____ technology called OFDMA.
35. A _____ of cells uses the whole available frequency spectrum.

(The answers to these questions are at the end of the book)

3.8 Mobile phone glossary

Term	Definition	Term	Definition
1/2/3/4 G	First/Second/Third/Fourth Generation. Generations of mobile communications systems	**BTS**	Base Transceiver Station. In 2G, the BTS, which includes the tower, antennas, and co-located processing equipment, conducts radio communications with mobile phones
Accelerometer	Tiny electromechanical device that senses movement	**Case**	The outer, protective covering of a mobile phone
ADC	Analog to Digital Converter. A chip, or part of a codec, that converts analog signals to digital signals	**CDMA**	Code Division Multiple Access. A multiple access technology that makes the whole frequency spectrum available to each user. Also, a 2G mobile communications system
A-GPS	Assisted GPS. A-GPS allows mobile phones to use information from the mobile phone network to quickly sync with GPS satellites	**CDMA2000**	CDMA2000 is the 3G evolution of CDMA
Analog signal	Continuous signal	**Cell**	One of the small areas that a mobile phone system coverage area is divided into
Antenna	A wire structure that receives and transmits signals.	**Cell cluster**	A group of cells that together use the whole available frequency spectrum
AuC	Authentication Center. A database used for authenticating mobile phone users	**Cell phone**	Same as mobile phone
Bluetooth	A short distance wireless connection technology	**Channel**	A frequency band
BSC	Base Station Controller. In 2G, a BSC controls and manages a group of adjacent BTSs, and handles the handoff of users between them	**Codec**	Coder Decoder. A chip that codes and decodes signals. A combination of ADC and DAC
BSS	Base Station Subsystem. In 2G, a BSS is a system comprised of multiple BTSs and their corresponding BSC	**DAC**	Digital to Analog Converter. A chip, or part of a codec, that converts digital signals to analog signals

Digital signal	Quantized, discrete-time signal	**Frequency spectrum**	A range of frequencies such as for a mobile communications service
Display	The screen of a mobile phone	**GGSN**	Gateway GPRS Support Node. The GGSN is the gateway of the GPRS network to other data networks such as the Internet
Downlink	The link from the base station to the mobile phone	**GMSC**	Gateway MSC. The MSC that is connected to the Public Switched Telephone Network (PSTN)
DSP	Digital Signal Processor. A high-speed chip for signal processing and manipulation	**GSM**	Global System for Mobile communications. 2G mobile communications system
EDGE	Enhanced Data rates for GSM Evolution. 2.75G evolution of GSM	**GPRS**	General Packet Radio Service. 2.5G evolution of GSM
EIR	Equipment Identity Register. A database used to check the validation of mobile phones	**Handoff**	The switching of a user's communication link from one base station to another base station
eNode B	Evolved Node B. In 4G, eNode B is the Radio Access Network single, consolidated element	**Handset**	A mobile phone device or unit
ESN	Electronic Serial Number. A unique number programmed into the phone when it is manufactured	**Headset**	Headphones
FDD	Frequency Division Duplex. The separation of the uplink and downlink on different frequencies	**HLR**	Home Location Register. A database that stores the permanent data about mobile phone users
FDMA	Frequency Division Multiple Access. A multiple access technology that allocates different frequency channels to different users	**HSDPA**	High Speed Downlink Packet Access. 3.5G evolution of GSM that offers a high data throughput downlink
Form factor	The outward design of a device. In the case of mobile phones, the form factors are candy bar, clamshell, flip, slider, swivel, twist	**HSPA**	High Speed Packet Access. 3.5G evolution of GSM that consists of HSDPA and HSUPA
Frequency reuse ratio	The inverse of the number of cells in a cluster	**HSUPA**	High Speed Uplink Packet Access. 3.5G evolution of GSM that offers a high data throughput uplink

Keypad	A small keyboard on a mobile phone	**Projector**	A promising feature on mobile phones that allows for the projection of data on any surface
Latency	The propagation delay of data through a communication system	**PSTN**	Public Switched Telephone Network. The traditional fixed phone network
LTE	Long Term Evolution. 4G mobile communications system	**RAN**	Radio Access Network. The network of antenna towers and associated equipment that provide network access to mobile phone users
Main board	A Printed Circuit Board that contains the main circuitry inside a mobile phone	**RNC**	Radio Network Controller. RNC in UMTS is the evolution of GSM's BSC
MIMO	Multiple Input Multiple Output. An antenna design that uses multiple antennas to attain a high data throughput	**RNS**	Radio Network Subsystem. In UMTS, an RNS is a system comprised of multiple Nodes B and their corresponding RNC
MME	Mobility Management Entity. An LTE core network control element	**RTOS**	Real Time Operating System. An operating system that supports real time data such as voice
MMS	Multimedia Messaging Service. An extension of text messaging that supports multimedia such as graphics, audio and video	**Sensor**	A small device that detects and measures a physical quantity, then converts it into a usable output signal
MSC	Mobile Switching Center. A core network facility that performs call switching between users	**SGSN**	Serving GPRS Support Node. SGSN is the GPRS network's switching element
Node B	Node B in UMTS is the evolution of GSM's BTS	**SGW**	Serving Gateway. An LTE core network switching element
OFDMA	Orthogonal FDMA. OFDMA is similar to FDMA in concept but uses a huge number of carriers, each one carrying part of the data	**SIM card**	Subscriber Identity Module. A small card which contains the identification and connection information needed to register a mobile phone with a mobile phone network and to make calls
PDN GW	Packet Data Network Gateway. An LTE core network element that connects to other data networks such as the Internet	**Smartphone**	A mobile phone that integrates the functions of a PDA or palmtop

SMS	Short Messaging Service. A data texting service	**UMTS**	Universal Mobile Telecommunications System. UMTS is the 3G evolution of GSM
Stylus	A small cylindrical or flat rod with a pointed end that is used for data input on a touch-screen	**Uplink**	The link from the mobile phone to the base station
TDD	Time Division Duplex. The time-wise separation of the uplink and downlink	**UTRAN**	UMTS Terrestrial Radio Access Network. The terminology for a UMTS RAN
TDMA	Time Division Multiple Access. A multiple access technology that allocates different time slots to different users	**VLR**	Visitor Location Register. A database that stores the temporary data about mobile phone users as they visit different cells
TD-SCDMA	Time Division - Synchronous CDMA. 3G technology mainly developed and supported by China	**WAP**	Wireless Application Protocol. A set of protocols to allow mobile phones to access the Internet
Touch-screen	A display that can sense physical contact from fingers or a stylus, and that can be used for information input	**WCDMA**	Wideband CDMA. The transmission standard used in UMTS. Also, synonymous with UMTS
UE	User Equipment, e.g. the mobile phone	**WiFi**	Wireless Fidelity. An Internet access wireless technology
UMB	Ultra Mobile Broadband. 4G evolution of CDMA2000	**WiMAX**	Worldwide Interoperability for Microwave access. 4G mobile communications technology

UNIT 4

MATHEMATICS

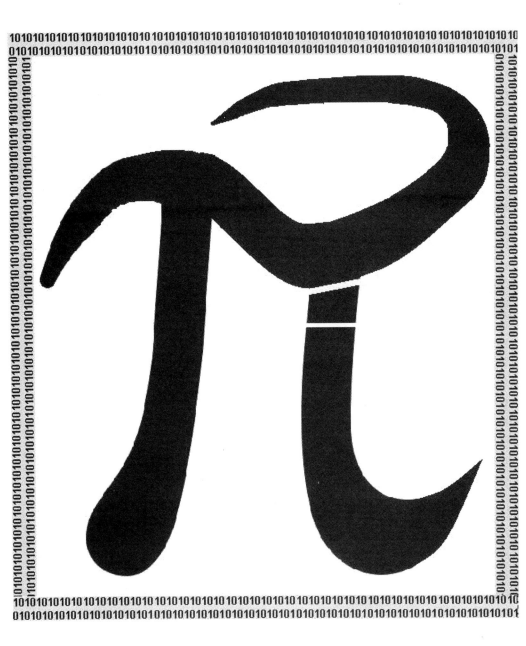

MATHEMATICS KEYWORDS

Absolute value	绝对值	Logarithm	对数
Addition	加法	Logic	逻辑
Algebra	代数学	Magnitude	大小／量
Angle	角	Matrix	距阵
Area	面积	Mean	平均数
Arithmetic	算术	Minus	减
Axis	数轴／坐标轴	Multiplication	乘法
Bar chart	条形图	Negative	负
Calculus	微积分学	Numerator	分子
Circle	圆	Odd number	奇数
Complex number	复数	Over	除
Coordinate	坐标	Parallel	平行
Cosine	余弦	Partial derivative	偏导数
Cube	立方体	Perpendicular	垂直
Decimal point	小数点	Pie chart	饼图
Denominator	分母	Plus	加
Derivative	导数	Positive	正
Dimension	维	Power	幂
Discrete mathematics	离散数学	Prime number	质数
Division	除法	Probability	概率
Equal to	等于	Quadratic equation	二次方程
Equation	方程式	Real number	实数
Even number	偶数	Rectangle	长方形
Exponential	指数	Root	根
Factorial	阶乘	Sine	正弦
Fraction	分数	Square	正方形
Function	函数	Standard deviation	标准差
Geometry	几何学	Statistics	统计学
Graph	坐标系	Subtraction	减法
Greater than	大于	Tangent	正切／切线
Horizontal line	水平线	Times	乘
Infinity	无限大	Triangle	三角形
Integer	整数	Trigonometry	三角学
Integral	整体	Truth table	真值表
Less than	小于	Vector	向量／矢量
Limit	极限	Vertical line	（铅）垂线
Linear equation	一次方程	Volume	体积

4.1 Introduction

Mathematics is the foundation of technology and is a universal language whose symbols are used all over the world. However, these symbols have different names in different languages; for example, the symbol "=" is referred to as "equal" in English, "égal" in French, and "deng yu" in Chinese. Thus, while visual communication using mathematical symbols is possible, verbal communication may not be. Since English has become the most commonly used language in the technical area, it follows that knowledge of mathematical symbols using the English language is essential.

4.2 Branches of mathematics

Mathematics is a vast area since it is used to describe many aspects of life, from simple counting to nuclear physics. The main branches of mathematics and their examples are as shown in the following figure.

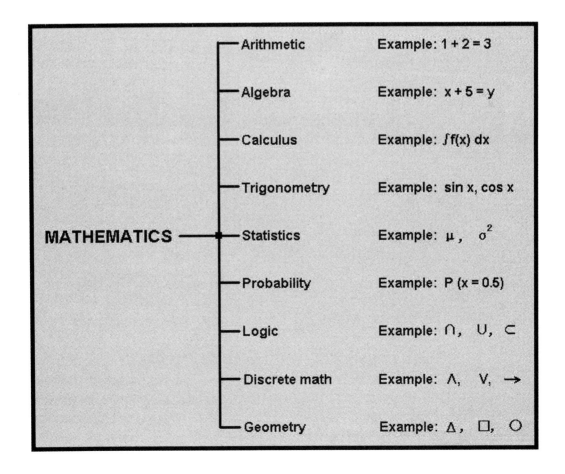

4.3 Arithmetic

Concept	Symbol	How to read the symbol	Examples
Addition	+	plus	1 + 2 = 3 One plus two is equal to three One plus two equals three
Subtraction	−	minus	3 − 2 = 1 Three minus two is equal to one Three minus two equals one
Multiplication	× * •	times (or multiplied by)	4 × 5 = 20 Four times five is equal to twenty Four times five equals twenty
Division	/ ÷	over (or divided by)	6 / 3 = 2 Six over three is equal to two Six over three equals two
Even numbers			2, 4, 6, 8, 10, 12, 14 … Two, four, six, eight, ten, twelve, fourteen … are even numbers
Odd numbers			1, 3, 5, 7, 9, 11, 13 … One, three, five, seven, nine, eleven, thirteen … are odd numbers
Prime numbers			11, 13, 17, 19, 23 … Eleven, thirteen, seventeen, nineteen, twenty three … are prime numbers

4.4 Algebra

Concept	Symbol	How to read the symbol	Examples
Complex Numbers	C	complex numbers	a + bi a plus b i is a complex number 3.5i Three point five i is an imaginary number
Real Numbers	R	real numbers	π Pi is a real number $\sqrt{2}$ Square root of two is a real number
Integers	Z	integers	-5 Negative five is an integer (Some read "–5" as minus five) +9 Positive nine is an integer (Some read "+9" as plus nine)
Natural Numbers	N	natural numbers	1, 2, 3, 4, 5, … One, two, three, four, five … are natural numbers
Decimal Point	.	decimal point	-3.5 Negative three point five is a decimal number 0.5 Point five is a decimal number

Concept	Symbol	How to read the symbol	Examples
Fraction	a / b	a over b a is the numerator b is the denominator (see examples in the next column on other ways to read "a over b")	1/2 One half is a fraction 1/3 One third is a fraction 2/3 Two thirds is a fraction 4/5 Four fifths is a fraction 99/77 Ninety nine over seventy seven is a fraction
Power	x^n or x^n	x raised to the n power x to the n power x to power of n x to the n	3^2 Three squared 2^3 Two cubed 10^6 Ten to the six
Root	$\sqrt[n]{x}$ or $x^{1/n}$	n^{th} root of x	$\sqrt{9}$ Square root of nine $27^{1/3}$ Cubic root of twenty seven $8^{1/7}$ Seventh root of eight

Concept	Symbol	How to read the symbol	Examples
Powers of ten prefixes	Y	yotta (= 10^{24})	1 GB = 10^9 Bytes One gigabyte equals ten to the nine (or one billion) bytes
	Z	zetta (= 10^{21})	
	E	Exa (= 10^{18})	1 MB = 10^6 Bytes One megabyte equals ten to the six (or one million) bytes
	P	peta (= 10^{15})	
	T	tera (= 10^{12})	1 km = 10^3 m One kilometer equals ten to the three (or one thousand) meters
	G	giga (= 10^9)	
	M	mega (= 10^6)	1 kg = 10^3 g One kilogram equals ten to the three (or one thousand) grams
	k	kilo (= 10^3)	
	h	hecto (= 10^2)	1 mg = 10^{-3} g One milligram equals ten to the negative three (or one thousandth of a) gram
	da	deca (= 10^1)	
	d	deci (10^{-1})	1 nm = 10^{-9} m One nanometer equals ten to the negative nine (or one billionth of a) meter
	c	centi (10^{-2})	
	m	milli (10^{-3})	
	μ	micro (10^{-6})	1 μs = 10^{-6} s One microsecond equals ten to the negative six (or one millionth of a) second
	n	nano (10^{-9})	
	p	pico (10^{-12})	
	f	femto (10^{-15})	
	a	atto (10^{-18})	
	z	zepto (10^{-21})	
	y	yocto (10^{-24})	

Concept	Symbol	How to read the symbol	Examples
Absolute Value	$\|x\|$	absolute value of x	$\|-3\|$ Absolute value of negative three
Inequality	$a \neq b$	a is not equal to b	$x \neq y$ x is not equal to y
	$a < b$	a is less than b	$-2 < 0$ Minus two is less than zero
	$a \leq b$	a is less than or equal to b	$x \leq y$ x is less than or equal to y
	$a > b$	a is greater than b	$-1 > -5$ Negative one is greater than negative five
	$a \geq b$	a is greater than or equal to b	$x \geq y$ x is greater than or equal to y
Approximate Equality	$a \approx b$	a is approximately equal to b	$\pi \approx 3.14$ Pi is approximately equal to three point one four
Exponential	e^x	exponential x	$y = e^x$ y equals exponential x
Logarithm	$\log x$	logarithm of x log of x	$\log 2$ Logarithm of two
	$\log_n x$	logarithm of x with base n	$\log_4 x$ Logarithm of x with base four
	$\ln x$	natural logarithm of x	$\ln 1$ Natural logarithm of one

UNIT 4   MATHEMATICS

Concept	Symbol	How to read the symbol	Examples
Factorial	$n!$	n factorial	$5!$ Five factorial
Linear Equation	$ax + b = 0$ $ax + by = c$	a x plus b equals zero a x plus b y equals c	$2x + 1 = 0$ Two x plus one equals zero
Quadratic Equation	$ax^2 + bx + c = 0$	a x squared plus b x plus c equals zero	$2x^2 + 3x + 1 = 0$ Two x squared plus three x plus one equals zero
Cubic Equation	$x^3 + bx^2 + cx + d = 0$	x cubed plus b x squared plus c x plus d equals zero	$x^3 + 5x^2 + x + 4 = 0$ x cubed plus five x squared plus x plus four equals zero
Polynomial	$x^n + x^{n-1} + x^{n-2} + \ldots + c$	x to the n, plus x to the n minus one, plus x to the n minus 2, plus …, plus c	$x^7 + x^2 + 7$ x to the seven plus x squared plus seven
Matrix	$\begin{bmatrix} a_{11}a_{12}\ldots a_{1n} \\ a_{21}a_{22}\ldots a_{2n} \\ \vdots \\ a_{m1}a_{m2}\ldots a_{mn} \end{bmatrix}$	m by n matrix	$\begin{bmatrix} 3 & -1 & 0 \\ 0 & 5 & 2 \\ -7 & 4 & 9 \end{bmatrix}$ This is a three by three matrix
Determinant	$\begin{vmatrix} a_{11}a_{12}\ldots a_{1n} \\ a_{21}a_{22}\ldots a_{2n} \\ \vdots \\ a_{m1}a_{m2}\ldots a_{mn} \end{vmatrix}$	m by n determinant	$\begin{vmatrix} 3 & -1 & 0 \\ 0 & 5 & 2 \\ -7 & 4 & 9 \end{vmatrix}$ This is a three by three determinant

Concept	Symbol	How to read the symbol	Examples
Summation	$\sum_{j=1}^{n} A_j$	the summation from j equal 1 to n of A sub j	$\sum_{m=1}^{3} C_m$ The summation from m equal one to three of C sub m
Product	$\prod_{j=1}^{n} A_j$	the product from j equal 1 to n of A sub j	$\prod_{k=1}^{5} T_k$ The product from k equal one to five of T sub k
Limit	$\lim_{x \to 0} f(x)$	the limit as x goes to zero of f of x	$\lim_{x \to 0} \log(x)$ The limit as x goes to zero of logarithm of x
Infinity	∞	Infinity	$1/0 = \infty$ One over zero equals infinity
Therefore	$\therefore$	therefore	a=b and b=c $\therefore$ a=c a is equal to b and b is equal to c, therefore a is equal to c
Implication	$\Rightarrow$	implies	A $\Rightarrow$ B A implies B
Proportionality	$\propto$	is proportional to	y $\propto$ x y is proportional to x

UNIT 4 MATHEMATICS

Concept	Symbol	How to read the symbol	Examples
Vector	↗	vector	A↗ A is a vector
Magnitude of vector	$|A|$	magnitude of vector **A**	A↗ The magnitude of vector A is $|A|$
Scalar Vector Product	·	dot	A . B A dot B [diagram of vectors A and B with angle α] $A \cdot B = |A||B| \cos \alpha$ A dot B equals the magnitude of A times the magnitude of B times cosine alpha
Cross Vector Product	×	cross	A × B A cross B
Gradient	∇	del	grad A = ∇A Gradient A equals del A
Divergence	∇·	del dot	div A = ∇ · A Divergence A equals del dot A
Curl	∇×	del cross	curl A = ∇ × A Curl A equals del cross A

Concept	Symbol	How to read the symbol	Examples
Graph		graph	This is an xy graph (it has two dimensions: x is the first dimension, y is the second dimension) This is an xyz graph (it has three dimensions: x is the first dimension, y is the second dimension, z is the third dimension) An xy graph has two axes, axis x and axis y The coordinates of point A are four and two

4.5 Calculus

Concept	Symbol	How to read the symbol	Examples
Function	$f(x)$	f of x	$y(x)$ y of x
Derivative	$\dfrac{df(x)}{dx}$	the derivative of f of x with respect to x	$\dfrac{dx^3}{dx} = 3x^2$ The derivative of x cubed with respect to x equals three x squared
N^{th} Derivative	$\dfrac{d^n f(x)}{dx^n}$	the nth derivative of f of x with respect to x	$\dfrac{d^2 x^3}{dx^2} = 6x$ The second derivative of x cubed with respect to x equals six x
Partial Derivative	$\dfrac{\partial f(x)}{\partial x}$	the partial derivative of f of x with respect to x	$\dfrac{\partial x^3 y}{\partial x} = 3x^2 y$ The partial derivative of x cubed y with respect to x equals 3 x squared y
N^{th} Partial Derivative	$\dfrac{\partial^n f(x)}{\partial x^n}$	the nth partial derivative of f of x with respect to x	$\dfrac{\partial^2 x^3 y}{\partial x^2} = 6xy$ The second partial derivative of x cubed y with respect to x equals six x y

Concept	Symbol	How to read the symbol	Examples
Integral	$\int_a^b f(x)dx$	the integral from a to b of f of x d x	$\int_1^3 x^3 dx$ The integral from one to three of x cubed d x
Double Integral	$\iint f(x,y)dxdy$	the double integral of f of x y d x d y	$\iint x^3 y\, dx\, dy$ The double integral of x cubed y d x d y
Triple Integral	$\iiint f(x,y,z)dxdydz$	the triple integral of f of x y z d x d y d z	$\iiint x^3 yz^2\, dx\, dy\, dz$ The triple integral of x cubed y z squared d x d y d z
Line Integral	$\oint f(x)\, dx$	the line integral of f of x d x	$\oint x^3\, dx$ The line integral of x cubed d x
Surface Integral	$\iint_S f(x)dx$	the surface integral of f of x d x	$\iint_S x^3 dx$ The surface integral of x cubed d x

4.6 Trigonometry

Concept	Symbol	How to read the symbol	Examples
Sine	sin	sine	sin 0 = 0 Sine zero equals zero
Cosine	cos	cosine	cos 0 = 1 Cosine zero equals one
Tangent	tan	tangent	tan 0 = 0 Tangent zero equals zero
Secant	sec	secant	sec = 1/cos Secant equals one over cosine sec 0 = 1 Secant zero equals one
Cosecant	csc cosec	cosecant	csc = 1/sin Cosecant equals one over sine csc $\pi/2$ = 1 Cosecant pi over two equals one
Cotangent	ctn cot	cotangent	ctn = 1/tan Cotangent equals one over tangent ctn $\pi/2$ = 0 Cotangent pi over two equals zero

Some functions, called "HYPERBOLIC FUNCTIONS", use a notation similar to trigonometric functions as shown below:

Concept	Symbol	How to read the symbol	Examples
Hyperbolic sine	sinh	hyperbolic sine	sinh 0 = 0 Hyperbolic sine zero equals zero sinh = 1/csch Hyperbolic sine equals one over hyperbolic cosecant
Hyperbolic cosine	cosh	hyperbolic cosine	cosh 0 = 1 Hyperbolic cosine zero equals one cosh = 1/sech Hyperbolic cosine equals one over hyperbolic secant
Hyperbolic tangent	tanh	hyperbolic tangent	tanh 0 = 0 Hyperbolic tangent zero equals zero tanh = 1/coth Hyperbolic tangent equals one over hyperbolic cotangent

4.7 Statistics

Concept	Symbol	How to read the symbol	Examples
Mean	μ	mean	$N(1, \sigma^2)$ This is a normal distribution with a mean equal to one and a variance equal to sigma squared
Standard deviation	σ	Standard deviation	$N(1, 4)$ This is a normal distribution with a mean equal to one and a standard deviation equal to two
Variance	σ^2	Variance	$N(1, 4)$ This is a normal distribution with a mean equal to one and a variance equal to four
Expected value	$E(x)$	expected value of x	$E(X) = 3.5$ Expected value of X equals three point five

Concept	Symbol	How to read the symbol	Examples
Pie chart		pie chart	This pie chart is divided into three slices equal to 20 percent, 30 percent and 50 percent of the total
Bar chart		bar chart	This bar chart shows components equal to five, fifteen, twenty and ten respectively. This bar chart illustrates a relative comparison of the areas of the world's largest countries

4.8 Probability

Concept	Symbol	How to read the symbol	Examples
Probability	P(x)	probability of x	P(x=0.5) Probability of x equal to point five $P(A \cup B) = P(A) + P(B) - P(A \cap B)$ Probability of A union B equals probability of A, plus probability of B, minus probability of A intersection B
Conditional probability	P(x/y)	conditional probability of x given y	P(x=0.5/y) Conditional Probability of x equal to point five given y
Normal distribution	$N(\mu, \sigma^2)$	normal distribution with mean μ and variance σ^2	N(1, 4)
Poisson distribution	Po(m)	Poisson distribution with parameter m	Po(1)
Binomial distribution	Bi(n,p)	binomial distribution with parameters n, p	Bi(1, 4)
Geometric distribution	Ge(p)	geometric distribution with parameter p	Ge(1)
Uniform distribution	Un(a,b)	uniform distribution with parameters a, b	Un(1, 4)

4.9 Logic

Concept	Symbol	How to read the symbol	Examples
Element	$\in$	belongs to set or is an element of set	$x \in A$ x belongs to set A
Not an Element	$\notin$	doesn't belong to set or is not an element of set	$y \notin A$ y doesn't belong to set A
Existence	$\exists$	there exists	$\exists x$ There exists x
Universal Quantifier	$\forall$	for all	$\forall x$ For all x
Element Definition	: |	such that	$\exists x: x<1$ There exists x such that x is less than one $\forall x \mid x<1$ For all x such that x is less than one
Set	{ }	set of (elements)	$A=\{x: x<1\}$ A is a set of elements x such that x is less than one

UNIT 4 MATHEMATICS 159

Concept	Symbol	How to read the symbol	Examples
Negation	¬	not	¬A Not A
Subset	⊂	is a subset of	A ⊂ B A is a subset of B
Not subset	⊄	is not a subset of	A ⊄ B A is not a subset of B
Union	∪	union	A ∪ B A union B
Intersection	∩	intersection	A ∩ B A intersection B
Empty set	∅	empty set or null set	
Logical OR	+	or	A + B A or B
Logical AND	×	and	A × B A and B

Concept	Symbol	How to read the symbol	Examples
Venn diagram	$\overline{A}$ (A)	Venn diagram	In this Venn diagram, the shaded area represents A intersection B (A ∩ B) In this Venn diagram, the shaded area represents A union B (A ∪ B)
Truth table	A|B|Output 0|0|α 0|1|β 1|0|γ 1|1|δ	truth table	A|B|A × B 0|0|0 0|1|0 1|0|0 1|1|1 This is a truth table for A and B (A × B)
Karnaugh map	A B \ 0 1 0 |α|γ| 1 |β|δ|	Karnaugh map	AB CD \ 00 01 11 10 00|1|0|0|1 01|1|1|1|0 11|0|0|0|0 10|1|1|1|1 This is an example of a Karnaugh map

Concept	Symbol	How to read the symbol	Examples
AND Gate		AND Gate	$C = A \times B$
NAND Gate		NAND Gate	$C = \overline{A \times B}$
OR Gate		OR Gate	$C = A + B$
NOR Gate		NOR Gate	$C = \overline{A + B}$
XOR Gate		Exclusive OR Gate, XOR Gate	$C = A \oplus B$
XNOR Gate		Exclusive NOR Gate, XNOR Gate	$C = \overline{A \oplus B}$
NOT Gate		NOT Gate, Inverter	$A \rightarrow \overline{A}$

Concept	Symbol	How to read the symbol	Examples
Numeration	101_2	binary	101_2 is a binary numeral One o one base two is a binary numeral
	357_8	octal	357_8 is an octal numeral Three five seven base eight is an octal numeral
	596_{10}	decimal	596_{10} is a decimal numeral Five nine six base ten is a decimal numeral
	$E7_{16}$	hexadecimal	$E7_{16}$ is a hexadecimal numeral E seven base sixteen is a hexadecimal numeral
Integrated Circuits	[S-R Latch block diagram with S, R inputs and Q, $\bar{Q}$ outputs]	S-R Latch	[NOR gate implementation with R, S inputs and Q, $\bar{Q}$ outputs]
	[Enabled S-R Latch block diagram with S, E, R inputs and Q, $\bar{Q}$ outputs]	Enabled S-R Latch	The S-R latch can be implemented with two NOR gates, with the output of each gate connected as input to the other gate

UNIT 4 MATHEMATICS 163

Concept	Symbol	How to read the symbol	Examples
Integrated Circuits	S, C, R / Q, Q̄	S-R Flip-flop	(S-R latch circuit diagram with R, E, S inputs and Q, Q̄ outputs)
	D, E / Q, Q̄	D Latch	The Enabled (or gated) S-R latch can be implemented with two NOR gates and two AND gates
	D, C / Q, Q̄	D Flip-flop	(D flip-flop circuit diagram with D, E inputs and Q, Q̄ outputs)
	J, C, K / Q, Q̄	J-K Flip-flop	The D latch can be implemented with two NOR gates, two AND gates and an inverter One application of flip-flops is as counters

4.10 Discrete mathematics

Concept	Symbol	How to read the symbol	Examples
Operator	¬	not	¬p, also written as "~ p" and "NOT p", is pronounced "not p"
	T	true	
			p | ¬p T | F F | T
	F	false	If p is true, then not p is false If p is false, then not p is true
	∧	and	p∧q, also written as "p & q" and "p AND q", is pronounced "p and q"
	∨	inclusive OR	p∨q, also written as "p OR q", is pronounced "p or q"
	⊕	exclusive OR	
	→	if … then …	The truth table of "if p then q" is as follows: p | q | p → q F | F | T F | T | T T | F | F T | T | T
	↔	if and only if, iff	

Concept	Symbol	How to read the symbol	Examples
Equivalence	$\Leftrightarrow$	are equivalent or is equivalent to	$p \Leftrightarrow q$, also written as "$p \equiv q$" and "p EQ q", is pronounced "p is equivalent to q" or "p and q are equivalent"
Sequence	$\{a_i\}$	sequence a sub i	$\{a_i\} = \{1/i\}$ Sequence a sub i is made of elements equal to one over i
Combination	$C(n,r)$	combination of n elements chosen r at a time or combination of n choose r	$C(n,r) = \dfrac{n!}{r!(n-r)!}$ Combination of n choose r equals n factorial over r factorial times n minus r factorial
Permutation	$P(n,r)$	permutation of n elements chosen r at a time or permutation of n choose r	$P(n,r) = \dfrac{n!}{(n-r)!}$ Permutation of n choose r equals n factorial over n minus r factorial $C(n,r) = P(n,r) / P(r,r)$ Combination of n choose r equals permutation of n choose r over permutation of r choose r

4.11 Geometry

Concept	Symbol	How to read the symbol	Examples
Point	•	point	Point B is between points A and C
Straight Line	/	straight line	Lines "L one", "L two" and "L three" are straight lines
Curved Line	⌒	curved line	Lines "L one" and "L two" are curved lines
Horizontal Line	—	horizontal line	"L one" is a horizontal line
Vertical Line	|	vertical line	"L one" is a vertical line

UNIT 4   MATHEMATICS   167

Concept	Symbol	How to read the symbol	Examples
Oblique Line	╲	oblique line	"L one" and "L two" are oblique lines
Angle	∠	angle	Angle ABC equals forty five degrees
Right angle	⌐	right angle	Angle ABC is a right angle
Parallel	∥	parallel	Lines "L one" and "L two" are parallel
Perpendicular	⊥	perpendicular	Lines "L one" and "L two" are perpendicular

Concept	Symbol	How to read the symbol	Examples
Length			A —— 3cm —— B The length of segment A B is three centimeters
Triangle	△	triangle	ABC is a triangle ABC is an **equilateral** triangle with all sides equal to five ABC is an **isosceles** triangle with sides AB and AC both equal to three
Right triangle	◹	right triangle, right-angle triangle, right-angled triangle	ABC is a right triangle

UNIT 4   MATHEMATICS

Concept	Symbol	How to read the symbol	Examples
Side			AB, BC and AC are the sides of the triangle
Hypotenuse		hypotenuse	AC is the hypotenuse
Circle	○	circle	This is a circle
Center	⊙	center	A is the center of the circle
Radius		radius	R is the radius

Concept	Symbol	How to read the symbol	Examples
Diameter	⊖	diameter	AB is the diameter
Arc	⌒	arc	BC is an arc
Circumference			"p" is the circumference
Ellipse	⬭	ellipse	This is an ellipse
Square	▫	square	ABCD is a square with each side equal to a

UNIT 4   MATHEMATICS

Concept	Symbol	How to read the symbol	Examples
Rectangle		rectangle	ABCD is a rectangle with the longer side equal to AD and the smaller side equal to AB
Diagonal		diagonal	AC is a diagonal in this rectangle ABCD
Parallelogram		parallelogram	ABCD is a parallelogram with side AD parallel to side BC, and side AB parallel to side CD
Trapezoid		trapezoid	ABCD is a trapezoid with the upper base AD and the lower base BC

Concept	Symbol	How to read the symbol	Examples
Pentagon	⬠	pentagon	ABCDE is a pentagon and has five sides
Hexagon	⬡	hexagon	ABCDEF is a hexagon and has six sides
Octagon	⯃	octagon	ABCDEFGH is an octagon and has eight sides
Area			The area of this rectangle equals a times b
Cube	▢	cube	This is a cube with the side equal to a

UNIT 4 MATHEMATICS 173

Concept	Symbol	How to read the symbol	Examples
Cylinder		cylinder	This is a cylinder
Cone		cone	This is a cone
Pyramid		pyramid	This is a pyramid
Sphere		sphere	This is a sphere
Volume			The volume of this cube equals a cubed

4.12 Mathematics exercises

4.12.1 Identifying mathematics branches

Which branch of mathematics does each of the following mathematical expressions represent?

1. $(2 + 1047) \times (308 - 52) - 66$
2. $x - 3.5 = 10$
3. $\iint x^3 y \, dx \, dy$
4. $\sin \beta = 0.5$
5. $N(\mu, \sigma^2)$
6. $P(X=0.5/Y)$
7. $x \in A$
8. $p \wedge q$
9. $\angle \; // \; \perp \; \triangle \; \square$

(The answers to these questions are at the end of the book)

4.12.2 Reading numbers

Read the following numbers.

1. 102
2. 3,506
3. 70,041
4. 255,689
5. 6,001,810
6. 27,000,000
7. 103,000,000
8. 1,344,000,005
9. 50,000,000,000
10. 457,000,635,000
11. 5,000,000,000,000

(The answers to these questions are at the end of the book)

UNIT 4   MATHEMATICS

4.12.3   Reading mathematical expressions

Read the following mathematical expressions.

1. $1 - 3/4$

2. -5.7

3. $2^3 - 3^4 + 7^2$

4. $4^{1/2} + 8^{1/3} - 7^{1/5}$

5. $|-9.2|$

6. $-1 > -2$

7. $\pi \approx 3.14$

8. e^{x+1}

9. $9!$

10. $2x^3 - 3x^2 + 6 = 0$

11. $\sum_{m=1}^{3} C_m$

12. $\lim_{x \to 0} \log(x)$

13. $\mathbf{A} \cdot \mathbf{B} = |A||B|\cos \alpha$

14. $\mathbf{A} \times \mathbf{B}$

15. $y(x)$

16. $d^2 x^3 / dx^2$

17. $\partial x^3 y / \partial x$

18. $\int_{1}^{3} x^3 \, dx$

19. $\sin 0$

20. $\cos 0$

21. $\sinh 0$

22. $E(X) = 0.5$

23. $P(X=0.2/Y)$

24. $x \in A$

25. $\forall x$

26. $\exists x: x<1$

27. $A = \{x: x<1\}$

28. $\neg A$

29. $A \not\subset B$

30. $A \cup B$

31. $A \cap B$

32. 101_2

33. $C(n,r)$

34. $P(n,r)$

(The answers to these questions are at the end of the book)

4.12.4 Describing geometric figures

Describe in words how to draw the following geometric figures.

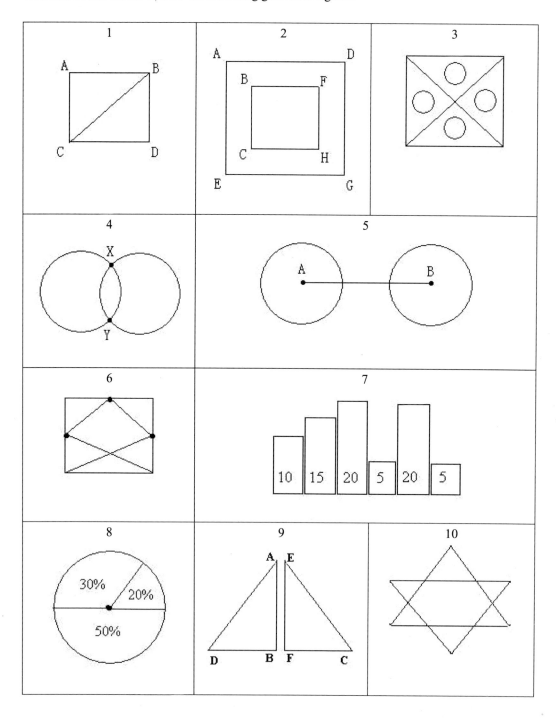

UNIT 4 Mathematics

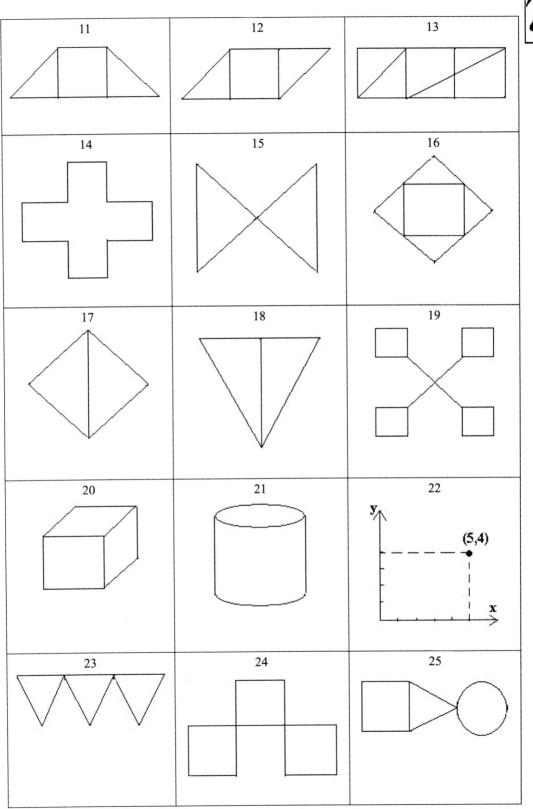

(The answers to these questions are at the end of the book)

4.12.5 Drawing geometric figures

For each of the following statements, draw the corresponding geometric figure.

1. Draw a horizontal straight line and segment it into three equal parts.
2. Draw two perpendicular lines with neither line being horizontal.
3. Draw two vertical parallel lines.
4. Draw an angle of 45° and label it with the Greek letter β.
5. Draw a square and label it ABCD clockwise starting from the upper right corner.
6. Draw two concentric squares and connect their corresponding corners to each other.
7. Draw a square and position it as if standing on one of its corners.
8. Draw four small equal squares and place them horizontally side-by-side and touching.
9. Draw a square and connect the middle point of its upper side to the lower right corner.
10. Draw two rectangles and place them perpendicularly so that they form a symmetric cross.
11. Draw a rectangle and show half of its diagonals similar to a letter envelope.
12. Draw a parallelogram with the longer side being horizontal.
13. Draw a right-angle trapezoid.
14. Draw a vertical bar chart illustrating the quantities 10, 15, 20, 5 respectively.
15. Draw an equilateral triangle with a side equal to 2.
16. Draw a right-angle triangle with a hypotenuse equal to 2.
17. Draw two triangles and connect them at one of their corners in a bow-tie shape.
18. Draw two equilateral triangles and place them on top of each other to form a six-corner star.
19. Draw a triangle with one of its angles greater than 90°.
20. Draw two concentric circles.
21. Draw two non-intersecting circles with centers A and B and connect their centers.
22. Draw a circle and show its vertical and horizontal diameters.
23. Draw two equal and intersecting circles such that the line connecting their centers is vertical.
24. Draw a square with each of its corners being the center of a circle with a radius half the side.
25. Draw a square with each side being the side of an equilateral triangle outside the square.
26. Draw a pie chart and divide it into slices of 30, 20 and 50%.
27. Draw a xy-graph and show the point with coordinates (3, 2).
28. Draw two vectors with the same origin and forming an angle of β between them.
29. Draw a cube with a side equal to 2.
30. Draw a cylinder with both height and radius equal to 2.
31. Draw a symmetric cone.

(The answers to these questions are at the end of the book)

4.12.6 Cloze

Fill in the blanks with the correct mathematical term.

1. The numbers 2, 4, 6, 8 are called _____ numbers.
2. The numbers 19, 21, 23, 25 are called _____ numbers.
3. The expression a/b is called a _____.
4. A number such as 11, which can only be divisible by 1 and itself, is called a _____ number.
5. A number of the form "a + bi" is called a _____ number.
6. A numerical expression with two rows and columns inside brackets is a two by two _____.
7. An equation of the form "ax +b = 0" is called a _____ equation.
8. An equation of the form "ax^2 + bx + c = 0" is called a _____ equation.
9. The _____ of vector **A** is |**A**|.
10. For vectors **A** and **B**, the product **A . B** is called a _____ product.
11. For vectors **A** and **B**, the product **A** × **B** is called a _____ product.
12. A xy graph is sometimes referred to as a 2D graph where "D" refers to _____.
13. In a graph, the projections of the location of a point on the axes are called the _____.
14. The symbol "∬" stands for a _____ integral while the symbol "∭" stands for a ____ integral.
15. In statistics, the _____ is usually represented with the Greek letter μ.
16. In statistics, the _____ is usually represented with the Greek letter σ.
17. A distribution of the form N(μ, σ^2) is called a _____ distribution.
18. A chart that looks like a circle divided into slices is called a _____ chart.
19. A chart that is made of rectangles of different lengths is called a _____ chart.
20. In mathematical logic, A+B is read A ____ B.
21. In mathematical logic, A×B is read A _____ B.
22. In mathematical logic, Venn _____ are used to show the intersection and union of sets.
23. In mathematical logic, a _____ table is used to show the result of logical operations.
24. For an _____ gate with inputs A and B, the output is A×B.
25. For an _____ gate with inputs A and B, the output is A + B.
26. A _____ gate inverts the input.
27. A numeral with base two is called a _____ numeral.
28. A numeral with base ten is called a _____ numeral.
29. A straight line that is neither vertical nor horizontal is _____.
30. If two straight lines in the same plane never cross each other, they are _____.
31. If two straight lines cross each other at a 90° angle, they are _____.
32. A triangle has three angles and three _____.
33. In a right triangle, the side opposite the right angle is called the _____.
34. A square has four _____ sides.
35. In a square or rectangle, the _____ joins opposite corners.

(The answers to these questions are at the end of the book)

UNIT 5

PHYSICS

PHYSICS KEYWORDS

Acceleration	加速度	Mechanics	力学
Acoustics	声学	Meter	米
Ampere	安培	Mile	英里
Anode	阳极	Momentum	动量
Battery	电池	Ohm	欧姆
Calorie	卡路里	Op-amp	运算放大器
Capacitance	电容	Optics	光学
Capacitor	电容器	Peak amplitude	峰值振幅
Cathode	阴极	Period	周期
Charge	电荷	Permeability	磁导率
Circuit	电路	Permittivity	电容率
Coulomb	库仑	Power	电力 / 功率
Current	电流	Pressure	压力
Degree Celsius	摄氏度	Radiation	辐射
Diode	二极管	Resistance	电阻
Distance	距离	Resistivity	电阻率
Electricity	电	Resistor	电阻器
Energy	能量	Saw-tooth wave	锯齿波
Farad	法拉	Signal	信号
Foot	尺	Sine wave	正弦波
Force	力	Speed	速度
Frequency	频率	Square wave	方波
Gram	克	Switch	开关
Gravity	重力	Temperature	温度
Heat	热	Thermodynamics	热力学
Henry	亨利	Transistor	晶体管
Hertz	赫兹	Triangular wave	三角波
Horsepower	马力	Unit	单位
Inch	英寸	Variable resistor	可变电阻器
Inductance	电感	Volt	伏特
Inductor	电感器	Voltage	电压
Kilometer	公里	Watt	瓦特
Length	长度	Wavelength	波长
Liter	升	Weight	重量
Magnetism	磁	Work	功

5.1 Introduction

Physics is the science that helps us study, understand and better use our environment. For example, the branch of physics that is called cosmology deals with studying the universe and exploring our origin as a living species. Another branch, quantum physics, allows us to understand the most infinitesimally small details of our world. Other branches, such as mechanics and electronics, allow us to devise machinery that makes our lives better.

5.2 Branches of physics

Physics has many branches and sometimes is divided into three main categories: classical physics, modern physics, and applied physics. Classical physics includes such aspects as Newtonian physics. Modern physics deals with such ideas as quantum mechanics and relativity. Applied physics constitutes a huge field and ranges from astrophysics to instrumentation such as electronics. If one were to enumerate all the physics branches in these three categories in detail, the list would be quite extensive and maybe confusing. However, there is a simple and generally accepted way to divide physics as shown in the figure below.

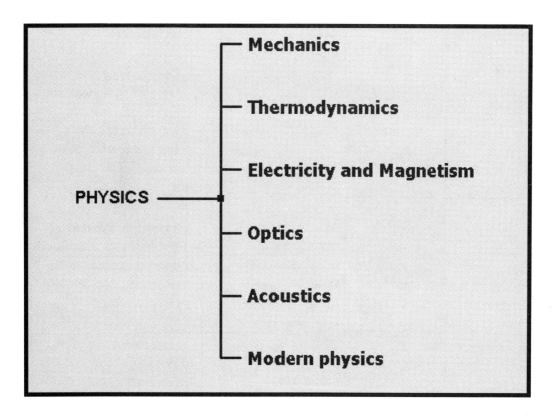

5.3 Mechanics and thermodynamics

Concept	Symbol	How to read the symbol	Examples
Distance, Length, Displacement	km m cm mm μm nm	kilometer meter centimeter millimeter micrometer nanometer	1 km = 1,000 m One kilometer equals one thousand meters 1 m = 1,000,000 μm One meter equals one million micrometers 1 m = 1,000,000,000 nm One meter equals one billion nanometers
	mi yd ft, ' in, "	mile yard foot inch	1 mile = 1.6 km One mile equals one point six kilometers 1 yd = 3 ft or 3' One yard equals three feet 1 ft = 12 in or 12" One foot equals twelve inches
Area	km^2 m^2 cm^2 mm^2 μm^2 nm^2	square kilometer square meter square centimeter square millimeter square micrometer square nanometer	$1\ km^2 = 1,000,000\ m^2$ One square kilometer equals one million square meters
	mi^2 yd^2 ft^2 in^2	square mile square yard square foot square inch	$A = 53\ mi^2$ A equals fifty three square miles

UNIT 5 PHYSICS

Concept	Symbol	How to read the symbol	Examples
Volume (gas)	m^3	cubic meter	$V = 25\ m^3$ V equals twenty five cubic meters
	ft^3 in^3	cubic foot cubic inch	Box volume = $9\ ft^3$ Box volume equals nine cubic feet Balloon volume = $3\ in^3$ Balloon volume equals three cubic inches
Volume (liquid)	l ml	liter milliliter	The coke bottle contains 600 ml The coke bottle contains six hundred milliliters
	gal qt pt oz	gallon quart pint ounce	1 gal = 4 qt One gallon equals four quarts 1 qt = 2 pt One quart equals two pints 1 pt = 16 oz One pint equals sixteen ounces
Time	yr dy hr min s ms µs ns	year day hour minute second millisecond microsecond nanosecond	1 hr = 3600 s One hour equals three thousand six hundred seconds $1\ s = 10^6\ µs$ One second equals one million microseconds

Concept	Symbol	How to read the symbol	Examples
Weight	t kg g mg	ton kilogram gram milligram	1 t = 1000 kg One ton equals one thousand kilograms 1 kg = 1000 g One kilogram equals one thousand grams
	lb oz	pound ounce	1 kg = 2.205 lb One kilogram equals two point two o five pounds 1 lb = 16 oz One pound equals sixteen ounces
Temperature	°C	degree Celsius degree centigrade	Water boils at 100 °C Water boils at one hundred degrees Celsius
	°F	degree Fahrenheit	Water freezes at 32 °F Water freezes at thirty two degrees Fahrenheit °C = (5/9) (°F − 32) Degree Celsius equals five ninths degree Fahrenheit minus thirty two
	°K	degree Kelvin	0 °K = −273.16 °C Zero degree Kelvin equals negative (or minus) two hundred seventy three point one six degrees Celsius

UNIT 5 PHYSICS

Concept	Symbol	How to read the symbol	Examples
Speed	km/h m/s	kilometer per hour meter per second	Speed of light = 3 x 10^8 m/s Speed of light equals three times ten to the eight meters per second
	mph	mile per hour	Highway speed limit = 65 mph Highway speed limit equals sixty five miles per hour Speed = |Velocity| Speed equals absolute value of velocity
Acceleration	m/s^2	meter per second squared	gravity = 9.8 m/s^2 Gravity equals nine point eight meters per second squared
Force	N	Newton	Force = mass x acceleration Force equals mass times acceleration
	lb	pound	F = m a F equals m a
Pressure	Pa	Pascal	1 Pa = 1 N/m^2 One pascal equals one newton per square meter
	psi	pound per square inch p s i	Pressure = 14.7 psi at sea level Pressure equals fourteen point seven pounds per square inch at sea level

Concept	Symbol	How to read the symbol	Examples
Work	N-m ft-lb	Newton meter foot pound	Work = force • displacement Work equals force dot displacement W = F • d W equals F dot d
Momentum	kg-m/s	kilogram meter per second	Momentum = mass x velocity Momentum equals mass times velocity P = m v P equals m v
Energy	J Wh kWh erg	Joule Watt hour kilowatt hour Erg	Kinetic energy = (1/2) mv^2 Kinetic energy equals half m v squared
Power	W hp	Watt horsepower	Power = $\Delta E / \Delta T$ Power equals delta e over delta t This V6 engine delivers 200 hp This v six engine delivers two hundred horsepower
Heat	cal kcal btu	calorie kilocalorie British thermal unit, b t u	A can of coke has 100 cal A can of coke has one hundred calories 1 btu = 252 cal One b t u equals two hundred fifty two calories

5.4 Electricity and magnetism

Concept	Symbol	How to read the symbol	Examples
Current	A mA μA	Ampere, Amp milliampere, milliamp microampere, microamp	I = 2 A I equals two amps
Voltage	kV V mV μV	kilovolt Volt millivolt microvolt	V = 220 V V equals two hundred twenty volts The AAA battery has 1.5 V The triple A battery has one point five volts
Current type	DC AC	direct current, DC alternating current, AC	A car battery provides a direct-current voltage of twelve volts, i.e. 12V DC In the US, homes are powered with a one-hundred-ten-volt alternating current at fifty hertz (110V AC, 50Hz) In China, homes are powered with a two-hundred-twenty-volt alternating current at sixty hertz (220V AC, 60Hz) Today's computers use universal power adapters that can work with both 110V and 220V AC

Concept	Symbol	How to read the symbol	Examples
Resistance	MΩ kΩ Ω	megaohm kiloohm Ohm	R = 100 Ω R equals one hundred ohms
Capacitance	F mF μF pF	Farad millifarad microfarad picofarad	C = 10 pF C equals ten picofarads
Inductance	H	Henry	L = 1 H L equals one henry
Resistivity	Ω/m	Ohm per meter	ρ = 1 kΩ / m rho equals one kiloohm per meter
Permittivity	F/m	Farad per meter	ε = 10 pF / m epsilon equals ten picofarads per meter
Permeability	H/m	Henry per meter	μ =.01 H / m mu equals point o one henry per meter
Charge	C	Coulomb	Q = 1 C Q equals one coulomb

UNIT 5 PHYSICS

Concept	Symbol	How to read the symbol	Examples
Voltage Source	—∣⊢— (+ −)	Cell, Battery	[12 V battery symbol] This battery provides a voltage of twelve volts
	(+/− in circle)	DC voltage source	
	(∿ in circle)	AC voltage source	[220V AC source symbol] This AC voltage source provides two hundred twenty volts AC
Resistor	—▭— —⋀⋀⋀—	Resistor	[circuit with R₁ and R₂ in series] Resistors R one and R two are (connected) in series [circuit with R₁ and R₂ in parallel] Resistors R one and R two are (connected) in parallel

Concept	Symbol	How to read the symbol	Examples
Variable Resistor		Variable resistor	This is a variable resistor. It is also called a potentiometer
Capacitor		Capacitor	1 pF This capacitor has a capacitance of one picofarad This is an R C circuit
Variable Capacitor		Variable capacitor	This is a variable capacitor
Inductor		Inductor	1 mH This is an R L circuit
Variable Inductor		Variable inductor	This is a variable inductor

Concept	Symbol	How to read the symbol	Examples
Transistor		Transistor	This is an npn transistor; b is the base, c is the collector, e is the emitter
			This is an FET transistor; g is the gate, d is the drain, s is the source
Diode		Diode	This is a bridge
		Light emitting diode, LED	This is an LED
		Zener diode	a is anode, c is cathode
		Photodiode	This is a photodiode

Concept	Symbol	How to read the symbol	Examples
Operational Amplifier	(op-amp triangle with +/−)	Op-amp	(single-ended op-amp diagram with input, output, +V, −V) This is a single-ended op-amp (differential op-amp diagram with input1, input2, output, +V, −V) This is a differential op-amp
Ground	(ground symbol)	Ground	(point A connected to ground symbol) Point A is connected to ground
Switch	(switch symbol)	Switch	(switch symbol) The switch can be open or closed
Fuse	(fuse symbol)	Fuse	(fuse symbol) The fuse acts as a safety mechanism

UNIT 5   PHYSICS

Concept	Symbol	How to read the symbol	Examples
Transformer	⌇⌇⌇	Transformer	A transformer has a primary side and a secondary side This is a step-down transformer This is a step-up transformer This is a variable transformer
Magnet	N □ S	Magnet	S ▭ N N is the north pole; S is the south pole

Concept	Symbol	How to read the symbol	Examples
Signals, Waves	～	Sine wave	This is the peak amplitude of the wave
	⊓⊔	Square wave	
	△▽	Triangular wave	This is the peak-to-peak amplitude of the wave
	⋁⋁⋁	Saw-tooth wave	This is the period of the wave
			Wave two has a higher frequency than wave one

5.5 Optics and acoustics

Concept	Symbol	How to read the symbol	Examples
Frequency	GHz MHz kHz Hz	gigahertz megahertz kilohertz Hertz	f = 2.5 GHz f equals two point five gigahertz
Wavelength	m cm mm µm nm Å	meter centimeter millimeter micrometer nanometer Angstrom	λ = 10 mm Lambda equals ten millimeters
Radiation	Gamma X-Rays UV Visible light IR Radar Microwave FM TV SW AM	gamma x-rays ultra violet visible light infrared radar microwave frequency modulation, FM Television, TV short wave amplitude modulation, AM	
Angle of incidence	α	angle of incidence	50° The angle of incidence equals fifty degrees

Concept	Symbol	How to read the symbol	Examples
Angle of reflection		angle of reflection	The angle of reflection equals fifty degrees
Angle of refraction		angle of refraction	The angle of refraction equals thirty degrees
Concave lens		concave lens	A concave lens is diverging
Convex lens		convex lens	A convex lens is converging
Luminous Intensity	cd	candela	
Sound	db	decibel d b	10 db Ten decibels or ten d b

UNIT 5 PHYSICS

5.6 Physics exercises

5.6.1 Reading physics notation

Read the following physics expressions.

1. $1 \; \mu m = 10^{-6} \; m$
2. $1 \; m = 10^9 \; nm$
3. $1 \; mi = 1.6 \; km$
4. $1' = 12''$
5. $1'' = 2.54 \; cm$
6. $A = 9{,}000{,}000 \; km^2$
7. $V = 137 \; m^3$
8. $1 \; gal = 4 \; qt$
9. $1 \; \mu s = 1000 \; ns$
10. $1 \; kg = 2.205 \; lb$
11. $1 \; lb = 16 \; oz$
12. $0 \; ^\circ C = 32 \; ^\circ F$
13. $0 \; ^\circ K = -273.16 \; ^\circ C$
14. $c = 3 \times 10^8 \; m/s$
15. $S = 65 \; mph$
16. $g = 9.8 \; m/s^2$
17. $F = 6 \; N$
18. $P = 100 \; Pa$
19. $P = 14.7 \; psi$
20. $W = 10 \; N\text{-}m$
21. $E = 3 \; J$
22. $P = 60 \; W$
23. $P = 200 \; hp$
24. $1 \; btu = 252 \; cal$
25. $I = 3 \; A$
26. $V = 110 \; V$
27. $R = 1 \; k\Omega$
28. $C = 1 \; pF$
29. $L = 1 \; H$
30. $Q = 1 \; C$
31. $f = 1800 \; MHz$
32. $\lambda = 10 \; \text{Å}$
33. $10 \; db$

(The answers to these questions are at the end of the book)

5.6.2 Identifying electronic symbols

Match the electronic symbols below to their corresponding names.

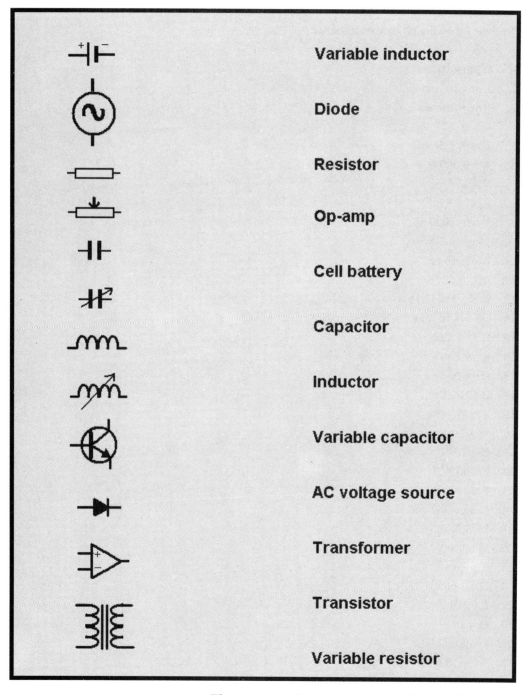

(The answers to these questions are at the end of the book)

5.6.3 Cloze

Fill in the blanks with the correct physics terms.

1. The meter is used as a unit to measure _____ or distance or displacement.
2. Today's chip technology allows CPUs to be built at the 45-_____ level.
3. The square meter is used as a unit to measure _____.
4. The cubic meter is used as a unit to measure _____.
5. The gallon and litter are used as units to measure _____ volume.
6. The second is used as a unit to measure _____.
7. The pound and kilogram are used as units to measure _____.
8. Degree Celsius and degree Fahrenheit are used as units to measure _____.
9. The meter per second is used as a unit to measure _____ or velocity.
10. The highest speed is that of _____ and is measured to be about 3×10^8 m/s.
11. The meter per second squared is used as a unit to measure _____.
12. The _____ or pull of the Earth is measured to be about 9.8 m/s^2.
13. The Newton and pound are used as units to measure _____.
14. The Pascal and psi are used as units to measure _____.
15. The Newton-meter and foot-pound are used as units to measure _____.
16. The kilogram-meter-per-second is used as a unit to measure _____.
17. The Joule and watt-hour are used as units to measure _____.
18. The Watt and hp are used as units to measure _____.
19. The calorie and btu are used as units to measure _____.
20. The Ampere is used as a unit to measure _____.
21. The Volt is used as a unit to measure _____.
22. The Ohm is used as a unit to measure _____.
23. The Ohm-per-meter is used as a unit to measure _____.
24. The Farad is used as a unit to measure _____.
25. The Farad-per-meter is used as a unit to measure _____.
26. The Henry is used as a unit to measure _____.
27. The Henry-per-meter is used as a unit to measure _____.
28. The Coulomb is used as a unit to measure _____.
29. The Hertz is used as a unit to measure _____.
30. The candela is used as unit to measure luminous or light _____.
31. The decibel is used as a unit to measure _____.

(The answers to these questions are at the end of the book)

UNIT 6

DATA COMMUNICATIONS

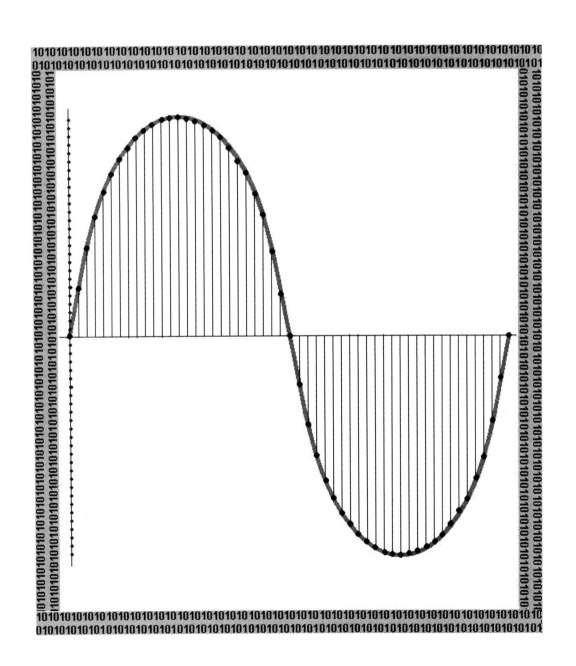

DATA COMMUNICATIONS KEYWORDS

Analog signal	模拟信号	Mbps	百万位每秒
Aperiodic	非周期性的	MBps	百万字节每秒
Asynchronous	异步	Modulation	调制
Band-pass filter	带通滤波器	MSB	最高位
Bandwidth	带宽 / 频带	Multiplexer	多路复用器
Binary	二进制的	Network	网络
Bit	比特 / 位	Packet	包 / 分组
Bridge	桥接器	Packet switching	包变换
Bus topology	总线拓扑	Parallel transmission	并行传输
Byte	字节	Parity bit	奇偶位
CDM	码分多路复用	Periodic	周期性的
Coaxial cable	同轴电缆	Phase	相 / 相位
Connector	连接器	Protocol	协议
Data rate	数据速率	Protocol stack	协议栈
Digital signal	数字信号	Quantizing	量子化 / 量化
Discrete signal	离散信号	Repeater	中继器 / 转发器
Encoding	编码	Ring topology	环形拓扑
Equipment	设备	Router	路由器
Error correction	差错纠正	Sampling	取样
Error detection	差错检测	Serial transmission	串行传输
Ethernet	以太网	Signal	信号
FDM	频分多路复用	Signal-to-noise ratio	信噪比
Fiber	光纤	Simplex	单工
Frame	帧	Star topology	星形拓扑
Frequency	频率	Start bit	启动位
Full duplex	全双工	Stop bit	停止位
Half duplex	半双工	STP	屏蔽双绞线
High-pass filter	高通滤波器	Switch	交换机
IP address	IP 地址	Synchronous	同步的
IP version	IP 版本	TDM	时分多路复用
LAN	局域网	Transmission	输送 / 传输
Laser	激光	UTP	非屏蔽双绞线
Low-pass filter	低通滤波器	Virtual circuit	虚电路
LSB	最低位	WAN	广域网
MAN	城域网		

UNIT 6   DATA COMMUNICATIONS

6.1   Introduction

The Internet, our home networks, our schools' and companies' intra-networks, and the inside of our computers and mobile phones work based on the principles of data communications. Data communications allows us to enjoy all kinds of electronic products such as the telephone, the radio, the television and the MP3 player. Understanding data communications is crucial if one is to have a good grasp of the information revolution.

6.2   Elements of data communications

Data communications deals with the nature, processing and transmission of signals. Signals can be anything from our voice to intergalactic signals. As signals are transmitted from source to destination, they go through different transmission media where they encounter all kinds of interference. Data communications deals with handling these problems and correctly extracting signals.

The main elements of data communications are as shown in the following figure.

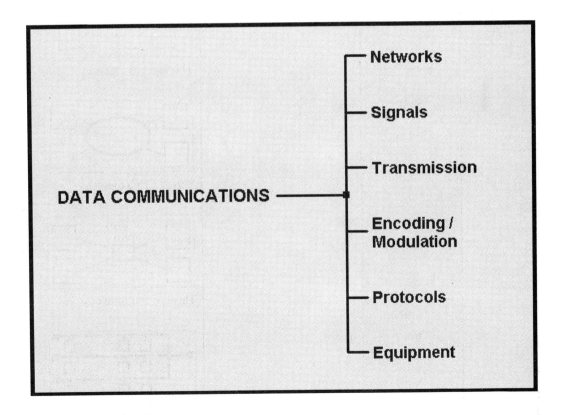

6.3 Networks

Concept	Symbol / Type	How to read the symbol	Examples
Network	LAN	local area network (or LAN)	The office installed a LAN to connect all its computers and servers
	MAN	metropolitan area network (or metro area network) (or MAN)	A MAN covers a whole city
	WAN	wide area network (or WAN)	The backbone of the Internet is an example of a WAN
LAN topology	bus	bus	This is a bus topology
	ring	ring	This is a ring topology
	star	star	This is a star topology
	tree	tree	This is a tree topology

Concept	Symbol	How to read the symbol	Examples
Ethernet	10B2	ten base two (or thin Ethernet)	This figure shows two groups of users, each group connected via a hub. The two hubs are then connected via a third hub. This is an example of a cascade configuration
	10B5	ten base five (or thick Ethernet)	
	10BT	ten base t	
	10BF	ten base f	
	100BT	one hundred base t (or twisted pair fast Ethernet)	
	100BF	one hundred base f (or fiber fast Ethernet)	
	1000BT	one thousand base t (or twisted pair gigabit Ethernet)	This figure shows an Ethernet frame. An Ethernet frame consists of the following fields. A Preamble of seven bytes. A Start of Frame Delimiter of one byte. A Destination Address of six bytes. A Source Address of six bytes. A Length field of two bytes. A Data field of up to fifteen hundred bytes. A Pad field of up to forty-six bytes. And a Frame Check Sequence field of four bytes
	1000BF	one thousand base f (or fiber gigabit Ethernet)	
	10000BT	ten thousand base t (or twisted pair ten gigabit Ethernet)	
	10000BF	ten thousand base f (or fiber ten gigabit Ethernet)	

6.4 Signals

Concept	Symbol / Type	How to read the symbol	Examples
Signal type	analog	analog	This **continuous** signal is analog
	digital	digital	This **discrete** signal is digital
	periodic	Periodic	This square wave is periodic with a period of T
	aperiodic	aperiodic	Signal s of t is aperiodic because it does not repeat itself
	binary	binary	This is a **binary** signal, which is a digital signal with two values

6.5 Transmission

Concept	Symbol / Type	How to read the symbol	Examples
Transmission medium	guided	guided	A guided transmission medium means one of the following: Unshielded Twisted Pair (UTP), Shielded Twisted Pair (STP), coaxial cable, or optical fiber
	unguided	unguided	An unguided transmission medium means one of the following: terrestrial microwave, satellite microwave, broadcast radio and TV, infrared and laser
Frequency	ELF	extremely low frequency	The unit of frequency is hertz (Hz)
	VF	voice frequency	
	VLF	very low frequency	The wavelength is inversely proportional to the frequency
	LF	low frequency	
	MF	medium frequency	FM radio signals are broadcast as VHF signals
	HF	high frequency	
	VHF	very high frequency	The human voice is a VF signal
	UHF	ultra high frequency	
	SHF	super high frequency	Transmission through optical fiber uses visible light
	EHF	extremely high frequency	
	IR	infrared	Submarine communication takes place in the ELF range
	Visible light	visible light	

Concept	Symbol	How to read the symbol	Examples
Bandwidth	BW	bandwidth	Even though speech frequencies extend from about 100 Hz to 7 kHz, most of the energy of the speech signal is confined to less than 4 kHz. Thus, the telephone bandwidth for transmitting voice is less than 4 kHz
Data unit	b B	bit byte	One byte has eight bits A "Mark" means a binary bit 1, whereas a "Space" means 0 In a byte, LSB means Least Significant Bit, whereas MSB means Most Significant Bit A "Parity" bit is used to check for errors In some transmissions, a "Start bit" and/or "Stop bit" are used
Data rate	Gbps GBps Mbps MBps kbps kBps bps Bps	gigabits per second gigabytes per second megabits per second megabytes per second kilobits per second kilobytes per second bits per second bytes per second	USB version 2 supports data rates of up to 400 Mbps

UNIT 6   DATA COMMUNICATIONS

Concept	Symbol / Type	How to read the symbol	Examples
Data package	frame packet	frame packet	To transmit a message on the Internet, the message data is broken into units, which are packaged into TCP/IP packets. The packets are then put into frames and transmitted
Packet switching	VC DG	virtual circuit datagram	In the TCP/IP protocol, TCP uses virtual circuits, whereas UDP uses datagrams
Transmission timing	SYNC ASYNC	synchronous (or synch) asynchronous (or asynch)	Some asynchronous transmissions use start and stop bits to allow the receiver to properly decode the data
Bit transmission mode	parallel serial	parallel serial	[diagram: CPU bit 1..bit n connected to RAM bit 1..bit n] The CPU and RAM in a computer communicate using a bus of n lines, such as 8 or 16 lines. This is an example of parallel transmission [diagram: CHIP 1 bit 1..bit n connected serially to CHIP 2 bit 1..bit n] In this example, the bits are transmitted serially on one line

Concept	Symbol / Type	How to read the symbol	Examples
Transmission direction	simplex	simplex	![simplex diagram] In simplex transmission, the transmission is unidirectional, from the transmitter to the receiver. One example of simplex transmission is TV or radio broadcasting, where the transmission goes from the station tower to the set at home
	half duplex	half duplex	![half duplex diagram] In half duplex transmission, the transmitter/receivers at both ends take turns transmitting. One example of half duplex transmission is radio used by taxi drivers to talk with their dispatchers
	full duplex	full duplex	![full duplex diagram] In full duplex transmission, the transmitter/receivers at both ends transmit simultaneously, one example being the phone

6.6 Encoding/modulation

Concept	Symbol	How to read the symbol	Examples
Digital to digital encoding	Unipolar	Unipolar	*[Graph: 0 1 1 0, +3/0/-3 axis, unipolar waveform]* This is unipolar encoding for the data string 0 1 1 0
	NRZL	Non return to zero level (or N R Z L)	
	NRZI	non return to zero inverted (or N R Z I)	*[Graph: 0 1 1 0, NRZL waveform]* This is NRZL encoding for the data string 0110. The NRZL signal is **polar**, i.e. it has a negative value and a positive value to represent bits 0 and 1
	Bipolar AMI	bipolar alternate mark inversion (or bipolar A M I)	
	Manchester	Manchester	
	B8ZS	bipolar with eight zero substitution (or B 8 Z S)	*[Graph: 0 1 1 0, NRZI waveform]* This is NRZI encoding for the data string 0110. The NRZI signal is polar. Bit 1 is represented by a transition in level; for bit 0 there is no transition
	HDB3	high density bipolar three zeros (or H D B 3)	
			[Graph: 0 1 1 0, bipolar AMI waveform] This is bipolar AMI encoding for the data string 0110. A bipolar signal has three values

Concept	Symbol	How to read the symbol	Examples
Digital to analog modulation	ASK	amplitude shift keying (or A S K)	This is the ASK modulation of the data string 0110. Bit 1 is represented by a bigger-amplitude signal than bit 0
	FSK	frequency shift keying (or F S K)	
	BFSK	binary F S K (or B F S K)	
	MFSK	multiple F S K (or M F S K)	This is the FSK modulation of the data string 0110. Bit one is represented by a higher-frequency signal than bit 0
	PSK	phase shift keying (or P S K)	
	BPSK	binary P S K (or B P S K)	
	DPSK	differential P S K (or D P S K)	
	QPSK	Quadrature P S K (or Q P S K)	This is the PSK modulation of the data string 0110. The signal's phase changes each time there is a bit 1. For bit 0, there is no phase change
	QAM	quadrature amplitude modulation (or QAM)	

UNIT 6 DATA COMMUNICATIONS

Concept	Symbol	How to read the symbol	Examples
Analog to digital encoding	PAM	pulse amplitude modulation (or PAM)	analog signal
	PCM	pulse code modulation (or P C M)	sampling
	DM	delta modulation (or D M)	PAM signal
			quantizing
			encoding
			PCM signal
			The analog-data-to-PCM signal encoding goes as follows: first, the analog signal is sampled to get the PAM signal; second, the PAM signal is quantized; third, the quantized values are encoded into binary data of zeros and ones; this is the PCM signal

Concept	Symbol	How to read the symbol	Examples
Analog to analog modulation	AM	amplitude modulation (or A M)	In AM modulation, if the carrier is a sinusoidal signal with amplitude A_c, frequency f_c and phase a, i.e. $A_c \cos(2\pi f_c t + a)$
	DSBTC	double sideband transmitted carrier (or D S B T C)	And the data signal is a sinusoidal signal with frequency f_m, i.e. $\sin(2\pi f_m t)$
	SSB	single sideband (or S S B)	
	DSBSC	double sideband suppressed carrier (or D S B S C)	Then, the AM modulated signal looks as follows in the time domain:
	VSB	vestigial sideband (or V S B)	
	FM	frequency modulation	And, the AM modulated signal looks as follows in the frequency domain: LSB, USB at $f_c - f_m$, f_c, $f_c + f_m$
	PM	phase modulation	In the above figure, LSB stands for lower sideband, and USB stands for upper sideband. This figure represents DSBTC. For DSBSC, the figure will only show LSB and USB. For SSB, the figure will either show LSB or USB

UNIT 6   DATA COMMUNICATIONS   217

Concept	Symbol	How to read the symbol	Examples
Multiplexing	MUX	multiplexer	
	DEMUX	demultiplexer	
	IMUX	inverse multiplexer	
	FDM	frequency division multiplexing (or F D M)	
	CDM	code division multiplexing (or C D M)	
	TDM	time division multiplexing (or T D M)	This is a MUX/DEMUX configuration. The MUX multiplexes the inputs onto one link; the DEMUX sorts them out
	STDM	statistical time division multiplexing (or S T D M)	An example of FDM is ADSL (Asynchronous Digital Subscriber Line). The ADSL modem allows both a telephone set and a computer to share one phone line simultaneously

Concept	Symbol	How to read the symbol	Examples
Filtering	LPF	low-pass filter	This is an ideal low-pass filter
	BPF	band-pass filter	This is an ideal band-pass filter
	HPF	high-pass filter	This is an ideal high-pass filter
Noise	S/N	signal to noise ratio	The signal to noise ratio is expressed in db
Error detection	Parity	parity	In error detection, even or odd parity can be used
	LRC	longitudinal redundancy Check (or L R C)	
	VRC	vertical redundancy check (or V R C)	
	CRC	cyclic redundancy check (or C R C)	
Error correction	BEC	backward error correction	In space exploration, spaceships must use forward error correction because of the huge distances involved
	FEC	forward error correction	

6.7 Protocols

Concept	Symbol	How to read the symbol	Examples
Protocol stack	TCP/IP	transmission control protocol, internet protocol (or T C P I P)	This figure shows the TCP/IP and OSI protocol stacks, side by side
	OSI	open systems interconnection (or O S I)	
TCP/IP applications	FTP	file transfer protocol (or F T P)	FTP is used when transferring large files, such as when downloading a movie or uploading a big file
	SNMP	simple network management protocol (or S N M P)	
	SMTP	simple mail transfer protocol (or S M T P)	Telnet allows for the login into a remote server
	HTTP	hypertext transfer protocol (or H T T P)	When we click on the link of a web page, our browser uses HTTP to communicate with the server where that web page resides and to show that web page in our browser window
	NFS	network file system (or N F S)	
	Telnet	terminal emulation protocol (or Telnet)	

Concept	Symbol	How to read the symbol	Examples
IP routing	RIP	routing information protocol (or RIP)	
	OSPF	open shortest path first (or O S P F)	
	EGP	exterior gateway protocol (or E G P)	
	BGP	border gateway protocol (or B G P)	
IP version	IPv4	I P version four	An IPv4 address has four bytes, whereas an IPv6 address has sixteen bytes
	IPv6	I P version six	
IP address	[0:netid:hostid]	class A I P address	
	[10:netid:hostid]	class B I P address	This is a class A IP address
	[110:netid:hostid]	class C I P address	
	[1110:Multicast]	class D I P address	
	[11110:Reserved]	class E I P address	This is a class B IP address

UNIT 6 DATA COMMUNICATIONS   221

Concept	Symbol	How to read the symbol	Examples
Wireless	Bluetooth	bluetooth	For its 3G, China developed its own technology, TD-SCDMA

Most of the world's mobile phone carriers use GSM instead of CDMA

WiFi, also called WLAN, is a technology for the wireless LAN. Its latest version, WiFi-n, provides high data rates

WiMAX can be used for longer distances than WiFi, and is seen as an option for the last mile to the home |
	CDMA	code division multiple access (or C D M A)	
	CDMA2000	C D M A two thousand	
	DVB-H	digital video broadcasting - handheld (or D V B H)	
	EDGE	enhanced data for GSM environment (or EDGE)	
	GPRS	general packet radio service (or G P R S)	
	GSM	global system for mobile communications (or G S M)	
	HSDPA	high-speed downlink packet access (or H S D P A)	
	HSUPA	high-speed uplink packet access (or H S U P A)	
	IR	infrared	
	TD-SCDMA	time division synchronous CDMA (or T D S C D M A)	
	3G	third generation (or 3 G)	
	WCDMA	wideband CDMA (or W C D M A)	
	WiFi abgn	Wi (as in why) Fi (as in fire) a b g n	
	WiMAX	Wi (as in why) MAX	

6.8 Equipment

Concept	Symbol / Type	How to read the symbol	Examples
Network equipment	bridge hub multiplexer repeater router switch	bridge hub multiplexer repeater router switch	A repeater works at the physical level. It amplifies the signal it receives and rebroadcasts it A hub works at the physical layer, amplifies the signal it receives, and sends it to the destination A bridge works at the network interface or data link layer and can connect LANs that use different technologies A router can be used to connect a LAN to an outside network such as the Internet The traffic on the Internet backbone is moved around the world using very fast routers
Connectors	RJ45 BNC ST SC	R J forty five B N C S T S C	An RJ45 connector is used with twisted pair wire such as UTP RJ stands for Registered Jack but we always read RJ45 as R J forty five A BNC connector is used with coaxial cable. A common type of BNC connector is the T-type ST and SC are fiber connectors

Concept	Symbol	How to read the symbol	Examples
Cabling	UTP	unshielded twisted pair (or U T P)	This is UTP cable
	STP	shielded twisted pair (or S T P)	
	COAX	coaxial	This is coaxial cable
	Fiber	fiber optic	This is fiber. The core is made of glass or plastic
Fiber type	SI	Step-index fiber -------→ (or step-index multimode fiber)	
	GI	graded-index fiber ------→ (or graded-index multimode fiber)	
	SM	single-mode fiber -----→	

6.9 Data communications exercises

6.9.1 Reading comprehension

1. Name the different types of networks.
2. What is the main difference between a LAN and a MAN?
3. Name the different LAN topologies.
4. What is the main difference between 10BT Ethernet and 10BF Ethernet?
5. What is the main difference between 100BT Ethernet and 1000BT Ethernet?
6. Is the human voice an analog or digital signal?
7. What do we call a sampled analog signal?
8. What do we call a sampled and quantized analog signal?
9. What do we call a signal that repeats itself at regular time intervals?
10. What do we call a digital signal that can have two values?
11. Name some examples of guided transmission media.
12. Name some examples of unguided transmission media.
13. What is the unit of frequency?
14. What do we call the frequency range of a signal?
15. How many bits are there in a byte?
16. What is a parity bit used for?
17. What are the names used to describe the data packages of bits?
18. Name the two modes of packet switching.
19. Name the two types of transmission timing.
20. Give an example of simplex transmission.
21. Give an example of half duplex transmission.
22. Give an example of full duplex transmission.
23. Name some examples of digital-to-digital encoding.
24. Name some examples of digital-to-analog modulation.
25. Name some examples of analog-to-digital encoding.
26. Name some examples of analog-to-analog modulation.
27. Name the different techniques of multiplexing.
28. Name the different types of signal filters.
29. What is the unit used to measure the signal-to-noise ratio?
30. Name some error detection and correction coding methods.

(The answers to these questions are at the end of the book)

6.9.2 Reading data communications acronyms

Complete the following table by showing how these data communications acronyms are pronounced and what they stand for.

Acronym	Pronunciation	Acronym expansion
LAN		
MAN		
WAN		
10BT		
100BF		
1000BT		
10000BF		
UTP		
STP		
VHF		
UHF		
BW		
Gbps		
GBps		
LSB		
MSB		
VC		
DG		
SYNCH		
ASYNCH		
FSK		
PSK		
PCM		
FDM		
CDM		
TDM		

(The answers to these questions are at the end of the book)

6.9.3 Identifying data communications signals

Match the words in the following table to their corresponding items in the figure below.

FSK modulation	Aperiodic signal
Binary signal	Continuous signal
PSK modulation	Full duplex transmission
Simplex transmission	Periodic signal

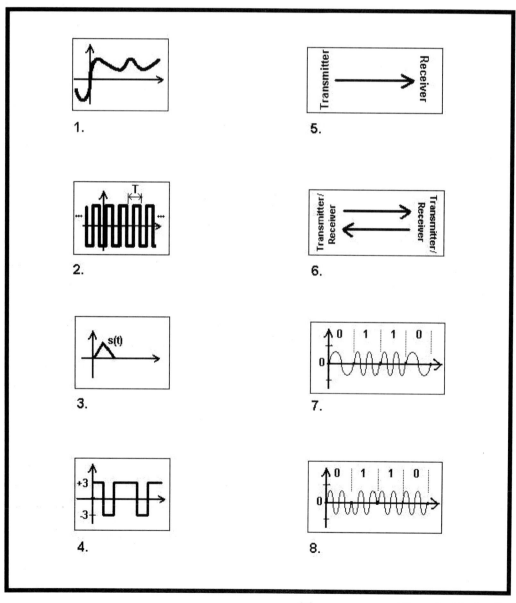

(The answers are at the end of the book)

6.9.4 Cloze

Fill in the blanks in the following statements with the correct data communications words.

1. The network used to connect the computers at home or in the office is called a ____.
2. The network that can cover a whole city is called a _____.
3. A network that can cover a whole country is called a _____.
4. An Ethernet segment uses a _____ topology.
5. Ethernet cabling uses twisted pair wiring or _____.
6. An analog signal is a _____ signal.
7. An analog signal that is sampled becomes a _____ signal.
8. An analog signal that is sampled and quantized becomes a _____ signal.
9. A digital signal with two possible values is called a _____ signal.
10. A signal that repeats itself at regular time intervals is called a _____ signal.
11. A signal that is not periodic is called _____.
12. _____ transmission media use some type of cabling such as fiber.
13. _____ transmission media mean the transmission is through space.
14. Transmission through optical fiber uses visible _____.
15. The telephone _____ for transmitting voice is less than 4kHz.
16. Data units are the bit and the _____, which contains eight bits.
17. A _____ bit is used to check for errors.
18. Groups of data bytes can be packaged into frames and _____ for transmission.
19. In packet switching, TCP uses _____ while UDP uses datagrams.
20. Timing in data transmissions can be synchronous or _____.
21. Data transmission between two chips can be either through _____ or parallel modes.
22. Data transmission that takes place in only one direction is called _____ transmission.
23. Simultaneous data transmission in both directions is called _____ transmission.
24. Multiplexing of data can use such techniques as _____, CDM, TDM and STDM.
25. ADSL uses ____ multiplexing to allow a telephone and a computer to share a phone line.
26. A _____ filter is used to filter out the higher frequencies in a signal.
27. The _____ ratio, measured in db, is used to express the quality of data transmission.
28. _____ error correction is used for very distant communications.
29. In data communications, the two main protocol stacks are _____ and OSI.
30. IP addressing is categorized into _____ called A, B, C, D and E.
31. The Internet traffic is moved around using equipment devices called _____.
32. The LAN port on a computer is called an _____ port.
33. Twisted-pair wiring can be either _____ or shielded.
34. The core of fiber cables is made of either _____ or plastic.

(The answers to these questions are at the end of the book)

APPENDIX

1. Greek letters

Greek letter		English Name
Lower case	Upper case	
α	A	alpha
β	B	beta
γ	Γ	gamma
δ	Δ	delta
ε	E	epsilon
ζ	Z	zeta
η	H	eta
θ	Θ	theta
ι	I	iota
κ	K	kappa
λ	Λ	lambda
μ	M	mu
ν	N	nu
ξ	Ξ	xi
o	O	omicron
π	Π	pi
ρ	P	rho
σ	Σ	sigma
τ	T	tau
υ	Υ	upsilon
φ	Φ	phi
χ	X	chi
ψ	Ψ	psi
ω	Ω	omega

2. The periodic table of the elements

The Periodic Table of the Elements

1 H																	2 He
3 Li	4 Be											5 B	6 C	7 N	8 O	9 F	10 Ne
11 Na	12 Mg											13 Al	14 Si	15 P	16 S	17 Cl	18 Ar
19 K	20 Ca	21 Sc	22 Ti	23 V	24 Cr	25 Mn	26 Fe	27 Co	28 Ni	29 Cu	30 Zn	31 Ga	32 Ge	33 As	34 Se	35 Br	36 Kr
37 Rb	38 Sr	39 Y	40 Zr	41 Nb	42 Mo	43 Tc	44 Ru	45 Rh	46 Pd	47 Ag	48 Cd	49 In	50 Sn	51 Sb	52 Te	53 I	54 Xe
55 Cs	56 Ba	57 La	72 Hf	73 Ta	74 W	75 Re	76 Os	77 Ir	78 Pt	79 Au	80 Hg	81 Tl	82 Pb	83 Bi	84 Po	85 At	86 Rn
87 Fr	88 Ra	89 Ac	104 Rf														

Lanthanide series: 57 La, 58 Ce, 59 Pr, 60 Nd, 61 Pm, 62 Sm, 63 Eu, 64 Gd, 65 Tb, 66 Dy, 67 Ho, 68 Er, 69 Tm, 70 Yb, 71 Lu

Actinide series: 89 Ac, 90 Th, 91 Pa, 92 U, 93 Np, 94 Pu, 95 Am, 96 Cm, 97 Bk, 98 Cf, 99 Es, 100 Fm, 101 Md, 102 No, 103 Lr

1 Hydrogen	2 Helium	3 Lithium	4 Beryllium	5 Boron
6 Carbon	7 Nitrogen	8 Oxygen	9 Fluorine	10 Neon
11 Sodium	12 Magnesium	13 Aluminum	14 Silicon	15 Phosphorus
16 Sulfur	17 Chlorine	18 Argon	19 Potassium	20 Calcium
21 Scandium	22 Titanium	23 Vanadium	24 Chromium	25 Manganese
26 Iron	27 Cobalt	28 Nickel	29 Copper	30 Zinc
31 Gallium	32 Germanium	33 Arsenic	34 Selenium	35 Bromine
36 Krypton	37 Rubidium	38 Strontium	39 Yttrium	40 Zirconium
41 Niobium	42 Molybdenum	43 Technetium	44 Ruthenium	45 Rhodium
46 Palladium	47 Silver	48 Cadmium	49 Indium	50 Tin
51 Antimony	52 Tellurium	53 Iodine	54 Xenon	55 Cesium
56 Barium	57 Lanthanum	58 Cerium	59 Praseodymium	60 Neodymium
61 Promethium	62 Samarium	63 Europium	64 Gadolinium	65 Terbium
66 Dysprosium	67 Holmium	68 Erbium	69 Thulium	70 Ytterbium
71 Lutetium	72 Hafnium	73 Tantalum	74 Tungsten	75 Rhenium
76 Osmium	77 Iridium	78 Platinum	79 Gold	80 Mercury
81 Thallium	82 Lead	83 Bismuth	84 Polonium	85 Astatine
86 Radon	87 Francium	88 Radium	89 Actinium	90 Thorium
91 Protactinium	92 Uranium	93 Neptunium	94 Plutonium	95 Americium
96 Curium	97 Berkelium	98 Californium	99 Einsteinium	100 Fermium
101 Mendelevium	102 Nobelium	103 Lawrencium	104 Rutherfordium	

3. Answers to questions

(1) Answers to computer questions

1.6.1 Reading comprehension

1. Enumerate all the types of computers and their main purposes.
   The various types of computers are supercomputers, mainframes, servers, workstations, desktops, laptops/notebooks/tablets, and palmtops. Supercomputers are the fastest of computers and are used in such complex applications as nuclear and meteorological simulations. Mainframes used to be the most powerful computers and were the main computers in data centers before servers displaced them. Mainframes still exist today and have adapted to remain competitive. Usually big companies buy mainframes and use them for all kinds of corporate computing such as database applications. The server has now become the most common computing device in data centers because it offers an ideal computing power to cost ratio. For example, the huge data centers of some Internet companies are stacked with servers. Workstations are used by engineers and scientists to perform technical tasks such as modeling and design. Desktops are used in offices and homes for daily computing tasks and gaming. Laptops/notebooks are gradually replacing desktops while offering portability. Tablets are laptops with touch-screens. Netbooks are small laptops. UMPCs and Palmtops are pocket-sized computers.

2. What are the main hardware components of a personal computer?
   The main hardware components of a personal computer include the motherboard, hard disk, optical drive, keyboard, mouse/touchpad, monitor/display, webcam and power supply. The motherboard contains the following parts: CPU, memory chips, GPU, chipset, buses, I/O ports, wireless components, slots and BIOS chip.

3. What is the basic three-step processing cycle of a CPU?
   The basic three-step processing cycle of a CPU is the fetch-decode-execute cycle.

4. Name some of the main parts of a CPU?
   Some of the main parts of a CPU are the Control Unit (CU), Arithmetic Logic Unit (ALU), Floating Point Unit (FPU), registers and cache memory.

5. What does Moore's Law state about the number of transistors inside a CPU?
   Moore's Law states that the number of transistors that can be crammed onto a chip doubles about every eighteen months.

6. What measurement unit is used to describe the speed of a CPU?
   The measurement unit used to describe the speed of a CPU is the Hertz (Hz).

7. What do the terms "Duo" and "Quad" mean when used in conjunction with a CPU?

When used in conjunction with a CPU, "Duo" means two cores, while "Quad" means four cores.

8. **What acronyms are used to refer to the amount of memory inside a computer?**
The acronyms used to refer to the amount of memory inside a computer are GB (gigabyte) or MB (megabyte).

9. **Which memory can the CPU access faster, the CPU cache or the hard disk virtual memory?**
The CPU accesses the CPU cache much faster because this cache is on the CPU itself.

10. **A gaming computer should come equipped with a GPU or an IGP?**
A gaming computer needs a GPU because games require intensive graphics processing. A computer with an IGP is not ideally configured for games.

11. **What is the function of the chipset?**
The function of a chipset is to control and manage the buses and interfaces that connect the various chips on the motherboard, such as the CPU and memory.

12. **What is the latest bus technology that is presently used in new computers?**
The latest bus technology is called PCI Express. This technology has replaced such older technologies as PCI and AGP.

13. **Presently, where is the memory controller located in the Intel and AMD designs?**
In the Intel design, the memory controller is located in the chipset North Bridge. In the AMD design, the memory controller is located in the CPU. The AMD design is more efficient and Intel is planning to adopt a similar design.

14. **What is another name for the chipset South Bridge?**
Another name for the chipset South Bridge is the I/O Controller Hub.

15. **Enumerate all the ports that a computer might have?**
The ports that a new computer might include are DVI or DisplayPort(for LCD monitors), HDMI (for LCD monitors), USB (for peripherals), Firewire (for peripherals), RJ45 (for Ethernet) and Audio (for line in, line out, microphone, earphones).

16. **What is an RJ45 port/jack used for?**
An RJ45 port or jack is used to connect to a LAN, which is usually an Ethernet.

17. **What is a DVI port used for?**
A DVI port is used to connect a computer to an LCD monitor. A DVI port is superior to the old VGA port because with DVI the video signal stays digital throughout and does not need to be converted to an analog signal.

18. **Enumerate all the wireless capabilities of a computer.**

The different wireless capabilities of a computer include IrDA, Bluetooth, WiFi, Wireless USB and WiMAX.

19. What are some differences between IrDA and Bluetooth? Between Bluetooth and WiFi?
    IrDA requires line of sight but Bluetooth does not. WiFi works over longer distances than Bluetooth.

20. What is the BIOS essentially used for?
    The BIOS is essential for booting up (starting) the computer. After the computer power button is pressed, the BIOS takes over to check that the computer's essential components are present and functioning properly. If the check is successful, the BIOS will then transfer control of the computer to the Operating System, which will finish the booting process and make the computer ready for the user.

21. What are some common form factors for today's Hard Disk Drives?
    The common form factors for Hard Disk Drives are 3.5" and 2.5". There are even smaller form factors but they may not become popular because of the rise of the Solid State Drive, which uses flash memory for storage.

22. What is the difference between an HDD and an SSD?
    An HDD uses platters that spin at high speeds, and heads that hover over those platters and read them. An SSD uses flash memory and has no moving mechanical parts. As of early 2008, SSDs were very expensive compared to HDDs. However, as the price of flash memory continues to drop, SSDs will become more popular.

23. What is the difference between a DVD-ROM and a DVD-R discs?
    A DVD-ROM is pre-recorded media. For example, when one buys software, the software may come on a DVD-ROM. A DVD-R disc is blank media that computer users can buy to record on.

24. What part of a laptop functions as the mouse?
    A laptop uses a touchpad and touchpad buttons for the functions of a mouse. Of course, if a mouse is needed, it could be used with a laptop by connecting it to the laptop via USB or Bluetooth.

25. What is the advantage of a wide-screen over the old 4:3 standard screen?
    A wide-screen is more suitable for watching movies since the whole screen is used.

26. What screen parameter is used to refer to numerical designations such as 1920 x 1200?
    The screen's parameter for numerical designations such as 1920 x 1200 is called the resolution.

27. What are the world's two available AC power supplies?
    Throughout the world, countries have adopted one of two types of AC power supplies: 220

V at 60 Hz as in China, and 110 V at 50 Hz as in the United States. This condition used to be a problem for users traveling between countries. However, nowadays this problem has been resolved since a computer's universal power adapter can work with either supply.

28. Enumerate all the types of computer software.
    The different types of software include: Firmware, Operating Systems, Utilities, Applications, Virtualization software, Middleware, Malware, and programming languages.

29. What are the four categories of Operating Systems?
    The four categories of Operating Systems are Real-Time OS (as in mobile phones and scientific devices), Single-user Single-task OS (as in regular mobile phones), Single-user Multi-task OS (such as Apple Mac OS X, Windows), and Multi-user OS (such as Linux and Unix).

30. What does multitasking mean? Multithreading? Multiprocessing?
    Multitasking means that an Operating System can run multiple programs concurrently. Multithreading means that an Operating System can run different parts of a program concurrently. Multiprocessing means that an Operating System can run on multiple processors, such as many CPUs or a CPU with many cores.

31. Name some popular Operating Systems.
    Presently, the most popular Operating Systems include Apple Mac OS X, Linux, and Windows.

32. Name some popular software applications.
    Some popular software applications include Media Player, Word Processing, Presentation, Spreadsheet, Database, Games, Security, Management and Webware. Webware includes such applications as Browser, Search engine, Email, P2P, IM, VoIP, RSS and online office applications.

33. What is the purpose of Virtualization software?
    The purpose of Virtualization software is to allow a computer to run more than one Operating System.

34. Name all the Malware that might infect a computer.
    The Malware that might infect a computer includes Viruses, Worms, Trojan Horses, Rootkits, Key Loggers, Spyware and Adware.

1.6.2 Reading and pronouncing acronyms

The following table shows how the computer acronyms are pronounced and what they stand for.

Acronym	Pronunciation	Acronym expansion
CPU	C-P-U	Central Processing Unit
BIOS	BYE-OSS (as in Oscar)	Basic Input Output System
RAM	RAM (as in ram)	Random Access Memory
GPU	G-P-U	Graphics Processing Unit
DVD-RW	D-V-D-DASH-R-W	Digital Versatile Disc Dash ReWritable
DVD+RW	D-V-D-PLUS-R-W	Digital Versatile Disc Plus ReWritable
HDD	H-D-D	Hard Disk Drive
SSD	S-S-D	Solid State Drive
LAN	LAN (as in lanyard)	Local Area Network
DRAM	D-RAM	Dynamic Random Access Memory
GB	GIGABYTE	Gigabyte
MB	MEGABYTE	Megabyte
GHz	GIGAHERTZ	Gigahertz
nm	NANOMETER	Nanometer
RJ45	R-J-45	Registered Jack 45
DVI	D-V-I	Digital Video Interface
WiFi	WHY-FI (as in five)	Wireless Fidelity
ESC	ESCAPE	Escape
GUI	GOOEY (as in gooey)	Graphical User Interface
C#	C-SHARP	C Sharp
C++	C-PLUS-PLUS	C Plus Plus
P2P	P-TO-P	Peer To Peer
VoIP	V-O-I-P	Voice Over IP
I/O	I-YO	Input Output
rpm	R-P-M	Revolutions Per Minute
DOS	DOS (as in dossier)	Disk Operating System
PCB	P-C-B	Printed Circuit Board
FSB	F-S-B	Front Side Bus
USB	U-S-B	Universal Serial Bus

1.6.3 Decoding computer jargon

The following text is a computer advertisement. It uses cryptic computer jargon that laymen would not understand. Its translation into plain English is shown below.

- Intel Core 2 Duo T9300
- Windows Vista Home Premium
- 1GB-4GB DDRII
- 15.4" WXGA screen
- NVIDEA GeForce 8600, 256MB
- 160/200GB Hard Disk
- SuperMulti
- 802.11 abgn
- 3Mpixel webcam
- 2.7 Kg

- **Intel Core 2 Duo T9300**

This item means this computer uses an Intel CPU called Core 2 Duo T9300. "Duo" means that the CPU has two cores. T9300 is a further detailed designation of this CPU meaning that it belongs to the latest Intel CPU family, "Penryn", which uses 45nm manufacturing.

- **Windows Vista Home Premium**

This item means that the computer's Operating System is Windows Vista Home Premium.

- **1GB-4GB DDRII**

This item means that the computer can have from 1 to 4GB of DDR2 memory.

- **15.4" WXGA screen**

The computer screen is wide-screen, its size is 15.4", and its native resolution is WXGA.

- **NVIDEA GeForce 8600, 256MB**

The computer uses an NVIDEA GeForce 8600 GPU and 256MB of dedicated video memory.

- **160/200GB Hard Disk**

The hard disk comes in two capacities, either 160 or 200 GB.

- **SuperMulti**

The optical drive supports the disc formats CD-ROM, CD-R/RW, DVD-ROM, DVD-RAM, DVD-R/RW, DVD+R/RW.

- **802.11 abgn**

The computer includes wireless technology WiFi and supports versions a, b, g, and n.

- **3Mpixel webcam**

The computer has a webcam with a resolution of 3 megapixels.

- **2.7 Kg**

The computer weighs 2.7 Kg.

1.6.6 Identifying computer parts

The following figure shows the different computer parts.

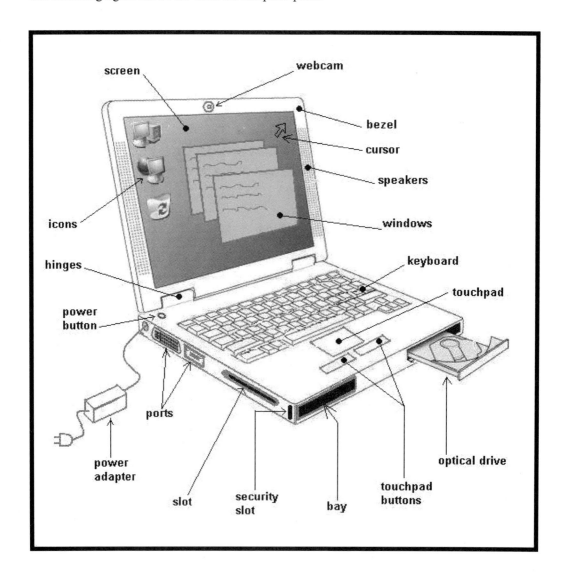

1.6.7 Cloze

The correct computer words are shown underlined.

1. The main chip on the motherboard is called a _CPU_.
2. The piece of software that serves to boot up a computer is called the _BIOS_.
3. The CPU is connected to the rest of the chips on the motherboard via a _bus_.
4. A laptop's cooling system is made of heat sinks and a _fan_.
5. The main storage in a computer is provided by a _hard disk drive_.
6. The fast memory provided on a CPU is called _cache_ memory.
7. In addition to a fast CPU, a good gaming computer should have one or more _GPUs_.
8. The chipset's _South_ Bridge connects all the I/O devices.
9. A Solid-State Drive uses _flash_ memory and has no moving mechanical parts.
10. On a laptop, the _touchpad and touchpad buttons_ take the place of a mouse.
11. After the BIOS boots up, it hands over the computer control to the _OS_.
12. DVI and USB are examples of _ports_ on a computer.
13. The small pictures representing different programs on the screen are called _icons_.
14. Double clicking on an icon on the screen will open a _window_.
15. For a C++ program to be understood by the CPU, it has to be translated into _machine language_.
16. Viruses and Trojan Horses are examples of _Malware_.
17. If an AC power supply is not available, a laptop can still operate using a _battery_.
18. The heart or core of an Operating System is called the _kernel_.
19. An Operating System relies on _device drivers_ to control and manage the hardware.
20. Software programs that add to the functionality of an Operating System are called _utilities_.
21. If a computer is to run two Operating Systems, it needs to have _Virtualization_ software.
22. A programming language translator could be an Assembler, Interpreter or _Compiler_.
23. If a computer is to be used for a video chat, it needs to have a _webcam_.
24. In some airports and cafés, a user could wirelessly surf the Internet using _WiFi_.
25. A screen that has a 16:9 or 16:10 aspect ratio is called a _wide-screen_.
26. Desktops provide a few PCI Express _slots_ for adding cards such as video cards.
27. A Hard-Disk Drive spins at high speeds, such as 7200 _rpm_.
28. A DVD-RW disc allows the user to both read and _write_ data.
29. The software application that allows a user to surf the Internet is called a _browser_.
30. An Operating System's ability to run on multiple-core CPUs is called _multiprocessing_.
31. An Operating System's ability to run multiple programs simultaneously is called _multitasking_.
32. The software application that allows for making slides is called _Presentation_ software.
33. When looking for information online, a user could use a _Search Engine_.
34. A CPU is mounted on a motherboard using a _socket_.
35. Devices, such as printers, that can be used with a computer are called _peripherals_.

1.6.8 Computer action words

Some possible answers are as follows.

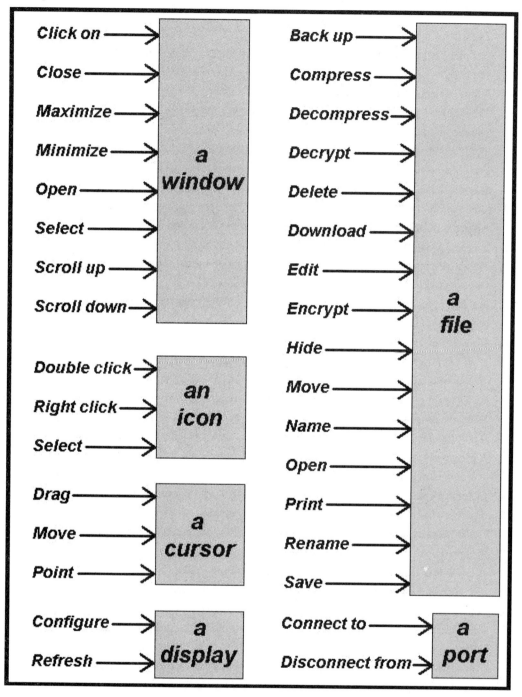

APPENDIX

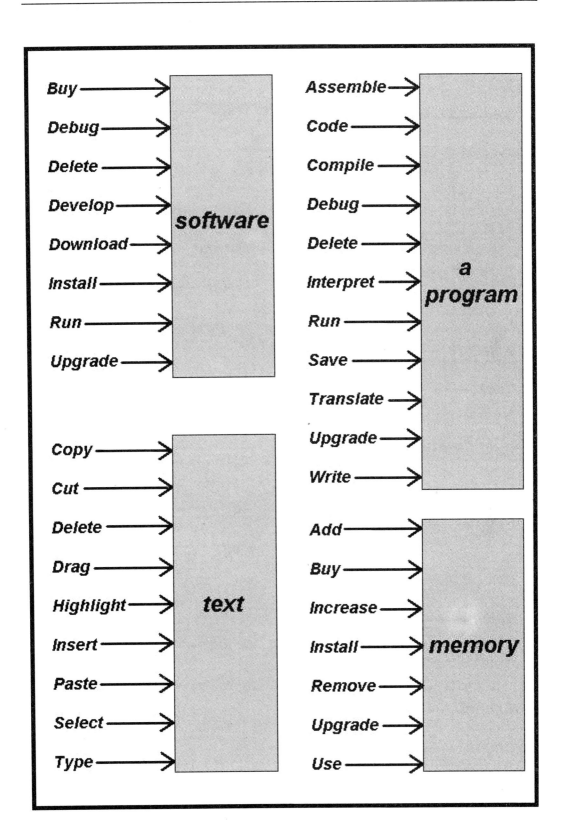

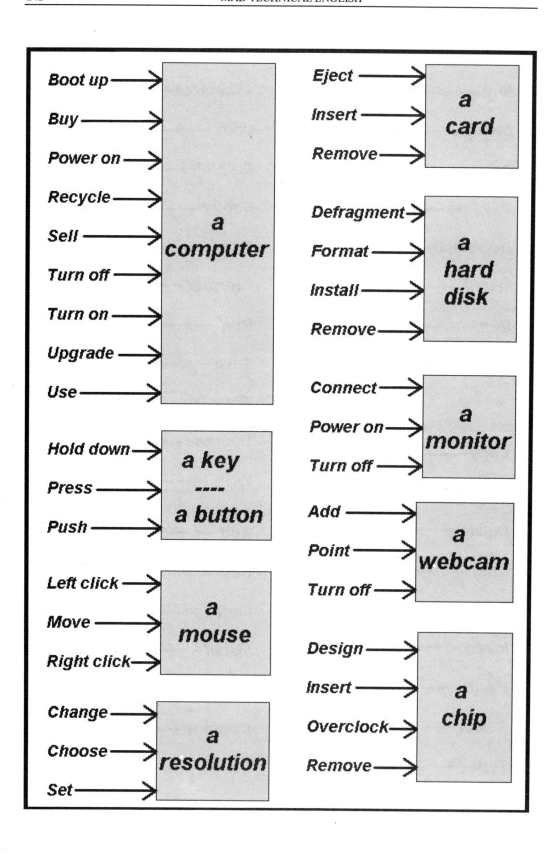

(2) Answers to Internet questions

2.8.1 Reading comprehension

1. **Which country deployed the original Internet?**
   The United States deployed the original Internet. This first Internet deployment was in the western part of the United States.

2. **What is the difference between the Internet and the Web?**
   The Web is part of and an application of the Internet. When the Internet was first deployed, there was no Web. At that time, the users' Internet interface was not as graphical and user-friendly as today's web browsers provide.

3. **What was the first Internet killer application?**
   The first Internet killer application was email. At its conception, email revolutionized the way that people corresponded, and quickly became an indispensable communication tool.

4. **What are the ways that netizens can chat with each other?**
   When netizens chat via Instant Messaging, such as when using QQ and MSN, they can chat via text, voice, and video.

5. **What is the name of the protocol suite on which the Internet is based?**
   The Internet is based on the TCP/IP protocol suite. The adoption of TCP/IP in the early days of the Internet was a key contributor to the early success of the Internet.

6. **The Internet architecture is usually divided into what three parts?**
   The Internet architecture is usually divided into three parts: the user equipment, the Internet access, and the Internet backbone. The user equipment could be computers, mobile phones and so on. The Internet access connects the user equipment to the Internet backbone. The Internet backbone is made of the various ISPs and their interconnections.

7. **What are the two ways that ISPs can peer with each other?**
   ISPs connect to each other through private peering or public peering. In private peering, two ISPs have a dedicated, one-to-one connection. In public peering, many ISPs connect to each other at a common connection point called an Internet eXchange (IX). An IX is also called an Internet eXchange Point (IXP) or a Network Access Point (NAP).

8. **Name the different types of Internet access.**
   Internet access could be either dial-up (slow and becoming more and more obsolete) or broadband. Broadband could be either wired or wireless. Wired broadband access can be through ADSL, cable or power line. Wireless broadband can be via WiFi and WiMAX.

9. **Name the four layers of the TCP/IP protocol stack.**
   The four layers of the TCP/IP protocol stack are from top to bottom: Application layer, Transport layer, Internet layer, and Network Interface layer.

10. **Name some of the TCP/IP Application layer protocols.**
    Some of the TCP/IP Application layer protocols are HTTP, DNS, DHCP, FTP, Telnet, SMTP, SNMP, POP and IMAP.

11. **Name the two main TCP/IP Transport layer protocols.**
    The two main TCP/IP Transport layer protocols are TCP and UDP.

12. **Name some of the TCP/IP Internet layer protocols.**
    Some of the TCP/IP Internet layer protocols are IP, ICMP, IGMP, ARP, OSPF and BGP.

13. **Name some of the TCP/IP Network Interface layer protocols.**
    Some of the TCP/IP Network Interface layer protocols are Ethernet, ATM, and WLAN.

14. **How is the TCP/IP protocol stack implemented on a computer?**
    The TCP/IP protocol stack is implemented on a computer as follows. The TCP/IP Application layer is part of the Operating System (OS) and can include third-party programs. The TCP/IP Transport and Internet layers are part of the OS. The TCP/IP Network Interface layer is implemented as part of the OS, firmware and hardware.

15. **What TCP/IP information is usually configured on an Internet user's computer?**
    An Internet user's computer is configured with the following TCP/IP information: IP address of the user's computer, net mask, default gateway, IP address of a primary DNS server, and IP address of a secondary DNS server.

16. **What is the most common type of LAN nowadays?**
    The most common type of LAN nowadays is Ethernet. Ethernet has basically vanquished the other LAN technologies such as Token Ring. Ethernet comes is various speed specifications up to gigabits per second, thus satisfying any LAN application, from small offices to data centers.

17. **How do the Transport and Internet layers package the data that they receive?**
    When receiving data from an upper layer, the Transport and Internet layers package that data by adding their headers, i.e. Transport header and Internet header respectively. When receiving data from a lower layer, the Transport and Internet layers strip away their respective headers from that data.

18. **Which Application layer protocol is used to download web pages?**
    HTTP is the Application layer protocol used to download web pages.

19. Which Application layer protocol is used to send email?
    SMTP is the Application layer protocol used to send email.

20. Which Application layer protocol is used to look up IP addresses of domains?
    DNS is the Application layer protocol used to look up the IP addresses of domains.

21. Which Application layer protocol is used to automatically configure networked computers?
    DHCP is the Application layer protocol used to automatically configure the computers on a network.

22. What are the two versions of the Internet that are currently deployed?
    The two versions of the Internet that are currently deployed are IPv4 and IPv6. IPv6 is slowly replacing IPv4 and is intended to eventually completely replace it.

23. What was the main reason for deploying IPv6?
    The main reason behind the deployment of IPv6 was the need for a larger address space. IPv6 provides a virtually unlimited number of IP addresses.

24. Name some of the main Top-Level Domains.
    Some of the Top-Level Domains are .com, .net, .org, .edu, .us, .cn and so on.

25. What network equipment device is used to route Internet traffic?
    A router is used to route Internet traffic.

26. What equipment device connects a user's computer to a phone line for Internet access?
    A modem connects a user's computer to a phone line for Internet access.

27. What Internet application is used to find information on the Internet?
    A search engine is used to find information on the Internet.

28. What Internet application is used to get web page updates?
    RSS is used to get web page updates.

29. What Internet application allows for making free or cheap phone calls on the Internet?
    VoIP allows for making free or cheap phone calls on the Internet.

30. What are some of the Internet disadvantages?
    The Internet's disadvantages include both technical and social problems. On the technical side, malware is a serious issue that threatens the security of the Internet. On the social side, the Internet has some problems such as addiction, pornography, and lack of real human interaction. Another problem, which is more of a political nature, is cyber terrorism.

2.8.2 Reading and pronouncing acronyms

The following table shows the pronunciation and expansion of some Internet acronyms.

Acronym	Pronunciation	Acronym expansion	
DNS	D-N-S	Domain Name System	
HTTP	H-T-T-P	HyperText Transfer Protocol	
POP	POP (as in popular)	Post Office Protocol	
IMAP	I-MAP (as in eye map)	Internet Message Access Protocol	
ARP	ARP (as in harp)	Address Resolution Protocol	
WiFi	WHY-FI (as in five)	Wireless Fidelity	
WiMAX	WHY-MAX (as in max)	Worldwide Interoperability for Microwave Access	
WAN	WAN (rhymes with man)	Wide Area Network	
MAN	MAN (as in man)	Metropolitan Area Network	
POTS	POTS (as in pots)	Plain Old Telephone System	
MAC	MAC (as in mac)	Media Access Control	
PPP	P-P-P	Point-to-Point Protocol	
IPv6	I-P-version-6	IP version 6	
IM	I-M (as in I am)	Instant Messaging	
TCP/IP	T-C-P-I-P	Transmission Control Protocol, Internet Protocol	
B2B	B-TO-B	Business To Business	
B2C	B-TO-C	Business To Consumer	
B2G	B-TO-G	Business To Government	
C2C	C-TO-C	Consumer To Consumer	
NIC	NIC (as in nick)	Network Interface Card	
.com	DOT-COM (as in combat)	Dot Com	(com = commercial)
.org	DOT-ORG (as in organ)	Dot Org	(org = organization)
.edu	DOT-E-D-U	Dot Edu	(edu = educational)
.us	DOT-U-S	Dot US	(US = United States)
.cn	DOT-C-N	Dot CN	(CN = China)
.biz	DOT-BIZ (as in business)	Dot Biz	(biz = business)
.mil	DOT-MIL (as in military)	Dot Mil	(mil = military)
.gov	DOT-GOV (as in govern)	Dot Gov	(gov = government)
.net	DOT-NET (as in net)	Dot Net	(net = network)

2.8.3 Cloze

The correct Internet words are shown underlined.

1. The Internet is a worldwide collection of interconnected networks.
2. The Internet was originally deployed in the United States.
3. Slow dial-up connections have been replaced by broadband connections.
4. In order to surf the Internet, a user needs to use a software program called a browser.
5. The company installed a firewall on its network to keep hackers away.
6. When looking for information online, a user can try one of the many search engines.
7. My mailbox is full of unwanted spam from advertisers.
8. A website can be reached by clicking on its link.
9. Today's chat software is comprehensive and allows for text, voice and video chatting.
10. Internet users should protect their computers by installing anti-malware software.
11. In order to test their systems, some companies hire hackers to try to break into them.
12. WiFi and WiMAX provide wireless access to the Internet.
13. An ADSL modem is used to provide broadband access over a phone line.
14. A layered-model of a communication protocol suite such as TCP/IP is called a stack.
15. DNS is used to find the corresponding IP addresses of domain names.
16. An ISP uses a DHCP server to automatically configure the users' computers.
17. VoIP allows an Internet connection to be used for making free or cheap telephone calls.
18. A browser uses a protocol called HTTP to get web pages.
19. Using RSS, an Internet user can stay updated with his/her favorite web pages.
20. Some Internet users write blogs as a sort of diary to be shared with other netizens.
21. Routers use the packets' IP addresses to send them to the proper destination.
22. Because it is much slower than email, post office mail is referred to as snail mail.
23. Very popular applications such as email and the Web are called killer applications.
24. A website's full domain name is called its URL or URI.
25. One of the major advantages of IPv6 over IPv4 is that it provides many more IP addresses.
26. An IPv4 address has 32 bits, whereas an IPv6 address has 128.
27. A computer that is connected to the Internet needs to be configured with a unique IP address.
28. A website that provides a comprehensive set of Internet services is called a portal.
29. B2B and B2C are examples of e-commerce.
30. Top-Level Domains can be Global, such as ".com", and Country-Code, such as ".us".
31. On a computer, TCP/IP is mainly implemented as part of the Operating System.
32. The most common type of LAN nowadays is Ethernet.
33. Online sex-related material such as pictures and videos is called pornography.
34. The illegal online posting and free downloading of copyrighted material is called piracy.

2.8.4 Internet action words

Some possible answers are as follows.

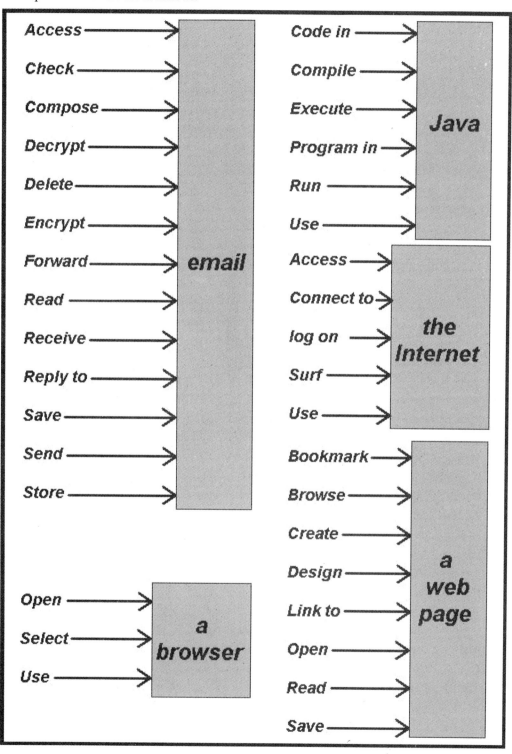

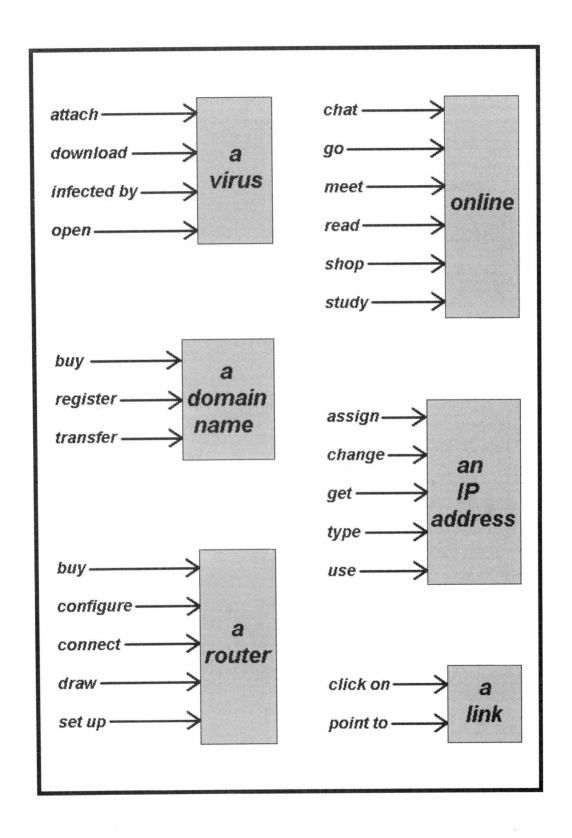

2.8.5 Identifying Internet elements

The figure below shows the names of some of the different Internet elements.

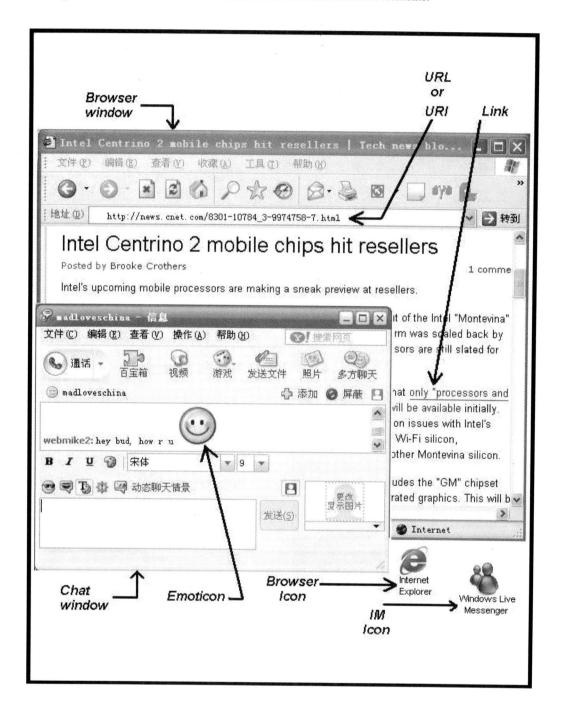

(3) Answers to mobile phone questions

3.7.1 Reading comprehension

1. What was the main reason for the transition from 1G to 2G mobile phone systems?
   The main reason for the transition from 1G to 2G mobile phone systems was to allow more users to use the limited frequency spectrum.

2. What is the difference between the access technologies of 1G and 2G systems?
   1G systems use analog technology while 2G systems use digital technology.

3. What was the main reason for the transition from 2G to 2.5/2.75/3G systems?
   The main reason for the transition from 2G to 2.5/2.75/3G systems was to provide faster data transfer rates.

4. What is the most widely deployed 2G mobile communications system in the world?
   The most widely deployed 2G mobile communications system in the world is GSM.

5. Name the two most widely used 3G mobile communications systems in the world.
   The two most widely used 3G mobile communications systems in the world are UMTS (WCDMA) and CDMA2000. A third 3G mobile communications system called TD-SCDMA is being deployed in China. Given China's huge mobile phone industry size, this system could become very competitive.

6. Enumerate the different form factors of mobile phones.
   Mobile phones come designed in the following form factors: candy bar, clamshell, flip, slider, swivel, and twist.

7. What are the main hardware components of a mobile phone?
   The main hardware components of a mobile phone are as follows: mainboard, SIM card, display, keypad, antenna, audio I/O, camera, memory cards, power supply, stylus, and case. The mainboard includes most of the chips and hardware circuitry, namely the processors, RF unit, ADC/DAC, memory, power management, Bluetooth/WiFi/USB, voice recorder, FM tuner, MP3/4 player, GPS receiver, accelerometers and sensors.

8. What hardware element manages both the voice and data interfaces of a mobile phone?
   The processor (or processors) manages the voice and data interfaces of a mobile phone.

9. What is the hardware unit that receives and transmits the antenna signals?
   The RF unit receives and transmits the antenna signals.

10. What hardware element changes analog signals to digital signals?
    The Analog to Digital Converter (ADC) changes analog signals to digital signals. The

ADC is part of a unit called the coder/decoder or codec.

11. What hardware element changes digital signals to analog signals?
    The Digital to Analog Converter (DAC) changes digital signals to analog signals. The DAC is part of a unit called the coder/decoder or codec.

12. What hardware element processes signals in real time?
    The Digital Signal Processor (DSP) processes signals in real time.

13. What type of memory is used for large-capacity storage inside a mobile phone?
    Flash memory is used for large-capacity storage inside a mobile phone.

14. What non-cellular wireless technologies may be present in a mobile phone?
    Non-cellular wireless technologies present in a mobile phone include Bluetooth and WiFi.

15. Why do mobile phones use Assisted GPS instead of simply GPS?
    Mobile phones use Assisted GPS instead of simply GPS because with Assisted GPS the mobile phones use information from the mobile phone network and thus can quickly home in on the GPS satellites.

16. What hardware element is used to rotate the display view when the phone is rotated?
    The accelerometer senses when the mobile phone is rotated and thus is used to rotate the display view accordingly to either portrait or landscape mode.

17. What hardware element is used to adjust the display clarity to the surrounding environment?
    The ambient light sensor is used to adjust the display clarity to the surrounding environment.

18. What hardware element holds a user's phone number inside a GSM mobile phone?
    The SIM card holds the user's phone number inside a GSM mobile phone.

19. Why did OLED displace LCD as the preferred display technology?
    OLED displaced LCD as the preferred display technology because of the following three factors. First, OLEDs emit their own light and thus unlike LCD displays do not need backlighting. Second, OLED displays use less power since they do not require backlighting. Third, they have a high contrast ratio and display rich colors with large viewing angles.

20. What are the various ways that information can be input into a mobile phone?
    Information can be input into a mobile phone via a keypad, a keyboard, a touch-screen, or voice.

21. Name the possible uses of a mobile phone.
    The uses of a mobile phone are numerous and include the following: communicating (voice/video phone calls, email, SMS, MMS, IM), serving as a time device (watch, alarm clock), serving as a Personal Information Manager (contacts, calendar, notes), surfing the

Internet, acting as a multimedia device (music, videos, movies, TV, radio, camera, games), acting as a GPS receiver, recording voice notes, storing data, serving as a calculator, serving as an education device (dictionary, e-books), serving as a credit card, and so on.

22. What type of operating system must run the communications software of a mobile phone?
    A Real Time Operating System (RTOS) is needed to run the communication software.

23. Name some of the most popular Open Operating Systems in use today.
    Some of the most popular Open OSs in use today are Linux and Symbian.

24. What are the three main parts of a mobile phone system architecture?
    The three main parts of a mobile phone system architecture are the user equipment, the access network (called the Radio Access Network or RAN), and the core network.

25. Name the different elements of a GSM Radio Access Network.
    A GSM Radio Access Network (RAN) includes Base Transceiver Stations (BTS) and Base Station Controllers (BSC).

26. Name the different elements of a GSM core network.
    A GSM core network includes Mobile Switching Centers (MSC), Gateway MSCs, and databases (Home Location Register (HLR), Visitor Location Register (VLR), Authentication Center (AuC), Equipment Identity Register (EIR)).

27. What are the main objectives of 4G systems?
    The main objectives of 4G systems are twofold: first, an all-IP infrastructure that supports both voice and data, and second, high data rates and low latency.

28. Which multiple-access technology allocates different frequency channels to different users?
    The multiple-access technology that allocates different frequency channels to different users is called Frequency Division Multiple Access (FDMA).

29. Which multiple-access technology accommodates multiple users by using time slots?
    The multiple-access technology that accommodates multiple users by using time slots is called Time Division Multiple Access (TDMA).

30. If a cluster of cells contains three cells, what is the frequency reuse factor?
    The frequency reuse factor for a three-cell cluster is 1/3.

31. What are some of the factors that users consider when selecting a new mobile phone?
    When selecting new mobile phones, users may consider such factors as usage, style, color, brand, features, price and so on.

32. What are some of the maintenance chores required by a mobile phone?
    Some of the maintenance chores include recharging the battery, downloading software

updates, cleaning the display, recharging the money balance and so on.

3.7.2 Reading and pronouncing acronyms

The pronunciation and expansion of the mobile phone acronyms are shown in the following table.

Acronym	Pronunciation	Acronym expansion
IMSI	IM-ZEE	International Mobile Subscriber Identity
DAC	DAC (rhymes with pack)	Digital to Analog Converter
ADC	A-D-C	Analog to Digital Converter
SIM	SIM (as in simple)	Subscriber Identity Module
RAN	RAN (as in ran)	Radio Access Network
3G	3-G	Third Generation
WAP	WAP (as in swap)	Wireless Application Protocol
PIN	PIN (as in pin)	Personal Identification Number
MIMO	MI-MO	Multiple Input Multiple Output
GSM	G-S-M	Global System for Mobile communications
GPRS	G-P-R-S	General Packet Radio Service
EDGE	EDGE (as in edge)	Enhanced Data rates for GSM Evolution
UMTS	U-M-T-S	Universal Mobile Telecommunications System
HSPA	H-S-P-A	High Speed Packet Access
LTE	L-T-E	Long Term Evolution
WiMAX	WHY-MAX	Worldwide Interoperability for Microwave Access
FDD	F-D-D	Frequency Division Duplex
TDD	T-D-D	Time Division Duplex
UE	U-E	User Equipment
MS	M-S	Mobile Station
HLR	H-L-R	Home Location Register
VLR	V-L-R	Visitor Location Register
MSC	M-S-C	Mobile Switching Center
FDMA	F-D-M-A	Frequency Division Multiple Access
DSP	D-S-P	Digital Signal Processor
RTOS	R-T-O-S	Real Time Operating System

3.7.5 Identifying mobile phone parts

The following mobile phone parts are illustrated in the figure below.

Battery charge icon	*Network signal strength icon*
Navigation key	*Keypad*
Case	*Display*
Antenna	*Stylus*
Bluetooth headset	*Earphones*
Power adapter / Charger	*SIM card*

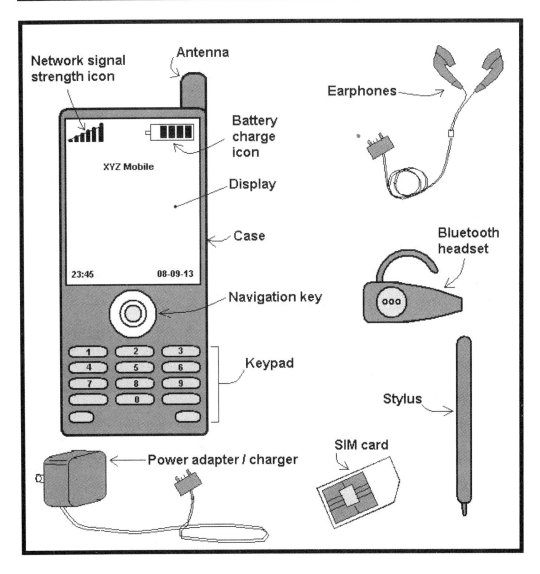

3.7.6 Cloze

The corect mobile phone words are shown underlined.

1. The 2G systems came about to allow more users to use the limited <u>frequency spectrum</u>.
2. Whereas 1G mobile phones used analog signals, 2G mobile phones used <u>digital signals</u>.
3. Whereas 1G systems used FDMA multiple-access, 2G ones introduced <u>TDMA and CDMA</u>.
4. The most popular 2G mobile communications system in the world is <u>GSM</u>.
5. The 3G mobile communications systems provide faster data <u>transfer rates</u>.
6. <u>UMTS</u> is the 3G evolution of GSM.
7. Mobile phone form factors include the candy bar, <u>clamshell, flip, slider, swivel, and twist</u>.
8. The processors in the smartphones manage both the voice and <u>data</u> interfaces.
9. Mobile phone processors are limited to <u>power</u> envelopes of less than 1W.
10. The RF unit on the main board transmits and receives <u>antenna</u> signals.
11. A user's voice is analog and is <u>digitized</u> using an Analog to Digital Converter (ADC).
12. <u>Signal</u> processing and manipulation inside a mobile phone is done by the DSP.
13. The type of memory used for large-capacity storage inside a mobile phone is <u>flash</u> memory.
14. Mobile phone wireless headsets use the wireless technology <u>Bluetooth</u>.
15. Mobile phones use a variation of GPS called <u>Assisted</u> GPS.
16. <u>Accelerometers</u> are used to automatically rotate the display view as the phone is rotated.
17. An ambient light <u>sensor</u> is used to adjust the display brightness to different environments.
18. A <u>SIM card</u> is used to keep the same phone number when switching GSM mobile phones.
19. A SIM card's sensitive information is password-protected with a <u>PIN</u>.
20. Since they don't need <u>backlighting</u>, OLED displays are more power efficient than LCD ones.
21. Some displays are <u>touch-screens</u> and are used for information input into mobile phones.
22. 4G systems will use a revolutionary multiple <u>antenna</u> design known as MIMO.
23. Today's mobile phone <u>batteries</u> are made of Lithium-Ion.
24. Mobile phone software consists of <u>communications</u> software and applications software.
25. Mobile phones use a <u>Real Time</u> Operating System to run the communications software.
26. The <u>Radio</u> Access Network is the bridge between the user equipment and the core network.
27. Cells are usually diagrammed as a honeycomb of <u>hexagonal</u> shapes.
28. The core network technology is evolving from circuit switching to <u>packet switching</u>.
29. The VLR database stores the temporary data of <u>visiting</u> mobile phone users.
30. The AuC database is used for <u>authenticating</u> mobile phone users.
31. The GPRS network is an IP-based <u>internal</u> backbone.
32. The goals of 4G systems include an <u>all-IP</u> infrastructure, and high <u>data rates</u> and low <u>latency</u>.
33. FDMA allocates different <u>frequency</u> channels to different users.
34. 4G systems will use a new <u>multiple-access</u> technology called OFDMA.
35. A <u>cluster</u> of cells uses the whole available frequency spectrum.

(4) Answers to mathematics questions

4.12.1 Identifying mathematics branches

The branches of mathematics that are represented by the following mathematical expressions are as follows.

1. $(2 + 1047) \times (308 - 52) - 66$ — Arithmetic
2. $x - 3.5 = 10$ — Algebra
3. $\iint x^3 y \, dx \, dy$ — Calculus
4. $\sin \beta = 0.5$ — Trigonometry
5. $N(\mu, \sigma^2)$ — Statistics
6. $P(X=0.5/Y)$ — Probability
7. $x \in A$ — Logic
8. $p \wedge q$ — Discrete mathematics
9. $\angle \; // \; \perp \; \triangle \; \square$ — Geometry

4.12.2 Reading numbers

The following numbers are read as follows.

1. 102 — One hundred two
2. 3,506 — Three thousand five hundred six
3. 70,041 — Seventy thousand forty one
4. 255,689 — Two hundred fifty five thousand six hundred eighty nine
5. 6,001,810 — Six million one thousand eight hundred ten
6. 27,000,000 — Twenty seven million
7. 103,000,000 — One hundred three million
8. 1,344,000,005 — One billion three hundred forty four million five
9. 50,000,000,000 — Fifty billion
10. 457,000,635,000 — Four hundred fifty seven billion six hundred thirty five thousand
11. 5,000,000,000,000 — Five trillion

4.12.3 Reading mathematical expressions

1. One minus three fourths — $1 - 3/4$
2. Negative five point seven — -5.7
3. Two cubed minus three to the four plus seven squared — $2^3 - 3^4 + 7^2$
4. Square root of four plus cubic root of eight minus fifth root of seven — $4^{1/2} + 8^{1/3} - 7^{1/5}$
5. Absolute value of negative nine point two — $|-9.2|$
6. Negative one is greater than negative two — $-1 > -2$
7. Pi is approximately equal to three point one four — $\pi \approx 3.14$
8. Exponential x plus one / e to the x plus one — e^{x+1}
9. Nine factorial — $9!$
10. Two x cubed minus three x squared plus six equals zero — $2x^3 - 3x^2 + 6 = 0$
11. The summation from m equal one to three of C sub m — $\sum_{m=1}^{3} C_m$
12. The limit as x goes to zero of logarithm of x — $\lim_{x \to 0} \log(x)$
13. A dot B equals magnitude of A times magnitude of B times cosine α — $\mathbf{A} \cdot \mathbf{B} = |A||B| \cos \alpha$
14. A cross B — $\mathbf{A} \times \mathbf{B}$
15. Y of x — $y(x)$
16. The second derivative of x cubed with respect to x — $d^2 x^3/dx^2$
17. The partial derivative of x cubed y with respect to x — $\partial x^3 y/\partial x$
18. The integral from one to three of x cubed dx — $\int_{1}^{3} x^3 dx$
19. Sine zero — $\sin 0$
20. Cosine zero — $\cos 0$
21. Hyperbolic sine zero — $\sinh 0$
22. Expected value of X equals point five — $E(X) = 0.5$
23. Conditional probability of X equal to point two given Y — $P(X=0.2/Y)$
24. X belongs to set A — $x \in A$
25. For all x — $\forall x$
26. There exists x such that x is less than one — $\exists x: x<1$
27. A is a set of elements x such that x is less than one — $A = \{x: x<1\}$
28. Not A — $\neg A$
29. A is not a subset of B — $A \not\subset B$
30. A union B — $A \cup B$
31. A intersection B — $A \cap B$
32. One o one base two — 101_2
33. Combination of n choose r — $C(n,r)$
34. Permutation of n choose r — $P(n,r)$

4.12.4 Describing geometric figures

1	2	3
Draw a square. Label it ABDC clockwise starting from the upper left corner. Draw the diagonal BC.	Draw two concentric squares. Label the outer square ADGE clockwise starting from the upper left corner. Label the inner square BFHC clockwise starting from the upper left corner.	Draw a square. Draw its two diagonals. In the middle of each of the four resulting triangles inside the square, draw a circle that does not touch any of the triangle sides.

4	5
Draw two equal and intersecting circles such that their centers are on an imaginary horizontal line. Label the upper intersection point X and the lower intersection point Y.	Draw two equal and non-intersecting circles such that their centers are on an imaginary horizontal line. Label the center of the left circle A and the center of the right circle B. Draw a line from A to B.

6	7
Draw a square. Draw a straight line from the middle point of the upper side to the middle point of the left side, and from this latter point to the lower right corner. Finish by drawing two similar and symmetric lines.	Draw a vertical bar chart with the bar lengths from left to right proportional to the quantities: 10, 15, 20, 5, 20, 5. Inside each bar write the corresponding quantity.

8	9	10
Draw a pie chart and divide it equally into a lower and an upper half. Label the lower half 50%. Divide the upper half into two slices, one 30% and one 20% of the pie, with the 30% slice on the left.	Draw a right angle triangle such that one of its right-angle sides is horizontal, the other side is vertical and the hypotenuse faces upper left. Starting from the upper corner and clockwise, label it ABD. Draw another horizontally-symmetric-to-it triangle on the right. Starting from the upper corner and clockwise, label this second triangle ECF.	Draw an equilateral triangle with one of its sides horizontal. Draw a second similar one, invert it vertically, then move it over the first triangle so that the two triangles form a six-corner, symmetric star (Star of David).

11 Draw a square. On its left and right sides draw right angle, isosceles triangles so that the whole figure looks like a trapezoid with the upper side being the small base.	12 Draw a square. On its left and right sides draw right angle, isosceles triangles so that the whole figure looks like a parallelogram with the sides slanting to the right.	13 Draw three equal squares, side by side and joined together in a horizontal arrangement. In the left square, draw the diagonal from the lower left corner. Draw a line from the lower left corner of the middle square to the upper right corner of the right square.
14 Draw two similar rectangles and place them perpendicular to each other in the form of a symmetric cross. Erase all the lines inside the cross.	15 Draw two vertical, parallel, straight-line segments at the same level. Join their opposite ends to form a bow tie figure.	16 Draw a square standing on one of its corners. Connect the middle points of the sides of this square to form an inner square.
17 Draw a square standing on one of its corners. Draw a straight line from the upper corner to the lower corner.	18 Draw an isosceles triangle standing on the corner formed by the equal sides. From this corner draw a line perpendicular to the third side.	19 Draw four small, equal squares and place them symmetrically at the corners of a big, imaginary square. Join their inner corners in a cross.
20 Draw a cube.	21 Draw a vertical cylinder.	22 Draw a xy-graph. Locate the point at coordinates (5,4) with dashed lines and write (5,4) next to it. Show the gradations on the axes.
23 Draw an equilateral triangle standing on one corner with the upper side horizontal. Draw two similar triangles and place all three next to each other so that their upper sides form a continuous straight line.	24 Draw three equal squares, side by side and joined together in a horizontal arrangement. Rotate the middle square 180° around its upper side.	25 Draw a square. Its right side is also the side of an equilateral triangle. At the triangle corner opposite this common side, draw a tangential circle with a diameter equal to the side of the square. The resulting figure looks symmetric around a horizontal axis.

4.12.5 Drawing geometric figures

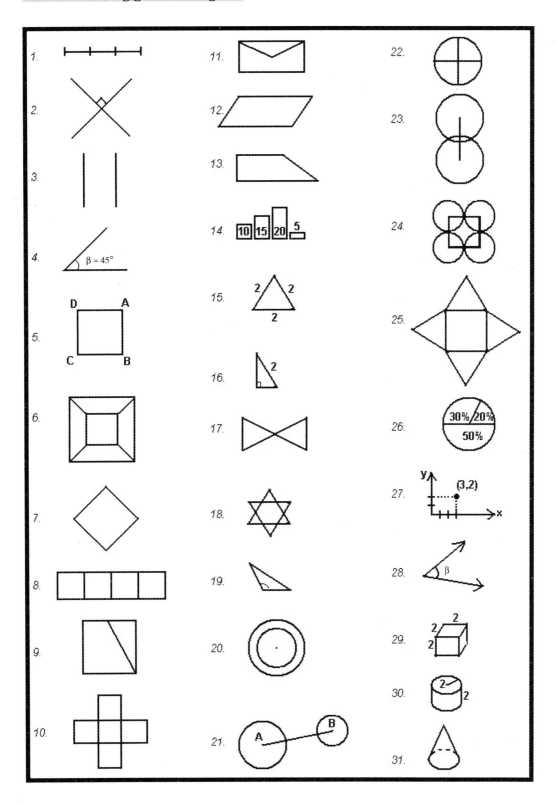

4.12.6 Cloze

The correct mathematical words are shown underlined.

1. The numbers 2, 4, 6, 8 are called <u>even</u> numbers.
2. The numbers 19, 21, 23, 25 are called <u>odd</u> numbers.
3. The expression a/b is called a <u>fraction.</u>
4. A number such as 11, which can only be divisible by 1 or itself, is called a <u>prime</u> number.
5. A number of the form "a + bi" is called a <u>complex</u> number.
6. A numerical expression with two rows and columns inside brackets is a two by two <u>matrix</u>.
7. An equation of the form "ax +b = 0" is called a <u>linear</u> equation.
8. An equation of the form "$ax^2 + bx + c = 0$" is called a <u>quadratic</u> equation.
9. The <u>magnitude</u> of vector **A** is |**A**|.
10. For vectors **A** and **B**, the product **A . B** is called a <u>scalar</u> product.
11. For vectors **A** and **B**, the product **A** × **B** is called a <u>vector</u> product.
12. A xy graph is sometimes referred to as a 2D graph where "D" refers to <u>dimension</u>.
13. In a graph, the projections of the location of a point on the axes are called the <u>coordinates</u>.
14. The symbol "$\iint$" stands for a <u>double</u> integral while the symbol "$\iiint$" stands for a <u>triple</u> integral.
15. In statistics, the <u>mean</u> is usually represented with the Greek letter μ.
16. In statistics, the <u>standard deviation</u> is usually represented with the Greek letter σ.
17. A distribution of the form N(μ, σ^2) is called a <u>normal</u> distribution.
18. A chart that looks like a circle divided into slices is called a <u>pie</u> chart.
19. A chart that is made of rectangles of different lengths is called a <u>bar</u> chart.
20. In mathematical logic, A+B is read A <u>or</u> B.
21. In mathematical logic, A*B is read A <u>and</u> B.
22. In mathematical logic, Venn <u>diagrams</u> are used to show the intersection and union of sets.
23. In mathematical logic, a <u>Truth</u> table is used to show the result of logical operations.
24. For an <u>AND</u> gate with inputs A and B, the output is A × B.
25. For an <u>OR</u> gate with inputs A and B, the output is A + B.
26. A <u>NOT</u> gate inverts the input.
27. A numeral with base two is called a <u>binary</u> numeral.
28. A numeral with base ten is called a <u>decimal</u> numeral.
29. A straight line that is neither vertical nor horizontal is <u>oblique</u>.
30. If two straight lines in the same plane never cross each other, they are <u>parallel</u>.
31. If two straight lines cross each other at a 90° angle, they are <u>perpendicular</u>.
32. A triangle has three angles and three <u>sides</u>.
33. In a right triangle, the side opposite the right angle is called the <u>hypotenuse</u>.
34. A square has four <u>equal</u> sides.
35. In a square or rectangle, the <u>diagonal</u> joins opposite corners.

(5) Answers to physics questions

5.6.1 Reading physics notation

The physics expressions are read as shown below.

1.	One micrometer equals ten to the negative six meters.	$1\ \mu m = 10^{-6}$ m
2.	One meter equals ten to the nine nanometers.	$1\ m = 10^9$ nm
3.	One mile equals one point six kilometers.	$1\ mi = 1.6$ km
4.	One foot equals twelve inches.	$1' = 12''$
5.	One inch equals two point five four centimeters.	$1'' = 2.54$ cm
6.	A equals nine million square kilometers.	$A = 9{,}000{,}000\ km^2$
7.	V equals one hundred thirty seven cubic meters.	$V = 137\ m^3$
8.	One gallon equals four quarts.	$1\ gal = 4\ qt$
9.	One microsecond equals one thousand nanoseconds.	$1\ \mu s = 1000\ ns$
10.	One kilogram equals two point two o five pounds.	$1\ kg = 2.205\ lb$
11.	One pound equals sixteen ounces.	$1\ lb = 16\ oz$
12.	Zero degrees Celsius equal thirty-two degrees Fahrenheit.	$0\ ^\circ C = 32\ ^\circ F$
13.	Zero degrees Kelvin equal negative two hundred seventy three point one six degrees Celsius	$0\ ^\circ K = -273.16\ ^\circ C$
14.	c equals three times ten to the eight meters per second.	$c = 3 \times 10^8$ m/s
15.	S equals sixty-five miles per hour.	$S = 65$ mph
16.	g equals nine point eight meters per second squared.	$g = 9.8\ m/s^2$
17.	F equals six newtons.	$F = 6$ N
18.	P equals one hundred pascals.	$P = 100$ Pa
19.	P equals fourteen point seven p s i (or pounds per square inch)	$P = 14.7$ psi
20.	W equals ten newton meter.	$W = 10$ N-m
21.	E equals three joules.	$E = 3$ J
22.	P equals sixty watts.	$P = 60$ W
23.	P equals two hundred horsepower.	$P = 200$ hp
24.	One b t u equals two hundred fifty two calories.	$1\ btu = 252\ cal$
25.	I equals three amps.	$I = 3$ A
26.	V equals one hundred ten volts.	$V = 110$ V
27.	R equals one kiloohm.	$R = 1\ k\Omega$
28.	C equals one picofarad.	$C = 1$ pF
29.	L equals one henry.	$L = 1$ H
30.	Q equals one coulomb.	$Q = 1$ C
31.	f equals eighteen hundred megahertz.	$f = 1800$ MHz
32.	Lambda equals ten angstroms.	$\lambda = 10$ Å
33.	Ten d b (or decibels).	10 db

5.6.2 Identifying electronic symbols

The electronic symbols and their corresponding names are as shown below.

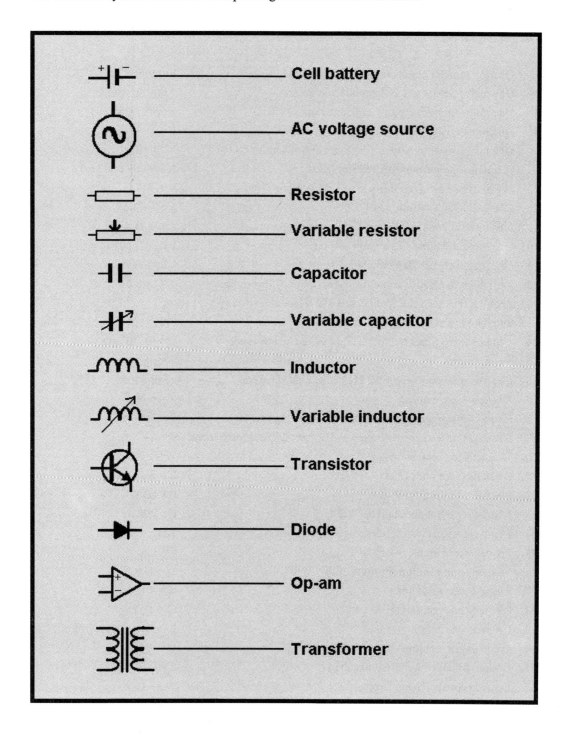

5.6.3 Cloze

The correct physics terms to fill in the blanks are as shown below.

1. The meter is used as a unit to measure <u>length</u> or distance or displacement.
2. Today's chip technology allows CPUs to be built at the 45-<u>nanometer</u> level.
3. The square meter is used as a unit to measure <u>area</u>.
4. The cubic meter is used as a unit to measure <u>volume</u>.
5. The gallon and litter are used as units to measure <u>liquid</u> volume.
6. The second is used as a unit to measure <u>time</u>.
7. The pound and kilogram are used as units to measure <u>weight</u>.
8. Degree Celsius and degree Fahrenheit are used as units to measure <u>temperature</u>.
9. The meter per second is used as a unit to measure <u>speed</u> or velocity.
10. The highest speed is that of <u>light</u> and is measured to be about 3×10^8 m/s.
11. The meter per second squared is used as a unit to measure <u>acceleration</u>.
12. The <u>gravity</u> or pull of the Earth is measured to be about 9.8 m/s^2.
13. The Newton and pound are used as units to measure <u>force</u>.
14. The Pascal and psi are used as units to measure <u>pressure</u>.
15. The Newton-meter and foot-pound are used as units to measure <u>work</u>.
16. The kilogram-meter-per-second is used as a unit to measure <u>momentum</u>.
17. The Joule and watt-hour are used as units to measure <u>energy</u>.
18. The Watt and hp are used as units to measure <u>power</u>.
19. The calorie and btu are used as units to measure <u>heat</u>.
20. The Ampere is used as a unit to measure <u>current</u>.
21. The Volt is used as a unit to measure <u>voltage</u>.
22. The Ohm is used as a unit to measure <u>resistance</u>.
23. The Ohm-per-meter is used as a unit to measure <u>resistivity</u>.
24. The Farad is used as a unit to measure <u>capacitance</u>.
25. The Farad-per-meter is used as a unit to measure <u>permittivity</u>.
26. The Henry is used as a unit to measure <u>inductance</u>.
27. The Henry-per-meter is used as a unit to measure <u>permeability</u>.
28. The Coulomb is used as a unit to measure <u>charge</u>.
29. The Hertz is used as a unit to measure <u>frequency</u>.
30. The candela is used as unit to measure luminous or light <u>intensity</u>.
31. The decibel is used as a unit to measure <u>sound</u>.

(6) Answers to data communications questions

6.9.1 Reading comprehension

1. Name the different types of networks.
   The different types of networks are Local Area Networks (LAN), Metropolitan Area Networks (MAN) and Wide Area Networks (WAN).

2. What is the main difference between a LAN and a MAN?
   The main difference between a LAN and a MAN is that whereas a LAN covers an office, building or campus area, a MAN can cover a whole city.

3. Name the different LAN topologies.
   The different types of LAN topologies are the bus, ring, star and tree.

4. What is the main difference between 10BT Ethernet and 10BF Ethernet?
   The main difference between 10BT and 10BF Ethernet is that 10BT uses twisted-pair wiring whereas 10BF uses fiber.

5. What is the main difference between 100BT Ethernet and 1000BT Ethernet?
   The main difference between 100BT and 1000BT Ethernet is the data rate of 100 Mbps for 100BT versus 1Gbps for 1000BT.

6. Is the human voice an analog or digital signal?
   The human voice is a continuous and thus analog signal.

7. What do we call a sampled analog signal?
   A sampled analog signal is a discrete signal.

8. What do we call a sampled and quantized analog signal?
   A sampled and quantized analog signal is a digital signal.

9. What do we call a signal that repeats itself at regular time intervals?
   A signal that repeats itself at regular time intervals is called periodic.

10. What do we call a digital signal that can have two values?
    A digital signal with two possible values is called binary.

11. Name some examples of guided transmission media.
    Some examples of guided transmission media are twisted-pair wiring, coaxial cable, and optical fiber. Twisted-pair wiring includes Shielded Twisted Pair (STP) and Unshielded Twisted Pair (UTP).

12. **Name some examples of unguided transmission media.**
    Some examples of unguided transmission media are terrestrial microwave, satellite microwave, broadcast radio and TV, infrared and laser.

13. **What is the unit of frequency?**
    The unit of frequency is the Hertz (Hz).

14. **What do we call the frequency range of a signal?**
    The frequency range of a signal is called its bandwidth.

15. **How many bits are there in a byte?**
    There are eight bits in a byte.

16. **What is a parity bit used for?**
    A parity bit is used to check for errors.

17. **What are the names used to describe the data packages of bits?**
    Bits are packaged in groups for transmission. Depending on the protocol, these data packages are called packets or frames.

18. **Name the two modes of packet switching.**
    The two modes of packet switching are virtual circuits (VC) and datagrams.

19. **Name the two types of transmission timing.**
    The two types of transmission timing are synchronous and asynchronous.

20. **Give an example of simplex transmission.**
    An example of simplex transmission is radio or TV broadcasting.

21. **Give an example of half duplex transmission.**
    An example of half duplex transmission is walkie-talkie or CB radio communication.

22. **Give an example of full duplex transmission.**
    An example of full duplex transmission is phone communication.

23. **Name some examples of digital-to-digital encoding.**
    Some examples of digital-to-digital encoding are Unipolar, Non Return to Zero Level (NRZL), Non Return to Zero Inverted (NRZI), Bipolar Alternate Mark Inversion (AMI), Manchester, Bipolar with 8 Zero Substitution (B8ZS), and High Density Bipolar 3 zeros (HDB3).

24. **Name some examples of digital-to-analog modulation.**
    Some examples of digital-to-analog modulation are Amplitude Shift Keying (ASK), Frequency Shift Keying (FSK), Binary FSK (BFSK), Multiple FSK (MFSK), Phase Shift Keying (PSK), Binary PSK (BPSK), Differential PSK (DPSK), Quadrature PSK (QPSK), and Quadrature Amplitude Modulation (QAM).

25. **Name some examples of analog-to-digital encoding.**
    Some examples of analog-to-digital encoding are Pulse Code Modulation (PCM) and Delta Modulation (DM).

26. **Name some examples of analog-to-analog modulation.**
    Some examples of analog-to-analog modulation are Amplitude Modulation (AM), Single Side Band (SSB), Vestigial Side Band (VSB), Frequency Modulation (FM), and Phase Modulation (PM).

27. **Name the different techniques of multiplexing.**
    The different types of multiplexing are Frequency Division Multiplexing (FDM), Code Division Multiplexing (CDM), Time Division Multiplexing (TDM), and Statistical TDM (STDM).

28. **Name the different types of signal filters.**
    The different types of signal filters are low-pass filters (LPF), band-pass filters (BPF), and high-pass filters (HPF).

29. **What is the unit used to measure the signal-to-noise ratio?**
    The signal-to-noise ration (S/N) is measured is decibels (db).

30. **Name some error detection and correction coding methods.**
    Some error detection coding methods are parity, Longitudinal Redundancy Check (LRC), Vertical Redundancy Check (VRC), and Cyclic Redundancy Check (CRC). Some error correction coding methods are Backward Error Correction (BEC) and Forward Error Correction (FEC).

6.9.2 Reading data communications acronyms

The following table shows the pronunciation and expansion of the data communications acronyms.

Acronym	Pronunciation	Acronym expansion
LAN	LAN	Local Area Network
MAN	MAN	Metropolitan Area Network
WAN	WAN	Wide Area Network
10BT	TEN-BASE-T	Ten Base T
100BF	ONE HUNDRED-BASE-F	One Hundred Base F, or Fiber Fast Ethernet
1000BT	ONE THOUSAND-BASE-T	One Thousand Base T, or Twisted Pair Gigabit Ethernet
10000BF	TEN THOUSAND-BASE-F	Ten Thousand Base F, or Fiber Ten Gigabit Ethernet
UTP	U-T-P	Unshielded Twisted Pair
STP	S-T-P	Shielded Twisted Pair
VHF	V-H-F	Very High Frequency
UHF	U-H-F	Ultra High Frequency
BW	BANDWIDTH	Bandwidth
Gbps	GIGABITS PER SECOND	Gigabits per second
GBps	GIGABYTES PER SECOND	Gigabytes per second
LSB	L-S-B	Least Significant Bit
MSB	M-S-B	Most Significant Bit
VC	V-C	Virtual Circuit
SYNCH	SYNCH	Synchronous
ASYNCH	ASYNCH	Asynchronous
FSK	F-S-K	Frequency Shift Keying
PSK	P-S-K	Phase Shift Keying
PCM	P-C-M	Pulse Code Modulation
FDM	F-D-M	Frequency Division Multiplexing
CDM	C-D-M	Code Division Multiplexing
TDM	T-D-M	Time Division Multiplexing

6.9.3 Identifying data communications signals

The words in the following table are matched to their corresponding items in the figure below.

FSK modulation	Aperiodic signal
Binary signal	Continuous signal
PSK modulation	Full duplex transmission
Simplex transmission	Periodic signal

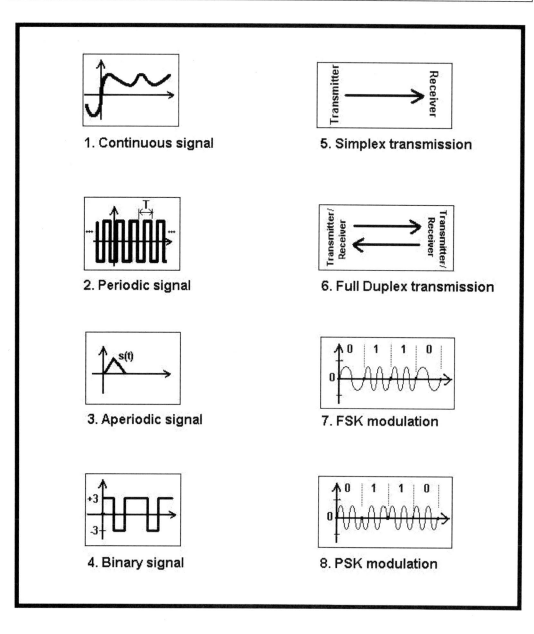

6.9.4 Cloze

The correct data communications words are shown underlined.

1. The network used to connect the computers at home or in the office is called a LAN.
2. The network that can cover a whole city is called a MAN.
3. A network that can cover a whole country is called a WAN.
4. An Ethernet segment uses a bus topology.
5. Ethernet cabling uses twisted pair wiring or fiber.
6. An analog signal is a continuous signal.
7. An analog signal that is sampled becomes a discrete signal.
8. An analog signal that is sampled and quantized becomes a digital signal.
9. A digital signal with two possible values is called a binary signal.
10. A signal that repeats itself at regular time intervals is called a periodic signal.
11. A signal that is not periodic is called aperiodic.
12. Guided transmission media use some type of cabling such as fiber.
13. Unguided transmission media mean the transmission is through space.
14. Transmission through optical fiber uses visible light.
15. The telephone bandwidth for transmitting voice is less than 4kHz.
16. Data units are the bit and the byte, which contains eight bits.
17. A parity bit is used to check for errors.
18. Groups of data bytes can be packaged into frames and packets for transmission.
19. In packet switching, TCP uses virtual circuits while UDP uses datagrams.
20. Timing in data transmissions can be synchronous or asynchronous.
21. Data transmission between two chips can be either through serial or parallel modes.
22. Data transmission that takes place in only one direction is called simplex transmission.
23. Simultaneous data transmission in both directions is called full duplex transmission.
24. Multiplexing of data can use such techniques as FDM, CDM, TDM and STDM.
25. ADSL uses FDM multiplexing to allow a telephone and a computer to share a phone line.
26. A low-pass filter is used to filter out the higher frequencies in a signal.
27. The signal-to-noise ratio, measured in db, is used to express the quality of data transmission.
28. Forward error correction is used for very distant communications.
29. In data communications, the two main protocol stacks are TCP/IP and OSI.
30. IP addressing is categorized into classes called A, B, C, D and E.
31. The Internet traffic is moved around using equipment devices called routers.
32. The LAN port on a computer is called an RJ45 port.
33. Twisted-pair wiring can be either unshielded or shielded.
34. The core of fiber cables is made of either glass or plastic.

Epilogue

TO MY FATHER